SUNSHINE
STATES

SUNSHINE STATES

Patrick Carr

DOUBLEDAY

Wild Times and Extraordinary Lives in the Land of Gators, Guns, and Grapefruit

NEW YORK   LONDON   TORONTO   SYDNEY   AUCKLAND

Published by Doubleday, a division of
Bantam Doubleday Dell Publishing Group, Inc.
666 Fifth Avenue, New York, New York 10103

Doubleday and the portrayal of an anchor
with a dolphin are trademarks of
Doubleday, a division of Bantam Doubleday Dell
Publishing Group, Inc.

LIBRARY OF CONGRESS CATALOGING-IN-PUBLICATION DATA

Carr, Patrick.
    Sunshine states : wild times and extraordinary lives in the land
of gators, guns, and grapefruit / by Patrick Carr. — 1st ed.
      p. cm.
    ISBN 0-385-24204-2
    1. Florida—Social life and customs. 2. Carr, Patrick—
Journeys—Florida. I. Title.
F316.2.C37   1990
975.9′063—dc20   89-35098
                                                     CIP

ILLUSTRATIONS AND DESIGN BY KATHRYN PARISE

For Cath

Acknowledgments

My thanks go first to all the Floridians who allowed me to observe and write about their lives in the Sunshine State: James Billie and Jim Shore of the Seminole nation; Lisa Voisard and the other Aquamaids and staff of Cypress Gardens; Cam Oberting, Dr. Garald Parker, "Buddy Buildit," Jan Platt, and Roger Stewart in America's Next Great City; Lovett Williams and David Austin of the Fisheating Creek hunting camp; alligator hunters Don Smith, Bill Shattuck, Eugene Rewis, and the Thomas family; Art Nehrbas, Walt Murphree, Dennis Reddington, Ed Howett, Russ Kubik, and other men and women of the Metro Dade Department of Public Safety; and Alfonso Lobo and his family and friends. I am deeply indebted to all these people for their time, attention, and trust.

Other people gave me their ideas, support, and advice. Among them are my old friends Michael Bane and Mary Ellen Moore and my newer friends Pete Cimino, Richard Kent, Guy King, Ernest Krehr, Steve Major, Fred and Ricky McColl, John Whitinger, Leonard and Cheryl Wood, Hank and Anne Wright, and Mike Young; and many writers, editors, agents, publicists, and other sources, most notably Jay Acton, Tammy Barden, Christa Deason, Joe Guidry, Gregg Holder, Madeline Morel, Jim Morgan, John Morthland, John Orbaugh, Gloria Raines, Dan Ross, Randy Wayne White, and Nick Wiley.

I owe my greatest debts to the people most intimately involved with the work of *Sunshine States:* Jim Fitzgerald, whose idea began the book, and Casey Fuetsch, Jill Roberts, and Herman Gollob, who helped finish it; and of course, finally and closest to home, my agent Kevin McShane and my wife Christopher Anne Wright.

Introduction

I love Florida. Like all transplants I love it for what it isn't, cold and old. I also appreciate it, and occasionally hate it as much as I love it, for what it is: crazy.

Florida is not normal. Many of us here try to pretend that it is, that we live in just another version of the Sunbelt dreamland, a place for giving thanks and snoozing, enjoying the relief of a sunshine state of life. But in our hearts we know we don't. Deep down we know we live on the frontier.

What frontier? Well, there's the frontier of nature. Florida is a place of blistering heat and frequent drought and just as frequent flood, of lightning strikes and sinkhole collapses and tornados and hurricanes, of organic life that can kill you just as surely as a tidal wave.

We are also on the frontier of American social interaction, the brave new world in action—cultures colliding, urban growth and rural decay seesawing wildly in a boom/bust economy, pollution tightening its stranglehold, education in ruins, racism rampant, corruption endemic, fortunes falling out of the sky, drugs everywhere, thievery and violence prospects you can plan on: the melting pot on high heat.

It is, I suppose, possible for us transplants to remain ignorant of the true nature of the forces at work around us, focusing tightly on the sunshine state of life we had in mind when we moved here—our gentle winters in our little piece of paradise, our lovely palms and beaches, our low taxation, our good housing, our worst memories fading behind us—but ignorance cannot be parlayed completely into bliss. Frontier dynamics have a way of getting one's attention.

The have captured mine on occasion. On the natural frontier there were the two summer months I spent ravaged by dysentery from drinking country well water, and the times I had to evacuate my home to wait out hurricanes on high ground, and the wrenching moment when I killed my first feral hog, and the morning when I learned that someone I knew had been eaten by a twelve-foot alligator. On the social frontier there was the night I heard a Miami drug dealer's bullet buzz above my head, and the morning when I opened the *Tampa Tribune* to discover that an acquaintance had shot three teenagers during a brawl in his yard. On another morning on another frontier— the final frontier, my TV calls it—I stood in another friend's yard and watched as the space shuttle *Challenger* scrawled a sudden white-smoke obscenity across the Florida sky. Another friend of mine, a tugboat driver, spent the next four months dragging the bed of the Atlantic for the debris of that communal nightmare.

These happenings, and many others of similar aspect during the five years of my personal sunshine state, were not aberrations. I am not an adventurer. I live a basically sensible life in a little pink stucco house in a good neighborhood in a medium-sized city. The craziness is not mine. It visits all us frontier lawn waterers. So while like most transplants I am glad to have left my former life behind me, and am appreciative of Florida's many soft and easy beauties, I can no longer even attempt to approach my environment as many others try to, as a sort of neutral new-life free zone. I can't reduce its natural and social character to background Muzak for my sunshine state.

Florida's real soundtrack, you see, is not as soothing as Muzak. It's the ultra-high-voltage din of cultures slapped together any old way, of people wired for everything from the fabulous to the fatal. Its melodies come from salsa, rap, reggae, rock & roll, gutbucket country, the blues, and the music of the spheres and the symphony of the sea. Its percussions are the jangle of coin, the thrum of a pickup tire, and the drum of a gun. It's wild.

Patrick Carr
Tampa 1989

SUNSHINE
STATES

The lives described in *Sunshine States* are set in the times between early 1986 and late 1988. They are likely to have changed by the time you hold the book in your hands.

1

The Thoughts of Chairman Billie

Under the smoke-blackened thatch of his chickee, deep in the heart of his people's ancient homeland with the light of his cook-fire dancing across the eyes of his retainers and the skulls of his kills, Chairman Billie speaks visions of the future. His voice booms, reverberates; a big, weird, rough-tough musical Irish/redneck/Indian amalgam of profanely poetic proportion.

"You walk out into this country right here, and look around," he says, sweeping broad dirty work-callused hands across the moonless mystery of swamp and hammock looming just yards beyond the firelight. "The nighttime atmosphere will equal or surpass any high mountain country. The silence of it is just as fabulous as any mountain range; the terrain is just as beautiful as anybody else's. I could build a high-class hunting resort or a trail-ride resort right here.

"It wouldn't have to be hunting to kill, either. It could be hunting just to see, or just the fascination of two lovers taking a tour through the jungle, screwing in the back of the truck, or a nice safe down-to-earth camping experience for the family. You could bring in people

from all over the world, let them see a wild panther, sleep in a chickee. I could do it all. A resort for executive lovers, dining and dancing. 'Course, we might have to invent some new music. Seminole reggae, maybe . . ."

You can see it. The Everglades vacation done right. Style amid the otherworldly strangeness, something far above and beyond the beat-up roadside airboat rides and sad little alligator farms along the roads white men have driven straight and hard through the Everglades' mystic ancient River of Grass; a tribute to Seminole sophistication. It's a natural concept. Chairman Billie has his head screwed on.

The snarl of a chain saw drives home the possibility. Already the Big Cypress Seminole Indian Reservation, forty-six thousand acres of agriculturally unpromising tribal land abutted to the south by the Alligator Alley highway, is undergoing relentless transformation. The massive cypress structural members of a new Seminole museum tower over the Chairman's little hunting camp (he erected them, and the camp, himself; a crew of workers from among the seventeen hundred Seminoles scattered across four reservations will finish the building). Across State Route 833, beside a five-thousand-foot excavation which will soon be a runway capable of handling the biggest and fastest jets of today or tomorrow, stands an almost-completed administration building and an enormous new bingo hall where the gamblers of Florida and the world play for the largest stakes in bingo history, stopping by the tax-free cigarette concessions between games to add a few more sawbucks to the tribal coffers.

The hall, and bingo, are central to the Seminoles of today, but perhaps not those of tomorrow. For while the two existing bingo halls and the tax-free cigarette concessions grouped around them on the tribe's Tampa and Hollywood reservations are the source of most of their growing wealth, these operations are insecure. They could continue indefinitely, or they could be closed down within twenty-four hours. So Chairman Billie, who personally introduced the bingo halls and smoke shops and a lot of other changes into Seminole life, must plan accordingly. Here by the fire where he cooks his meat and tells his tales and talks on his telephone, he explores the possibilities.

He shifts abruptly from contemplation of the tribal lands as locations for leisure spending. "Then again," he muses, "if I don't make a resort, I can go into defense contracts. That's why I'm building the big runway. But I don't know; I have to look at the academic mentality of my youth and see where they all fit. Are they all good in vocabulary and English? Are they all good in the mathematical field? The mechanical field? There must be some field where they're absolutely good, better than anybody else in this god-damned world. Who knows? They might become the main guys in intercontinental ballistic missiles; they don't need no goddam machines, all they do is look at it and go 'Phhhhhhhhew! Hit it!' I've watched 'em play those video games, and man, they're so good they're spooky. They've got some kind of gift for that kind of shit that white men don't. . . . Whatever it is, though, the stone has not been flipped by anybody yet, and I'm damn sure looking to be the guy that flips it."

And there you have James Billie, leader: fourth-term chairman of the Seminole Council at the age of forty-four, agent of the future and medium for the revitalization of the traditional past, free-spirit dreamer, gut-cunning schemer, and hands-on authoritarian. Also folk singer, gator wrestler, Harley Davidson rider, guerilla warrior, sex symbol, "sorry-ass bowlegged half-breed" (his description), and "uppity Injun motherfucker" (predominant white Floridian opinion); alive and dangerous, a great chief in a great tradition.

A century and a half ago in Florida, at approximately 1 P.M. on December 29, 1835, Private Ransome Clarke looked around at the other white soldiers still alive and fighting in the open pinewoods sixty-five miles east of Tampa, and noted to himself that his comrades were "as cool as if they were in the woods shooting game."

That they were. Half their number had died in the first sudden lash of fire, but the fifty-odd survivors had regrouped quickly, dug and scratched for cover, formed a perimeter, and begun a long, disciplined fight for their lives. These were not cooks or clerks, soft rear echelon personnel. Their young commander had acted foolishly in marching them through potentially hostile country without scouts or outriders, but now the rank and file were acting like the hard United States infantry regulars they were. These were good men.

As only Private Clarke lived to testify, however, the Seminoles were just as good, and considerably more prudent. By nine o'clock that evening, despite the white men's courage (and more significantly their cannon), the warriors had done as much feinting and probing and fire-drawing, exercised as many of their infernal now-you-see-'em-now-you-don't-and-pretty-soon-you're-out-of-ammunition tactics, as they needed to. There was a final assault, and then a final tally: three dead and five wounded Indians, one hundred and nine dead white men. Private Clarke, wounded by two bullets, escaped and hid in the woods.

Such was Dade's Massacre, the opening engagement of the Second Seminole War and an evil portent for the whites in more ways than one. A massacre was bad enough, but this was an intelligent, carefully executed massacre, the work of sophisticated fighting men, and its concluding act was even more ominous. The Indians did not flee the scene in guilt or fear; they cleaned up the battlefield and buried their dead. Neither did they mutilate or loot the bodies of their victims. The uniform of the foolish Major Dade was taken, as were many scalps and usable weapons, but otherwise the vanquished soldiers were left to rot in peace.

The men who found them were impressed. "Osceola is a master spirit and must have gained a wonderful influence over the minds of his followers to induce them to forego . . . articles of which they are so notoriously fond. Our men were struck with awe and astonishment at the circumstances," wrote one officer, betraying an almost touching naïveté about the nature of his new adversaries in the supposition that charismatic leadership must alone be responsible for the scene before him. Osceola, the brilliant but by no means unique young tactician under whose leadership the polyglot Seminoles were uniting, was in fact not present at the fight.

The officer's conclusion, however, was very much to the point: "We fear that many a tragic event must be recorded before the close of this war with an enemy capable of such determination and self-control."

The tragic events came quickly. Dade's Massacre was followed by the first battle at the Withlacoochee River (Indians' casualties eight of two hundred; whites' one hundred and fifty-seven of two hundred and thirty), and, during the malaria-free winter months of the next seven

4

years, many similar fights, including the marathon second engagement on the Withlacoochee in which seven hundred Seminoles kept eleven hundred of General Gaines's best fighting men pinned down for seven terrible days before the arrival of a relief force prompted them to fade away into their swamps and cypress hammocks. To use the slang of a very similar jungle war in which United States soldiers found themselves embroiled and embarrassed a hundred and thirty years later and half a world away, the Seminoles were kicking ass. The whites' war for ownership of all Florida was not working out as planned.

In a rational world this should not have come as any great surprise, for the Seminoles of 1835 were the survivors of a rich, well-organized, stable society based on a thousand years of agriculture and urbanization, and moreover the dominant peoples among them had established their rule over all Florida precisely as the whites intended to do: by conquest over powerful and sophisticated societies whose lands they had initially penetrated in relative peace.

The whites' blind (and now dangerous) ignorance of these facts was betrayed by the very word they used for their enemies. "Seminole" was a term both artificial and inaccurate. An Anglicization of a corruption of an Indian term, "isti-se-mo-le," meaning "wild men," it had once referred only to the Creek Indians, who during the seventeenth century began filtering into Florida from their traditional territories to the north.

These strangers were accepted in friendship at first by the once-mighty Calusa, whose unique agricultural/maritime culture still pervaded the lower regions of the peninsula (and whose canals thread the seacoast reaches of the Everglades to this day), by the more conventionally Southern upper-peninsula Ocale and Timucua, and by the Apalachee and Apalachicola of the Panhandle. Gradually, however, as the strangers' numbers and needs increased, disputes arose and were settled, in favor of the invaders, by violence. The power of Florida's first kingdoms was broken and their people assimilated into the new order. A "Seminole nation" could not therefore be correctly said to exist until the time of Cowkeeper, the great Creek chief whose enormous cattle herds so impressed naturalist William Bartram when that gentleman visited his capital near what is now Gainesville on the eve of the American Revolution.

In reality, then, the "Seminoles" of 1835 were Creeks, Calusas, Apalachees, Ocales, Timucuas, and other Indians—and also Spaniards, French, Britons, Ibos, Mandingos, Ashantis, and more; intermarriage with and absorption of successive generations of Europeans had been a fact of life since the early sixteenth century, and the Indian practice of sheltering and adopting escaped slaves had added a significant African ingredient to the Seminole patchwork. ("The Indian loves his negro as much as one of his own children," a staff officer once observed, correctly, to General Gaines; he failed to add that the affection was mutual, and that the black Seminoles, products of combative kingdoms just as skilled and resourceful in the art of war as their bronze brothers and a good deal more familiar with the ways of the enemy whites, contributed greatly to the Indian cause. In fact, Osceola himself was part black—and part white.)

Through much of their history, the aboriginal Florida Indians who eventually became Seminoles lived in relative peace with the new peoples of Europe and Africa. The first contacts, quite naturally, had been unsettling—Ocale arrows darting across the wide low dunes at the mouth of Tampa Bay to puncture the armor of crucifix-wielding, gold-hungry Iberians; mammoth seagoing Calusa dugouts emerging from the lower coastal mangroves to trouble the ambitions of poxed and scurvied English privateers—but subsequent relations between the Florida Indians and their slave-equipped visitors were, on the whole, cordial. The Indians, initially outnumbering the whites by a wide margin, were necessarily to be respected.

They were also to be learned from. The early settlers in their grimy little villages could probably not have survived without helpful hints and more from the denizens of large, complex towns and cities surrounded by fields from which they had learned to extract crop yields far in excess of those made possible by European methods. Like most Southeastern Indians, the tribes of Florida were farmers whose economy had been built around the efficient cultivation of maize for a thousand years. Hunting and gathering had a significant place in their lives, but it was supplemental rather than central to their survival.

Their good favor was to be courted. In the succession of wars and police actions between the Portuguese, the French, the British, variously affiliated Americans, and free-lancing pirates, slavers, and rogue Indians which constituted Florida history prior to the mid-nineteenth century, the ability of any one faction to call upon superior numbers of highly competent indigenous troops was as often as not a deciding factor in whatever dead-serious disagreement happened to be at issue. The maintenance of harmonious relations with the various aboriginal factions (including the subtle diplomatic art of manipulating them into conflict with each other during white peacetimes, then uniting them when the outbreak of hostilities necessitated their cooperation) was therefore a task to which successive generations of colonial administrators applied considerable effort.

In this regard the Spanish excelled, which talent was at least partly responsible for the fact that Madrid's hold over the Florida peninsula was not completely broken, by either the British or the Americans, until 1821. It was then that the Spanish king finally ratified a treaty forced upon his ambassador in 1819 by the diplomacy of John Quincy Adams and the guns of Andrew Jackson's rapaciously effective Tennessee/Georgia volunteers.

The British too had their own kind of affection for the Indians, and their own way of expressing it. While the Catholic Spanish concentrated (not exclusively, but with fervor) on winning the aboriginals' souls, the nation of shopkeepers sought and won their business. Guns and farm implements and good cotton cloth and whiskey and a thousand and one different kinds of solid, reliable luxuries and labor savers traveled west across the Atlantic; Indian furs and skins and feathers traveled east.

It was an elegant arrangement, the usual British industrial/imperial equation in which the Crown defrayed the cost of whatever occupation forces were necessary by taxing the merchants whose trade was the whole point of the game, and it worked well. And once the writing on the American wall had been emphasized in bold relief over New Orleans by Andrew Jackson and his Tennesseans, it in fact worked even better. Unburdened by defeat of the costly business of overcompetitive colonization, Britannia simply encouraged its unbeatably efficient and self-sustaining merchants. These gentlemen took the place of her tax-hungry soldiers, the profit flowed, and her revenue agents did the rest.

For the most part, the Indians were happy. The Britons among them, worldly and convivial sorts eager to please in the manner of salesmen of all ages and races, were not only nonthreatening (what danger did they pose—they no longer had any interest whatsoever in Indian land, blood, or fealty) but actively useful. Even today the Seminoles look with particular affection on those tourists and bingo players who hail from the land of the Purdy shotgun and the Sheffield steel skinning knife and the malt elixir of the clear cold Grampian streams.

Relations between Indians and Americans in Florida, however, were another matter entirely. Basically it was hate at first sight. As soon as Andy Jackson set eyes on the Seminoles in 1815 (actually, long before that moment), he was filled with a consuming desire to be rid of them. Jackson, then governor of Tennessee, was on a mission—America for Americans, specifically the hundreds of thousands of vital white immigrants choking the republic's cities as they burned for land of their own—and anybody who got in his way, be he a Royal Scots Guardsman or a Barcelona Jesuit or a tribal landholder or a lily-livered Washington politician, was going to get hurt.

Jackson's route to his date with the Indians of Florida was circuitous but lively. Acting on his own initiative and funds, he took the lives (and twenty-three million acres) of several hundred Creeks who had killed two hundred and fifty whites at Fort Mims in Alabama, then moved on the British in Mobile, then the neutral Spanish in Pensacola, and then the British again (conclusively) in New Orleans.

Then he went home, but not for long. He was conscious of unfinished business. Florida was still not American. It was still alive with blacks and Brits and Spaniards and angry Indians (including refugees from his Alabama mission, the angriest of them all), and these obstacles to American settlement just had to go. Therefore Jackson had General Gaines attack the "Negro Fort" on the Apalachicola River (which Gaines did with spectacular results; one fateful shell from a gunboat penetrated the fort's powder magazine, and it rained blacks and Indians), and then he himself moved. Although President Monroe authorized him to proceed only as far as Georgia, he and the Georgia militia scythed into Florida and went to work. Indian villages were burned, troublesome chiefs and Englishmen shot or hanged, Spanish forts taken—and then Jackson made his second, definitive, unauthorized move on the Spanish capital of Pensacola. It was not an assault that could be resisted, and the Spanish governor surrendered his town and his flag.

All hell broke loose in Washington, but Jackson held his ground, threatening to continue his invasion all the way south through Florida and on to Spanish Cuba even though the cost of such an undertaking was anathema to his government, and Washington decided to take him seriously. The Spanish king spent three years backing and filling, but in the end he reached the same conclusion.

Florida was now no longer Spanish, though neither was it quite all-American yet. Jackson was installed, much against his wishes, as provisional governor, and the settlers flowed in to take from all comers. It was then that the long Indian hell began in earnest.

It was brutal, and it had the force of law. All chiefs and subchiefs were ordered to appear at Fort Moultrie in Charleston, South Carolina, in 1823, and there, surrounded by the bayonets of the United States Army, they were stripped of their lands and all future claims thereto. They were compensated with cash and promises of food and annuities to be delivered over the next twenty years (at which time, it was planned but not revealed, they would all be evicted from the four million acres of useless scrub country to which the Fort Moultrie treaty confined them, and shipped west to reservations in Oklahoma).

Only a few of the illiterate Indians actually made their marks on the documents before them, but it didn't matter; the whole affair was just a sap to the conscience of Congress anyway.

Predictably, very little of the promised money was ever received by the Indians. Their food rations were shorted if distributed at all, and slavers and thieves preyed on their people and livestock. Written permission to hunt outside their assigned territory was seldom granted (a legal lashing or worse awaited those who hunted anyway); permission for chiefs to beg on the streets of St. Augustine was dispensed more freely. The Seminoles, denied the means with which to continue their amply sustaining urban/agricultural way of life, descended into poverty, starvation, and death.

These conditions were not accidental. One member of the Florida Legislative Council explained them succinctly in 1824 when he wrote, "The only course, therefore, which remains for us to rid ourselves of them, is to adopt such a mode of treatment toward them, as will reduce them to acts that will justify their expulsion by force."

And so it came to pass. The final provocation was the Treaty of Fort Gibson, in which seven unfortunate chiefs, transported under lugubrious conditions to far Oklahoma, somehow ended up with their marks affixed to a document promising that all Florida Indians would emigrate posthaste. When these sorry souls came home, their hangovers were compounded by the wrath of the people in whose name they had spoken (there remains some doubt as to whether the seven did actually sign anything; they swore to their fellows that they didn't remember doing any such thing, while the recollections of their hosts attested otherwise), but it was too late for remedial action. The United States government, now headed by *President* Andrew Jackson, had a paper in hand and intended to enforce it. As Jackson put it in a letter to the Seminoles on February 16, 1835, "I tell you that you must go and that you will go."

But they didn't. In April a hundred and fifty of their chiefs were given one day to make up their minds by General Clinch. Eight agreed to go west. Osceola was not one of them. He was thrown in jail. When released, he disappeared. A few days later, so did all the other Indians, but not before they had bought all the shot and powder in the store at Fort King.

Some farms were burned, some councils held, some dire issues debated by both Indians and free Negroes, and then it really happened. On December 28 General Wiley Thompson and Lieutenant Smith, the former a veteran of a notoriously corrupt career as an Indian agent, succumbed to gunfire as they walked outside Fort King. The next day, Private Ransome Clarke and his comrades found themselves at the end of their road in the Central Florida pinewoods.

❂

The war was a mess. When Osceola told General Clinch in the days before hostilities commenced that given time to prepare his position he could maintain it "for five years against the whole United States forces," he had been scorned. But now his words were coming true. The very real problems involved in fighting superb, highly mobile, disciplined guerrillas on their home turf were making themselves bloodily apparent.

The problems were not just tactical, either. Osceola was adhering to another of his statements—"It is not upon women and children that we make war and draw the scalping-knife; it is upon men; let us act like men"—while the whites were not. So issues of morality were beginning to trouble the nation. Paeans to the virtue of Osceola (who did, it must be said, cut a fine figure; young, handsome, a great dandy and dancer and ball player as well as a fearsome war chief, he was made-to-order for the role of charismatic victim) appeared in both Northern and Southern newspapers; hard congressional questions about atrocities in the field harassed the Administration. Overall the war was growing unpopular, as ruthless but inconclusive campaigns against dubiously threatening but manifestly courageous underdogs have a way of doing in these United States.

For their part, the struggling soldiers were beginning to doubt both their cause and their competence. One officer, looking back on four years of frustration, of burning villages and stealing livestock and killing women and children between desperate fights with skilled and fearless warriors who refused to wage war on anybody but combatants, voiced the feelings of many of his comrades when he wrote of his enemies that "if they have the courage of men, they will die with arms in their hands. The white man will not deny them the privilege of sleeping out their death sleep on the soil upon which we cannot endure their living presence."

A complex statement, that; one soldier's tribute to another, and a tacit aknowledgment of both the venality and the inevitability of the end to which his own arms were turned. Unlike the many citizens of his nation who thought that sufficient protest might deflect the determination of the Florida settlers, this man knew that the whites would not cease their depradations until, by whatever means, they had the Seminoles' rich and beautiful lands for their own. Nothing could stop them in the end, and so perhaps death and extinction were a kinder fate than the banishment the Indians were resisting.

The Seminoles were not so clearheaded on this issue. Two years into the war, Osceola himself had thought that perhaps, after so much bloodshed and with no clear victory in sight, the whites might feel an honorable compromise to be in order.

He was mistaken. On October 22, 1837, he was taken prisoner when he arrived at Fort Marion to negotiate under a flag of truce. He and one hundred sixteen captured warriors and their families were sent to Fort Moultrie, and shortly thereafter he died of malaria. The Indians with him were sent west to reservations, while the blacks, who had lived and fought with them as an integral and fully assimilated ingredient in the Seminole patchwork, were sold back into slavery in the Bahamas.

Osceola himself was also divided and transported. The physician attending his death cut off his head and caused it to be exhibited at circus sideshows around the nation, discarding the trunk of the great warrior into a poor man's grave beneath Fort Moultrie's outer wall.

That unsavory little piece of business had not, as the Army brass had hoped, deprived the Seminoles of either the will or the means to resist effectively. It had in fact confirmed the suspicions of many tribal powers who had counseled against Osceola's peace initiative, and other chiefs had filled his fighting shoes very nicely. Moreover, the perfidious capture and its gothically horrid aftermath had inflamed the already-troubled consciences of the public, the press, and many members of the Van Buren Administration. Then as now, you did not neutralize a cause by martyring its figurehead.

And the war went on. Florida's land-hungry crackers insisted on it. The press and the Yankees could go hang, and the Seminoles could either die where they were or go to Oklahoma. Men and money were poured on the problem until some fifty thousand United States soldiers were involved in operations against warriors whose total number had never exceeded eighteen hundred. The pressure began to tell. Battle-hardened, Seminole-experienced forces under the shrewd and able General Zachary Taylor drew the Indians into a major battle on a cypress hammock east of the Kissimmee River and beat them in a fair fight, driving the survivors south into the Everglades. Then Taylor offered transportation west under conditions of truce if the Indians would assemble peacefully in Tampa; four hundred accepted and like thousands before them were gone from Florida forever.

The war entered its final and, for the white combatants, its most excruciating phase. For two years soldiers, marines, and sailors went Indian hunting in the ravening Glades, slashed by saw grass and infected by mosquitos and bitten by snakes and debilitated by hunger, with little to show for their pains. They caught mostly old men, women, and children while the warriors hid and sniped and vanished. (This, not the more conventional large-scale encounters earlier in the war, is the memory which survived in the lore and legend of the United States Army; "Seminole," a dirty word, haunted its tactical and logistical thinkers for a hundred and thirty years, at which point the word "Charlie" began to suggest a more current body of guerrilla-warfare nightmares.)

In the end the numbers were against the Seminoles. The United States' supply of soldiers was relatively inexhaustible, just as the supply of European immigrants and African slaves had been in the early days of contact. Then, the shifting dynamic of the numerical balance between outlanders and aboriginals had been set in motion by the diseases the strangers brought with them, the power and glory of the great Southeastern Indian civilizations eroded by an infernal array of novel microbes. Now the more deliberate application of the .54 caliber Minié ball and the firebrand and the slaver's shackles accelerated the equation, and every Seminole or free slave killed or transported represented the dwindling of a finite resource.

By June 1842, seven years after Private Clarke's ordeal in the Central Florida pines, there were only some three hundred Indians left in the Glades. And that, it seemed, was acceptable. Finally bowing to public pressure and the order of his president, Colonel William J. Worth called off his troops.

Armed crackers settled the arable lands around the Glades, ever vigilant and eager for Indian blood, and the Seminoles (now under the ancient Billy Bowlegs) were told that finally they could rest in peace so long as they remained in their valueless wilderness.

That, however, was not that. Land lust and fear and hatred continued, and pressure on Bowlegs's people mounted until, having refused to be transported in 1854, he lashed out and killed some soldiers who, legend has it, deliberately destroyed his banana patch. The Third Seminole War was declared and federal troops joined the Florida volunteers engaged in transportation at a bounty of two hundred and fifty dollars a head.

Again the Indians did well, but again the numbers were against them. When his infant granddaughter was captured, Bowlegs submitted to transportation and began the long journey west with a hundred and twenty of his people and forty-one led by Chief Tiger Tail, who killed himself en route to New Orleans.

And that *was* that. In the nineteen years since 1835, the number of Indians in Florida had been reduced from over five thousand to less than a hundred, at a cost of some forty-five million dollars and the lives of more than fifteen hundred soldiers. The crackers had the land, while the remaining Seminoles went on living in their hidden places, guided by the spiritual leadership of an ancient by the name of Abiaca who clung to life in the Glades until the age of a hundred and eleven.

The seventeen hundred Seminoles of today—men, women, and children scattered across four reservations in Florida and at large in the nation and the world—are descended directly from Abiaca's people. They are correct when they say that they are unvanquished; the Seminoles of the nineteenth century never signed a peace treaty or document of surrender to the United States. There might therefore be an interesting case to be made for the proposition that technically, they are still at war.

❁

Jim Shore finds such a notion amusing, but hardly worth the attention of his legal mind. As chief counsel of the Seminole Tribe of Florida and its various corporations, he has little time for such frivolity. For while it is ludicrous to imagine that the United States and the Seminoles of today could be at war, it is all too easy to picture them in all manner of other time- and budget-sapping conflict.

The key word here is "sovereignty": the all-pervasive convoluted question of who is in authority to decide what rights and restrictions apply to the activities of the tribe. A million fascinating little confusions hurtle around the legal vacuum between the propositions that on the one hand the Seminole Tribe of Florida is a sovereign nation unto itself, while on the other its people are in many ways wards of the larger state, adult children to be sustained and disciplined by the Great White Father's Bureau of Indian Affairs.

For the first half of this century the sovereignty issue was moot. The Seminoles lived an obscure existence in the untraveled places and unexamined fringes of a relatively unpopulous white man's Florida, participants in an illiterate rural subsistence economy far removed from the mainstream of modern America. The post-World War II Florida land boom and population explosion invaded the Seminole world in all manner of ways, however, so in 1957 a new generation of leaders created both a tribal constitution and the corporate-umbrella Seminole Economic Council to address the issue of the tribe's survival in an increasingly voracious but also potentially beneficent economy.

Since then, the sovereignty issue has pervaded every aspect of the Seminoles' communal activity, most importantly the often-interrelated fields of land use and corporate enterprise: the tribe's long-standing cattle business, its catfish farms, the development of its various tourist attractions, its ventures into light industry and real estate and stock market speculation, the wildly profitable but ever tenuous cash machine of its bingo and cigarette businesses. Exactly how free are the Indians to decide what to do with the land they live on and the money they make, and who exactly has the ultimate authority to decide? What benefits can be realized from the fact that while the Seminoles are accountable under an enormously intricate body of federal law, they are not bound by many of Florida's state, county, and municipal ordinances?

The ongoing exploration of these questions complicates tribal affairs with endless paperwork and bureaucratic obfuscation, provides loopholes-of-opportunity such as the gambling and tax-free cigarette bonanzas, and consumes an annual Seminole legal department budget of some one million dollars.

The money has been spent on various irons in the fire. Some, virtually all of them Seminole victories, are now cold. A suit begun in 1957 against the United States for land compensation—belated payment for the historical theft of tribal lands—ended in 1976 with the receipt of sixteen million dollars. The fracas over a tribal burial site uncovered in downtown Tampa during excavation for a new bank building resulted in the tribe's acceptance, and subsequent highly intelligent development, of fourteen acres of land on the eastern fringe of the city. And after much to-ing and fro-ing on the issue, the Seminoles now have their own police force fully empowered to enforce the criminal laws of the state of Florida on reservation lands.

Other irons still radiate considerable heat. The issue of water rights on the Big Cypress Reservation, long assumed by the state but challenged by the tribe in 1977, is still edging toward what Jim Shore hopes will be a reasonable conclusion, the tribe's formal ceding of fourteen thousand acres to the state in exchange for cash. And then of course there is the explosive Bingo Question, currently answered by the 11th United States Circuit Court's 1982 decision in favor of the Seminoles' right to conduct gambling on their reservations. That issue could achieve critical mass the moment any of the Seminoles' adversaries manage to escalate the conflict in the direction of the Supreme Court. Lots of folks, both organizations philosophically opposed to games of chance and entities annoyed by native American competition in their traditional domain, are deeply motivated to close down the Indian bingo halls in Tampa, Hollywood, Big Cypress, and indeed the nation at large.

In effect, then, significant proportions of Jim Shore's budget and energy go into maintaining what is essentially an economic house of cards. Without a bingo- and cigarette-generated cash flow providing both weekly paychecks for a hefty proportion of tribal members and capital accumulation for better-than-subsistence housing, social services, and diversification into "legitimate" businesses, the tribal economy would simply collapse. And understandably, that little home truth —the knowledge that the rap of some federal judge's gavel could propel them straight back into a Third World-like subsistence economy—lends an almost literally lethal edge of insecurity, not to mention annoyance, to the Seminole weltschmerz.

Jim Shore doesn't have to struggle too hard to imagine how such a catastrophe would translate into daily reality, or to call up the bitterness he feels when he considers his people's possible future; he just has to remember his own past. As a member of the first Seminole generation to achieve literacy and experience the changes wrought by the original post-World War II wave of "modern" tribal leaders—Bill Osceola, Billy Osceola, Mike Osceola, Frank Billie, Laura Mae Osceola—he can compare and contrast at the drop of a memory: today's modern, well-funded Big Cypress medical center *versus* the almost total lack of health care which robbed him of many of his childhood friends; the commonplace of starvation and destitution during his formative years *versus* the relative rarity of such blight at present; and of course there's the existence today of electricity, telephones, automobiles, winter heat, and other basics necessary to a people whom history has deprived of the means and resources with which to survive without them.

Jim Shore's personal case is particularly poignant on this front. He is a lawyer today because the loss of his sight in an automobile accident early in manhood prevented him from becoming a cowboy like most of his peers on the Brighton Reservation. Had he been born in his parents' generation, he wouldn't have had the basic education even to begin struggling through Braille textbooks and audio study aids toward any sort of career, and he would have lived out his life in a very small world.

As it is, here he is in his workman-like little office in the Seminole Tribe of Florida's Hollywood headquarters, talking about the issues at the heart of his work.

"What does it mean to be a sovereign nation within a nation?" he asks. "Do we really have sovereignty, or is the government just playing around with the words?

"You see, it's not a clear-cut issue as to what we can do and what we cannot do, but we'll never know what authority we have unless we take the steps to find out. We can't just sit back and wait for the government to come along and say, 'Here; here's what's good for you.' We can't sit here mild and meek and docile, waiting for opportunities to come to us, and we can't afford to be subject to the yo-yo effect of the federal government's ups and downs. We don't want to be in good times when one particular party is in office, and bad times otherwise. We want to be able to at least level off our own development. And really, whatever we do for ourselves eases the burden on the state, county, and federal governments; if we're self-sufficient, they don't have to support us. But they don't see it that way. They want to take everything we've done so far and put us back in a 1950s-type situation.

"I don't know," he sighs. "I don't understand it. What do they want? Do they really want us living on welfare, sitting by the railroad tracks selling beads and trinkets?"

The central problem having been stated, Shore progresses into operational frustrations. "You see, for us economic development is insanely complicated," he says. "If we want to develop a reservation or get into a new business, we have to deal with the federal government, and then we have to deal with the state, and then we have to deal with the local communities, and *then* we have to deal with the purely business issues. Our competitors just have to do the last part. And then, whenever we go into some money-making proposition, the people in that business raise a ruckus, legitimately or illegitimately. And they can always get enough movement going to undo us. We can be legislated out of existence in the first place, so if we aggravate enough people they can undo us up in Tallahassee or even at the Washington level."

He sighs again, shakes his head slowly. "You want to know the bottom line?" he asks. "I'll tell you. White people just don't like to see Indians making money, and there are a lot more of them than there are of us."

There are indeed, and Shore is correct about the main thrust of white Floridian attitude toward the Seminoles; overlying the usual all-American combination of scalp-itching fear and cultural fascination is the same kind of resentment enjoyed in Florida today by Latin real estate entrepreneurs, Vietnamese fishermen, Pakistani motel operators, and other obviously viable and therefore threatening racial minorities.

It's tough. It rankles a businessperson or bureaucrat that the Seminoles must now be approached as skilled negotiators rather than easy marks. It's hard for a liberal to watch a favorite underdog transcend the need for paternalistic compassion, become an equal or superior competitor for health and wealth and services. It hurts a good ole boy to know that when these days he aims his rifle through his pickup truck window at some goddam swamp Injun, that person may have more cash in the bank than he does.

●

Most of Jim Shore's work is civil-law litigation of one sort or another, but occasionally a criminal matter engages his attention. Such was the infamous Panther Case, James Billie's chief claim to national fame.

The panther was a problem. When James shot it on reservation land in 1983, he had no inkling that his act would embroil him in one of the more protracted and contentious struggles of his career as an Indian leader. But once the cat was out of the bag, so to speak—once an unidentified snitch had alerted Florida game officers to the fact that the hide of a protected animal was hanging in the Chief's hunting camp—the dimensions of his problem became immediately apparent.

The cat he had slain, it was claimed, was an example of the subspecies of cougar known as the Florida panther. And if in fact that were the case—if James had shot a Florida panther as opposed to one of the other varieties of cat at large in the Glades and elsewhere—then he had not killed just any old endangered, protected animal. He had shot a celebrity. For in Florida, panthers are very definitely the ecosymbol of choice. Pelicans and pink flamingos are of course well up there in a dime-a-dozen, souvenir-store sort of way, and the threatened manatees certainly have their peaceloving-brothers-and-sisters-of-the-ocean appeal, but in terms of sheer scarcity and pure animal magnitude, the panthers are incomparable. So whenever some poor tourista's Oldsmobile pounds one to pulp as it tries to get from one side of Alligator Alley to the other, it's an Event. Official statements are issued, talking heads are bowed throughout the state and even the nation, and workers mount the road signs around the Glades to conform them with newly doleful reality: PANTHERS REMAINING, 8 (OR 7, OR 6).

To actually kill a panther on purpose in Florida is therefore somewhat worse than unwise. One *will* be pilloried in the press, villified by the citizenry, and prosecuted to the full extent of the law: jail time is a distinct possibility. And so it was in the case of the Seminole chief. He was indicted by the state, then by the federal government.

At this point Jim Shore faced two distinct problems. First, James had to be somehow extricated from a trip up the river. Second, the sovereignty of the Seminoles had to be defended, for James's act was committed both on reservation land, traditionally though not legally off-limits to Florida game-law enforcement officers, and in compliance with Seminole spiritual beliefs and religious practices.

On the latter point the tradition is clear. Basically, the Seminoles believe that in creation, certain animals stand as high as man, or higher, in the regard of Yaweh, the Supreme Being. The eagle, which soars above man in the space between him and the heavens, is paramount, plainly a higher power. On earth, entities such as the bear and the deer and the otter are man's spiritual brothers at least (a fact acknowledged in the naming of the matriarchal Seminole clans which are the basis of their social organization). Man may take the lives of these creatures—indeed he must, if he is to survive both in body and spirit—but he must do it for a purpose, and with full recognition of the power of the life he is taking.

In this hierarchy the highest animal on earth is the panther (and so the Panther Clan is supreme in Seminole society). Therefore, if Yaweh sees fit to cross the life-path of a male Seminole with such a power, He is offering the ultimate gift of strength and spiritual advancement. If the man is worthy, he must accept it. And when the deed is done, he must provide the tribal medicine men with those parts of the beast which are an essential ingredient of the religious rituals of the tribe.

Thus James's prosecution could be, and was, interpreted by Jim Shore as the latest move in a long history of governmental assaults on tribal sovereignty rather than as a reasonable response to an alleged individual criminal act. On that broader front, his fight did not go well. Though conceding that the occasional killing of a panther and provision of panther parts to the tribal medicine men might indeed be an important ingredient of Seminole religious life, the federal judge denied the validity of Shore's religious-freedom defense motions in pretrial hearings. The survival of an endangered subspecies, he opined, took precedence over the tribe's constitutional rights. The same judge also ruled irrelevant the Seminoles' own stated concern for the cats' continued existence in a natural state and Shore's pretrial argument that white overdevelopment and pollution (for example the environmentally disastrous four-laning of Alligator Alley through Seminole and Mikasuki land) are in fact the overwhelmingly destructive forces in the feral feline survival equation.

These decisions cleared the way for both the federal and state cases to be fought on the facts alone—did James Billie knowingly kill a Florida panther?—and so, although as it happened their leader didn't end up in jail (the state jury delivered a Not Guilty verdict, while in the federal case the jury was hung), the Seminoles had suffered a defeat in the overall sovereignty war.

All of which caused Jim Shore to remark with some weariness, "It's the same old story. They're just out to get us, box us in," and add a final thought: "If they want to start all over again, we could make it real easy for them. We could draw a line through the center of Florida. We'd take back all the land south of that line, we'd take care of the panthers and everything else, and they could keep their damn bingo and cigarettes."

James Billie himself was less articulate on the subject, partly because Shore had advised him not to comment on the panther case and partly just because of what kind of man he is. "I did right," he growled. "The medicine men tell me I'm cool, so all the Feds can hurt is my body. Let 'em try. I don't care. Fuck 'em."

James did, however, admit to killing a panther of some sort; recalled the occasion, in fact, with characteristic zest.

The deed was accomplished with one .223 round from a single-shot Thompson Contender pistol (hardly the ideal weapon and caliber with which to confront large fast predatory carnivores, and therefore, the way the man-versus-beast macho game works, a most appropriate if imprudent choice). In the ideal scheme of things Seminole and spiritual, James said, he would have touched the cat before nailing it; as it happened he got almost close enough, but had to settle for laying hands on the beast in its twilight interval between impact and death.

He regretted the compromise. "Yeah, that would have been perfect," he mused. "To reach out and grab him by the balls, let him know who I was. I always do that, let 'em know it's me. Even in Vietnam, I'd try to get 'em to look at me—Hey!—before I pressed the trigger."

●

It is probable that many components of the adult James Billie were forged in Indochina, where like most young male Seminoles of his generation he went voluntarily to learn about the taking and giving of human life. Certainly he learned his leadership style there: "Keep it small, keep it tight, and keep it moving. When everybody else is figuring out what to do, you're doing it."

He came by that knowledge as a scout, long-range recon, leader of an eight-man team operating however far into enemy turf that the Air Force's high-altitude infrared cameras detected human-sized heat sources worth investigating afoot. He also learned something else. "This is the thing," he says. "There has to be just one leader, and that's got to be the man who knows his shit and has it together better than anybody else. Otherwise everybody dies."

People did die, too. In all his time as a recon squad leader, James says, he never failed to bring every one of his men back alive, but all the members of his first team died anyway. They went out with another leader one day, and he took them up a trail they had used just a few weeks before. They were found on their knees, with their heads buried in the ground.

So James is not much of a committee person. He has his lieutenants, a small hard core of experienced warriors much like himself, and he has an ever-present aide-de-camp (Brian Cohen, a young white lawyer with the neutral but vigilant demeanor of an extremely discerning attack dog), but he takes his responsibility personally. When he talks of "my museum" and "my bingo hall" and "my village," it sounds odd, but really it's not so strange. He built the museum and parts of the show village on the Hollywood Reservation with his own hands, and the Bingo hall was his idea, his baby. And when he talks of "my people," he doesn't really mean "the tribal entity to which I belong"; he means "the people who depend on me, and of whom I am in charge."

All of which implies that James Billie is a powerful person both in the world and in himself, and indeed he is. He is also poetic, funny, cunning, outrageous, sentimental, and egotistical; part Charles Bronson, part Don Corleone, part Huey Long, part Dylan Thomas, and part your favorite steel-fisted movie slum priest, he's a wonderful show.

Here, for instance, he sits in full regalia, lovely color-bursting hand-made finery that even Osceola would have worn with pride, at the side of a little bridge connecting the rodeo/food-concession and the ceremonial/craft-booth areas of the Hollywood Reservation. It's the Seminoles' big show weekend, the climax of their annual public festival, and James is seeing and being seen.

All sorts of outsiders flow around and to him: snowbirds from Ohio and Michigan, cowgirls from distant Omaha and Okeechobee only fifty miles north up Highway 441, long gray Brahmins from the Bureau of Indian Affairs, the stern suntanned soldiers of the Florida Highway Patrol, the varied and various aides and employees of the Seminole Economic Council and other tribal enterprises. Indians too: shy soft young women in the flower of their Asiatic beauty, older ladies more substantially graceful in costume and knowing in look, exotic Aztec and Apache dancers, responsible Commanche educators, the BIA's compact bronze Sioux, the sharp-eyed warriors of the Seminole Police and all the assorted humanity of James Billie's tribal constituency: administrating Seminoles, politicking Seminoles, supplicating Seminoles, wheeling and dealing Seminoles, hardworking God-fearing child-raising Seminoles and, sadly but not surprisingly, a couple of young male shabby Seminoles too far gone into the bottle too early in the day to fit into any apparent arrangement of the greater tribal good.

James receives each of them con brio, with all the familial concern of a Little Italy patriarch and the instant extrovert instincts of a Tammany politician. He is quick to laugh and banter and sympathize sincerely, but he is also wired for analysis and action, alert for nuance and opportunity.

A smooth matronly lady glides toward him with a teenage girl who is obviously her daughter a step behind, and wiggles her fingers in coy greeting.

"Hi there, darlin', how're you?" the Chairman responds, smiling hugely; his broad dark coarse-boned Irish/Indian face, at rest a deceptive mask of almost sulky indolence, opens instantly to joyful lust in the smile, then switches just as quickly to raptly interested attention.

The adults chat briefly in their native tongue, then James turns to the daughter. This time the communication of lust is different, more a B-movie-Valentino parody than the real thing.

"How old are you gettin' to be, you cute thing?"

Seventeen, says the girl.

"Damn! You ain't gonna be jailbait much longer, girl. You better watch out; I might come lookin' for you like I did for your momma. You remember that, momma? Me on my Harley, lookin' for a ride?"

"I certainly do, you poor old thing," says Momma. "You didn't get one, though, did you?"

"Ain't that the truth," James sighs, "and now I'm just an old married man." He winks at his wife sitting beside him (she smiles indulgently, obviously an old hand at this particular game), and then he inquires after the health and progress of various members of the lady's family, scoring a good seventy-thirty on correct locations and relationships, if not names. A sister up on the Brighton Reservation is going for her Registered Nurse certificate; an aunt is working the bingo tables in Tampa; a nephew is looking at the Marine Corps and polishing his gator-wrestling skills on the side; another nephew is having trouble staying in touch with his parole officer . . .

Mother and daughter move on. James has time to note that "Yeah, I gotta keep those wimmin interested, keep 'em thinking 'bout me; election's comin' up fast" before his next guest, a tall, skinny, weatherbeaten country hippie type, looms before him. This guy wants to check out the Chief's handmade silver jewelry. While he examines it and makes approving noises, James's eyes travel down his legs and stop at his ankles.

"Bellbottoms!" he exclaims. "All right!"

"Never wear anything but," says the stranger.

"Me neither," says James. "Only kind of pants to wear when you're wrestling gators. You just roll 'em up before you start, and roll 'em down when you're done."

"Where do you find 'em?"

"I got a closet full of 'em. Went around the stores just before they went out of style, bought up two or three hundred pair."

The old hippie laughs delightedly, praises the Chief's foresight, moves on, and is replaced by a personage of entirely different aspect: the pale gray bulk of Steve Blad, the flashiest, the testifyingest, the motivatingest, and far and away the most successful bingo host ever in the history of the whole wide world. Blad, previously an evangelist, is the handsomely paid front man of Seminole bingo, and an individual James Billie holds in the highest professional regard.

You expect thunderbolts, tremors of the holy hip-shaking ear-popping high-stakes Force, but Blad off the job is not even vaguely intense. He just smiles quietly and asks, "Read the paper today?"

No, says James.

"Well, we came out lookin' good. Real good, in fact."

He is referring to a *Miami Herald* article about himself, James, the new bingo hall out at Big Cypress, and the state of Seminole bingo in general. The piece did indeed turn out okay, despite the recent history of Seminole coverage by the Florida press and more specific fears Blad experienced when the *Herald* reporter asked him for his Social Security number and the full name on his birth certificate. "I don't understand," he says. "Why would they want to do a positive piece about us? What's going on? How did they let that get by?"

"Makes you wonder, doesn't it?" says James. "But y'know, I had a good feeling about that reporter. After she ripped us that one time, then came around again, I think she was starting to feel bad about it. . . . It really was good, huh? How'd they handle the Oklahoma thing?"

The "Oklahoma thing" is one of James's problems, an involvement in a bingo operation with the Otoe-Missouria Indians which ended badly after the loss of around a million dollars of the Seminole tribal funds. It was by far the most spectacular failure of James's eight-year chairmanship, and quite obviously it bothers him a lot.

"It was okay," says Blad. "They said you lost the money, but they had you in there talking about learning your lesson. It was fair."

James pauses. "Sonofabitch!" he exclaims quietly. "I ain't never gonna do deals with other Indians again!"

Blad laughs, waves good-bye, and moves on. He's been taking a two-hour vacation, but now he's headed back into a full day and likely most of a full night of organizing and promoting and motivating. Flyers have to be stuck under windshield wipers throughout South Florida, senior citizens' groups must be alerted throughout the nation, buses and airplanes have to be chartered, and his staff needs to be indoctrinated with Faith, Enthusiasm, and a Positive Mental Attitude. Blad has Energy.

The parade past James Billie goes on: a lovely dreaming newborn to be held and cooed over, her future as a young buck's lust object to be speculated on with relish; a fine elkhorn-handled knife to be admired; a deal for next year's festival to be struck with the Apache dancers; a date for a discussion about copyrighting James's song lyrics to be made for tonight; some jovial pleasantries to be exchanged with Cecil Johns, the current president of the Seminole Economic Council, and some more intimate, operational communication to be shared with Jacob Osceola, an ex-marine helicopter door gunner now one of James's inner circle and a candidate for Cecil's job in the upcoming elections; and an equally brief and businesslike exchange, involving the passing of money from the Chairman's pocket, with a split-nosed, barefoot young Indian reeking of grime and alcohol.

And finally, before James goes back to work as master of ceremonies for another round of tribal stomp dancing, his past comes to visit in the person of a gnarled old Indian in a wheelchair. This ancient seems more than a touch standoffish; in fact, his whole being projects barely controlled anger. For his part James is friendly, even charming, but the old man remains aloof as they talk in their native tongue.

Afterward, James explains: "I can afford to be nice to that sonofabitch," he says. "He's the one who worked all the Christianity into our people, got 'em thinking the old ways were sinful; he played it smart, waited till the people were low and scared and confused and guilty, then hit them with all that 'Repent and Ye Shall Be Saved!' shit. And man, that was one tough bastard. He put the moves on me when I was comin' up, did everything he could to keep me down; I've still got the scar he put on my skull."

But now the "sorry-ass bowlegged half-breed" is the Chairman, and the medicine men and the old ways are once again becoming as important to Seminole youth as Christianity and MTV. The old man has reason to be bitter.

"Look at him now," says James, "all twisted up in that chair; look what God gave him to live with. So I'm pleasant with him, I treat him with respect. I used to hate that motherfucker. Now I love him."

❂

Like most of his peers in the Seminole tribe and virtually every other
Native American society, James Billie grew up in the grip of a central
confusion: "Was I a white man, or was I an Indian? I didn't think of it
in those terms—all I knew was that I always felt different—but yeah,
that's what was going on; I just didn't have any idea who the fuck I
was supposed to be." In his case the question was especially relevant;
he was after all a real half-breed, genetically as Irish as he was Indian.

As a kid he wasn't a good student of the things they taught in
school—he spent a great many school days off in the swamps, sling-
shot hunting—but when he was nine, the death of the mother who
had raised him alone had the eventual effect of turning him around.
"It really broke me up," he says. "I really went far down, and when
my grandmother died when I was thirteen, it was the same shit: all
alone, real angry, real sorry for myself. But I had this teacher, Miss
Bird, and she took an interest in this little orphan kid. She taught me
to read. I don't know. Maybe she wouldn't have if I hadn't been an
orphan, so maybe if it hadn't been for my ma dying, I'd still be down
there, still ignorant."

The next great event in his education was of course Vietnam,
where the field skills he'd learned in the Florida swamps added
greatly to both his worth and his survivability as a scout, with subsequent benefits to his self-esteem. Also, his work with Montagnard
tribesmen triggered a new kind of thinking about his Seminole heri-
tage. There on the other side of the globe was a whole separate
society of people still functioning like the Seminoles had before the
whites arrived in Florida. They even built their huts and cooked their
food the same way. Montagnard society would cease to exist after the
Americans left Indochina, eradicated by Pol Pot's murderous regime,
but the intimacy of James's experience with it while it still thrived—a
once-removed but nonetheless very affecting kind of homecoming—
opened his eyes to the potential warmth of a Seminole society built
around rekindled tradition. It also reminded him of a Seminole legend
he had heard as a boy. Before the whites arrived in Florida there had
been other visitors, people who told the Seminoles that one day they
would come back and look into the Indians' eyes. If they saw that

they had taken up the ways of the white man, they would kill them immediately. If on the other hand they saw that they had maintained their own culture, they would leave them in peace.

When he came back from the war, James wanted to "get something started in the tribe." He began at the bottom, as a maintenance man. Apart from the fact that the job was available, the education in politics he had received from prime tribal mover Laura Mae Osceola (whose family took him in after his grandmother died) told him that if maintenance men keep their eyes and ears open, they are in a unique position to learn all sorts of useful things about the landscape of tribal power, the reality of tribal economics, and the location of various leverage-yielding skeletons in the tribal closets. He moved up until he was named the director of the tribe's federally funded Community Youth Corps, then he became an employment specialist in the Manpower program, then he was the administrator of the tribe's show village on the Hollywood Reservation.

Along the way he learned all sorts of stuff about how to run things and whom he was dealing with—"their good habits, their bad habits, their working habits, their piss-poor habits, their criminal habits; everything I needed to know about all twelve hundred of them." Two particular items were seminal to the character who runs the whole store today.

The first he learned in jail, at the end of a period when he'd "gone out on my own." He'd been fishing for a living and his outboard motor had died, so with no cash and no credit and a family to support, he stole a new one and got caught.

"I'd gotten to the point where I really didn't want to be around my own people anymore," he remembers. "It got boring. It wasn't war, it wasn't Vietnam. It was just everyday living, everyday problems. And the biggest of those was something called 'apathy.' Somebody taught my people that they couldn't be anybody or go anywhere. Their mothers had problems, and they probably weren't disciplined, so the poor kids grew up with no guidance, no discipline, no religion, no stories, no nothin'; ended up not even knowing how to boil water. And I got to the point where I didn't even want to know that type of person. They'll drag you down without you even realizing it. And then I didn't want to be no fuckin' bureaucrat anyway, so I got away."

Sitting in jail, though, he realized that he himself was all too similar to the people he'd been trying to get away from: just another dumb Indian, despite all his experience.

"Getting caught like that was probably the best thing that ever happened to put my head in gear," he says now. "It taught me that if you need something, you don't go out like a fool and steal it. You work for it, no matter what it takes—picking up Coke bottles, whatever— or you sit yourself down and learn what it takes to go to a goddam bank and borrow it. So today it don't matter if somewhere down the line someone threw my ass in jail; I've got credit, and when I go to a bank, they know for a fact I'm gonna pay my debts."

Thus enlightened by this personal transcendence of Third World thinking, James returned to work for the tribe when he got out of jail, and he sought out an education in the ways of finance and other areas —insurance, promotion, sociology, psychology, the arts—where a person can't get ahead and influence people if he doesn't "know the language." He kept moving forward.

He doesn't remember exactly when the second great revelation of his leadership career came to him ("Maybe I was riding my Harley, maybe I was taking a shit, who knows?"), but he has full recall of the force of the idea.

"All of a sudden, out of nowhere, it dawned on me: the only thing that's ever going to get me anywhere in my life is my own culture. That's the only thing that's unique about me: my grandma, my grandpa, being a Mikasuki or a Seminole or whatever I am, living that way down to the stinking root of what I am. It doesn't matter if I have to use modern things; as long as I know the stories and I can pass them along to the next generation, I'm doing right. And I'll be goddamned if that has not been my fortune—if not in money, just in mental wealth."

That realization had profound consequences, both on James himself and on the flavor of Seminole life under his leadership, for along with it came a basic diagnosis of what, more than anything, was wrong with his people: "Indians do not want to be Indians. They want to look like what they see in the movies, they want to be the star. They want to be Randolph Scott, the Three Musketeers, John Travolta. But they don't realize the work behind becoming a star. Do they realize when they see a ballerina on TV, doing all those incredible moves, that she can only do them because of practice, practice, practice? Fuck, no! And what's behind that is lack of discipline; three generations of lack of discipline, and three generations of trying to get away from what being an Indian is all about.

"It's like when I was running the village. I got condemned, I got laughed at, people were saying I was stealing all the money. . . . It got to the point where the top-notch people were saying the way to make the village make money was to buy a new cash register; that would surely bring it in. I said, 'Fuck, no it won't! The village needs promotion, and it needs you people acting like what you're supposed to act like. Wear authentic clothes. You say you want to be Indians, but you're wearing Levi's, tennis shoes, cowboy boots, and calling that 'Indian.' It's not. It's just a Westernized look over a brown skin. You're walking around looking like that, and you can't even talk your own language!' Oh, man, that offended their ass. . . ."

James can carry on for hours like this, and indeed he sometimes does. Long into the night beside his campfire at the edge of the swamp, his resentments and dreams and schemes and compassion and cunning tumble together in a wildly alternating current of energy. The man is driven, voracious, almost desperate in his hunger for knowledge, understanding, and wisdom. And he's okay. He's doing well. Most of the time he makes sense, and even when he doesn't, there's little doubt that he really truly gives a damn.

As the necessity for rest makes itself felt in the hunting camp, James reduces himself to a final few essential words: "You know, what I'm trying to do is give my people hope. That's why the fire always has to burn at this camp, even if it's just an ember; to keep the hope alive. So if it just happens to die because a full-blooded Indian sitting out here doesn't respect what that feeling is, I'll call way ahead of time and say, 'I want that fire burning. I want to see smoke going up!'

"I don't know. Maybe that Indian's another hollow man, maybe he'll never know the feeling. But maybe his kids will. On weekends they come in here around me—I use all sorts of different baits to get 'em here—and I tell 'em the stories of their people, try to introduce them to themselves. And really, they're great stories. It's one hellacious culture. Ever since I realized I was a part of it, I've loved every fucking minute of my life."

On a Monday afternoon in South Florida, with the public responsibilities of the Seminole's festival behind him, James Billie is keeping it small, tight, and moving. He and his shadow Brian Cohen have been meeting with representatives of a New York investment house, talking real estate ventures and high-tone Seminole entertainment complexes all morning—James playing the funky-exotic good cop tempting whitebread-weary customers onto Brian's more familiarly sophisticated bad-cop hook—and then he's been home to his Hollywood house to talk on the telephone—stipulating drug tests for his potential new business partners, ordering a probe into a plot of land down the road from the existing show village, eliminating any confusion as to ownership of copyrights on the part of the people producing his new album of Seminole folk songs—and finally he's picked up his hunting dog and his rifle and bought himself a powerful new chain saw. In forty-eight hours he and Cohen will be pointing the tribal Cessna toward Tampa to deal with the BIA about their new hotel operation, and later in the week they'll fly to Sarasota for a concert engagement, but right now they're out on the Big Cypress Reservation, blasting in their pickup truck through a pleasant but infertile landscape of palmetto scrub and trash timber stands and cleared cow pastures and modest mobile homesites occupied by the Seminole rank and file.

The conversation, as usual, is reeling energetically through politics, religion, economics, psychology, philosophy, sociology, history, warfare, sex, whatever, and it happens to be in the realm of marital conflict (James relating, with great amusement and admiration, the time his wife drew down on him with a .38 Special revolver, pulled the trigger on an empty chamber, paused a heartbeat, then kept going hopefully through each of the other five chambers before dropping the gun and turning tail) when suddenly the subject jumps tracks into the area of drugs.

"Ain't that where them boys were landing them drug planes a few years back?" James wonders, indicating a certain unusually flat, unobstructed cow pasture. "Yup, that's it. I remember that thicket right there, see?"

"What happened to them?" I ask.

"Ooooh, they learned better of it. Someone came out here one dark night and caught 'em at it and had a word with them, you might say. They figured it would hurt a lot more if they did it again."

"And who might that someone have been? You?"

The question triggers Brian Cohen's icy guard-dog reflexes; his interjection is instant. "Someone," he says, with a frigid little smile.

James looks at him, eyebrows up in question. Brian looks back, nods affirmatively.

"Right," says James. "Someone. Definitely not me."

Correct. Never in your wildest dreams could you imagine a respectable, mild-mannered administrator like James Billie practicing Bronsonism, sneaking silent through the night to crack skulls and demonstrate the error of antisocial activities.

Now that we're on Seminoles-and-drugs turf, though, we must press forward. Here we have a core issue, a subject intimately connected with the classic twentieth-century Indian biography of dispossession, dependence, depression, alienation, and sporadic lawlessness. Such a drug- and alcohol-aided fate still awaits every young Seminole; it is perhaps the darkest of the clouds James has been trying to burn off the communal horizon ever since he first began lighting fires under his people.

He has had some success: "When I came back from Vietnam in '79, drugs were all over the place. Nowadays I see more clear eyes among my young people. And you know, once we somehow overcame the contraband business on the reservation, the people who'd been threatening my life became my friends. They're the ones who'll come and buy me a cup of coffee, just for the idea of me keeping them alive or something. Then again, sometimes they'll want to slug it out with me—you know, 'Why didn't you let me die? The world's too cold. Goddam, I don't know, I don't know how to feel good.' So I say, 'Let me show you how to build a fire.' That's the beginning of an education. That's the start of teaching them they don't have to be like the people in the goddam TV ads. They can be Indians!"

It's a fact, not just rhetoric. James sticks close to the "low Indians" among his people, does his damnedest to bolster them through the queasy transition from obscure second-class citizenhood to cultural reenrichment and economic dynamism. All the time, amid the deluge of people with whom he has to deal on matters of business and politics and administration, you see him huddled intimately with disoriented young drunks, outlaws of one sort or another, people with fear and pain and lonely defiance in their eyes. He intercedes on their behalf with white and tribal authorities, provides them with work on his personal payroll, holds the paychecks of the most incorrigible drinkers and drug addicts who might otherwise blow a week's wages on just one high.

These relationships have a personal component—James himself does after all know how it feels to go bad, and to be targeted for disdain and discrimination in both the white and Indian worlds—and of course his compassion for the more troubled members of his constituency fits naturally within his overall vision of the tribal future ("It's the hardest thing in the world, bringing a million dollars into a Third World economy"), but the arrangement is also politically intelligent. In return for his help and loyalty, the people James sponsors personally act as his eyes and ears, his message bearers, his grassroots barometers; they will tell him how he's doing, voice the vitriolic gossip and legitimate complaints that accompany the doings of the full-throttle chief and his allies and enemies around the little chickees and bungalows and mobile homes of the reservations. And essentially, while James must of course curry favor or at least avoid provoking united ire among the established hierarchy of the tribe (many of whom lean toward the "sorry-ass bowlegged half-breed" rather than the "great chief" vision of their Chairman), the low Indians are his real power base.

Today for instance, though the primary purpose of his visit to Big Cypress is to patch the hull of his airboat in preparation for a music video to support his record album, James is also on an errand of personal sponsorship. There is a young woman out here who is experiencing hard times in her struggle for a Registered Nurse certificate, and could use some help. Specifically, she could use some household furnishings for the shabby little chickee she's living in; a mattress, a cooker, some pots and pans and stuff. And thus it is that late afternoon finds the fourth-term chairman of the Seminole Council and his personal aide-de-camp picking through the housewares section of a secondhand-everything store in the worn little migrant worker town of Immokalee just north of the reservation.

James does well. He selects solid if not beautiful goods at bargain prices, and loads them on the truck nice and shipshape. Then, singing happily along with the Shirelles on his dashboard radio, he and Brian drive off to buy lunch for the future nurse and her female kin. They spend a pleasant hour or so gathering intelligence from and issuing soft-core sexual flattery to these ladies, then deliver the household goods to the chickee, and finally roar off toward James's hunting camp with the feeling of a job well done. "Voters," says James with a wink.

●

The airboat hull has now been patched, a tedious operation conducted in the day's dying light and featuring more than occasional bearishness on James's part, and now it's time for rest and recreation.

Which unsurprisingly is not a tranquil affair. James and Brian suit up in warm clothing, load their rifles, summon their hunting dog, and go roaring and laughing through the thick dark landscape, screaming dirty jokes at each other over the unsilenced blast of their homebuilt Road Warrior ATV's big-block Chevy. They find no sign of interesting wildlife, hog or bear or what have you, but no matter. They return happily to camp in the wee hours, and James settles in: sits by the fire, grills some bass and mudfish, plays some guitar, entertains us with tales of legends and ghosts and plots and pussy and caretaker corporations and combat.

And there in the firelight this crafty, competent carnival of a man who holds the welfare of Florida's natives in his hands pauses in mid-description of the feats of a warrior forebear and reflects on his own approach to leadership.

"I love challenges, I love trouble," he growls. "If the bombs are dropping, the bullets flying, the gossip goin' around, my wife beatin' the shit out of me, people tryin' to stab me in the back, I know something's happening, I know I'm doing my goddam job. 'Cause you see, I'm what my people need, man; I'm a fuckin' troublemaker, and I'm having a ball.

"And I'll tell you something else," he says from the center of his old-time alive and dangerous Seminole self. "If you're comin' after me, boy, I'll give you a little advice. You'd better finish the job. You see me go down, you'd better be damn sure I'm dead before you walk away."

2

The Aquamaids

Nancy and Lisa and I are zooming happily across the limpid sundrenched surface of lovely Lake Eloise, the thick soft breeze in our hair, the sleek powerful little Mastercraft responding perfectly, the stately old cypress swamps and million-dollar homes blurring smoothly past ashore, the other Lisa—Lisa Voisard, the star today—gorgeous and graceful in our wake, a fine bright cover-girl pearl set in the oyster shell of spume kicked up by her swivel ski. Oh, my. This is the life. At a moment like this, a person has no trouble understanding why he moved to Florida.

Let's savor that thought, linger on its stimuli.

The sunshine, of course, needs little comment except a statement of the obvious: the sun shines more on Florida than other places, promoting green subtropical abundance, the casting off of restrictive clothing, the building of swimming pools and "Florida rooms" from which its benevolence can be enjoyed in coolish comfort, the taking of a certain ease, and the overall availability of, well, warm feelings. In a world of trouble, the great dome of a clear blue sky can render the same service as that often ascribed to the realization of imminent death. It can clear the mind most wonderfully.

That goes for the water, too. We need say nothing about the amply advertised appeal of beachfront property on Florida's fourteen hundred miles of semitropical Atlantic Ocean and Gulf of Mexico coastline, but perhaps we do need to remind the reader that Florida is also a place of inlets and bayous and rivers and lakes, thousands of lakes. Infinite acres of inland shoreline pleasure.

Lake Eloise, the location of our pleasure today, is fairly typical, a shining blue-green dimple, forty feet deep in its center and fourteen miles in circumference, which receives its water from rainfall drainage and shares it with thirteen other lakes in its Central Florida chain, sending it eventually through the limestone layers of the Floridan Aquifer southward to Lake Okeechobee and the Everglades.

Eloise is beautiful, and beautifully framed. The houses on the large lots on its banks—here a carefully angular aqua-colored contemporary stucco showpiece, there a smoked glass and cedar A-frame abutting a pristine all-white antebellum mansion across rich smooth St. Augustine lawn grass curving downward into a stand of four- or five-hundred-year-old cypress trees—are aesthetic additions to, not subtractions from, the gentle grace of the land and waterscape. With their little boat docks and expansive swimming pools and lovingly tended landscaping, Eloise's dwellings murmur a convincing testament to the rightness of what every red-blooded American knows it's Really All About: the goal achieved, a fortune (not necessarily enormous) amassed, a home and a lifestyle very close indeed to heaven right here on earth. Mostly the lucky homeowners are mature people, Yankee-corporate noblemen and retired physicians and self-made Florida boom-boosters and the like, but there are some younger folk. Several Cincinnati Reds baseball players live on Eloise, as do a couple of families rumored to have realized their dream in the wholesale end of the recreational drug business.

So yes, leisured contemporary upper-middle-class perfection ashore, and out here on the water something else that's powerfully desirable.

Just look at these women, two in the boat and one on the slalom ski behind: firm swimsuited bodies, golden tans, clear vital eyes, the casual athletic confidence of Lisa Jackson's driving, Nancy Daley's vigilance at the ski mast, Lisa Voisard's seemingly effortless mastery of backbreaking water ballet. Here is not a model's or starlet's beauty, but a less conventional, more individually characteristic glow, health and muscle tone and competence and spirit shining through. They're wonderful women, these: America's best, the very incarnation of life as it ought to be. They could make you move to Florida in a heartbeat, or at least bring you back again to visit.

And that's exactly as it should be, for although these women and this place are one hundred percent real—they're working women, and Eloise is a more or less typical Central Florida lake—they're also a very special kind of illusion. They're a lure. They're a living advertisement, a beacon whose light has shone from Florida into the winter darkness of the world for more than forty years. They are the fabled Cypress Gardens Aquamaids.

○

The Aquamaids are exceptional, all right, but Cypress Gardens, two hundred and twenty-three acres on Eloise's eastern shore, is unique.

Today perhaps it seems normal, a corporately owned theme park distinguished from its many competitors only by the nature of its theme, a combination of Southern-plantation ambiance, exotic gardens, and athletic entertainments as opposed to giant mice or high technology or head-spinning rides or African animals or baseball. When you visit Cypress Gardens, then, you go expecting just about what you'd expect from Disneyland in Anaheim or Opryland in Nashville or Busch Gardens fifty miles away in Tampa—cleanliness, efficiency, photo opportunities, overpriced fast food served by college students and senior citizens, oodles of sublimely undemanding family entertainment, some mildly interesting insights into worlds you don't often visit, maybe a few real thrills, and eventually the awareness of very sore feet ameliorated by a distinct sense of accomplishment. And unless you're somehow attuned to wavelengths beyond the usual well-trafficked leisure-time frequencies, that's exactly what you get. Cypress Gardens comes through for you nicely.

If on the other hand you are a themeologist, or a Florida historian, or a professor of public relations, or if you possess the kind of sensibility that finds the careers of creators like Michael Deaver and Colonel Tom Parker and Walt Disney more enlightening than those of products such as Ronald Reagan and Elvis Presley and Mickey and the gang, your experience of Cypress Gardens is likely to take on the flavor of a pilgrimage.

Cypress Gardens, you see, is not just the farthest-flung outpost in Harcourt Brace Jovanovich's strategy of ringing the mighty tourist magnet of the Disney World/Epcot Center complex with competing/benefiting entertainment emplacements (in HBJ parlance, "Surrounding the Mouse"). It is, rather, the original. It predates not just Disney World and any other Central Florida theme park, but Disneyland in California and the term "theme park" itself. In fact, it predates even the phenomenon of tourism in Florida.

In further fact, a very good case can be made for the proposition that Cypress Gardens actually created that phenomenon; that rather than being just the first large-scale Florida institution designed expressly to help tourists spend their vacation money once in the locality, the original sixteen acres on the banks of Lake Eloise were what began drawing Yankees and foreigners and the like to the state in the first place. Which is why Cypress Gardens' founder, Mr. Dick Pope—whose mortal remains should by rights be disinterred and either enshrined in the lobby of the state capitol or cast anonymously into what's left of the natural swamps, depending on your point of view—lived and died in full and righteous sole ownership of the title "Mr. Florida."

He was of course not born with that honorable handle, and before he acquired it, a cynical Florida press bestowed upon him some considerably less flattering characterizations. "Swami of the Swamp," for instance, and "The Barnum of Botany" and "Maestro of Muck."

In a way, you can't really blame those long-dead copy hacks, for what Pope was attempting, the enhancement of a typical middle-of-nowhere Central Florida lakeshore to the point where people would actually travel significant distances and hand over real money to view it, was at that time a notion verging beyond optimism into lunacy, for (1) Who cared about swamps, except to eliminate the damn things so you could farm or build or otherwise make a living? and (2) Who would pay to see something they could drive half a mile off any

Central Florida highway and see for free? Add these arguments to the accumulated history of the private-sector swamp drainage and land development businesses in Florida at that time, basically a story of a few minor successes overwhelmed by a long litany of bankruptcies and broken hearts that culminated in the godawful real estate crash of the late 1920s, and you had a quite convincing portrait of just another fool.

But Dick Pope was no ordinary fool. For one thing, his basic vision made perfect sense under the prevailing circumstances ("For the last 10 years it has been rather hard to sell a visitor $5,000 or $10,000 worth of Florida," he wrote, "so now we are going to sell 10,000 of them 25 cents' worth"), and moreover the idea had at least one commercially successful antecedent; Pope had read in *Good Housekeeping* about a man making good money by throwing open the gardens of his family home to the public at a quarter a head. And then, too, he himself had qualities and experience beyond the norm, assets ideally suited to his task. His father was a realtor in Winter Haven, and he and his brother were competitive power-boat racers on the local lake chain when they were teenagers, and being the kind of person he was, he had taken more than the usual degree of interest in both fields. From hanging around his father's office he had learned to wheel and deal, and in power-boat racing he had learned how to stage events. To which education, being the person he was, he added the magic ingredient that would make him, Cypress Gardens, and his tourist-heaven good-life vision of Florida complete: an uncanny instinct—nay, a *genius*—for the effective application of promotional and public relations techniques.

Consider for instance the man's most significant single insight into the getting-the-word-out business, the formula which he invented and which became the cornerstone of Cypress Gardens' and a lot of other people's and places' fame: OPM Squared, or Our Photographic Materials times Other People's Money.

The fact that Mr. Pope chose to make a quick-quip formula out of this idea, and to bandy it about with as much glee as he did, tells you something about the man (that he really, genuinely, shamelessly enjoyed his work). So does the zeal with which he practiced what he preached. The basic idea was simplicity itself—rather than paying for advertising, you stage some outrageous or dangerous or supercute or star-studded stunt, then you photograph it, and then you send out the resulting pictures to newspaper and magazine and moving-picture editors only too glad to have something free and fun to run on slow or gloomy news days. Its manifestations were wondrous in their variety, ingenuity, and complexity, the products of a truly unique and supercharged imagination.

The Mr. Florida stories are legends now, told and retold for decades by awestruck PR persons and appreciative journalists and other delighted aficionados of pomp and cunning and illusion: how Dick Pope never tired of crowning beauty queens against the backdrop of his exotic gardens, inviting all comers and even inventing new thrones for the young lovelies to occupy if he'd exhausted the existing market, always making damn sure that the location of the resulting drab-day pictures appeared in their captions; how he was always finding novel poses for the girls, against a mound of "twenty-seven thousand, three hundred and eighty-three" grapefruit (in a typical touch, he made that number up) or skiing across Lake Eloise while he tickled the ivories of a barge-borne grand piano, keeping pace with the lovely young things; how he wasn't content with any old water-skiing show but demanded the best there possibly could be, constantly pushing the athletes he attracted to advance the sport into uncharted waters, to stage new stunt after photogenic new stunt and set world record after headline-grabbing new world record; how he thought small as well as big, pioneering the use of giveaway promotional placemats and arranging for exactly the kind of plantings a film or TV crew wanted in their backgrounds after he'd enticed them to shoot their features and specials and series episodes in his gorgeous made-over swamp; how for the paying customers all that press drew into his kingdom he provided "photo directors" to suggest optimal views and angles and even exposure settings so that when the folks got home and gave their Sunday night slide shows, blurred, badly composed pictures of other places would frame images of Cypress Gardens as perfect as postcards; how he always took and made his staff take "citrus breaks" instead of coffee breaks, and insisted they dress as he did like Joe Tourist in floral shirts and lurid jackets and plaid pants, and how he convinced local weathercasters to refer to overcast days as "partly sunny" instead of "partly cloudy"; how he spewed out thousands of letters of invitation to celebrities and wrung every ounce of publicity from the visits of those who accepted, persuading Carol Burnett and Johnny Carson and King Hussein of Jordan, though not King Edward VII or Wallace Simpson or the Shah of Iran ("There's no business like Shah business," he told the reporters) to ski for his cameras with the Aquamaids; how, understanding the paramount importance of the associations he must encourage in the public mind *(Cypress Gardens* meant *sunshine* meant *water* meant *beautiful wholesome women* meant *THE GOOD LIFE!* meant *FLORIDA!!!),* he chose Esther Williams as the one public figure whose endorsement could say it all, and got her; pestered her until she made the trip from Hollywood, worked tirelessly on her once she entered his domain, photographed her everywhere she went, talked her into making not one but two full-length movies at Cypress Gardens (1948's *On an Island with You* and *Easy to Love* in 1953), and finally, when she turned the tables on him and agreed to make a TV special that would cement the connection only if he would build her a special swimming pool as good or better than the one she had in Hollywood, he went ahead and did that too.

These transactions show you that the man was tireless and that he would go to any lengths, and their final outcome shows you more: that he really, *really* knew his business. Once Ms. Williams had talked him into the project, you see, the pool he built for her was of the specified depth and dimensions, and it had the required underwater camera ports—everything was perfect, just what the star had ordered —but it was also something else. Dick Pope had built it in the shape of the place of your dreams, the balmy and beautiful Sunshine State of Florida you owed it to yourself to see. And of course, naturally, that lovely exotic pool itself (and therefore Cypress Gardens, the good life, and Florida) turned out to be the real star of the show. Filled with healthy young women and tanned young men, set in a corona of bright beautiful flowering shrubs, shaded by mighty moss-draped cypresses rising from the rim of the gentle lake into which it thrust just as the peninsula after which it was modeled caressed the waters of the semitropical seas, that pool was an enormously seductive image.

So certainly Dick Pope was a genius, and obviously he was a great success. Cypress Gardens' status as Florida's prime inland tourist lure was not surpassed until the building of Disney World, which Pope himself had enticed to Central Florida, in the 1970s.

Equally obviously, he was what they call a character. Something of a fanatic, definitely an obsessive, a man absolutely absorbed by the strategies and details of his dream. When he built his office, for instance, he built it without windows, which might distract him from his work—but he was also a man absolutely in love with his dream made real, so finding himself unable to live without looking upon it when he wanted to, he had a periscope installed through the roof above his desk. Such was the intensity of the energy this five-foot-five cannonball spent on the broad strokes and tiny touches which made Cypress Gardens so peculiarly magnificent and magnificently peculiar (those Southern Belle hostesses, for instance, sitting out there on those sunny lawns cool as cucumbers in ninety-five-degree heat because—ha!—cool air from hidden blowers was circulating beneath their picture-perfect hooped skirts) that he didn't even seem affected by the sedatives with which his long-suffering staff would occasionally lace his drinking water.

Dick Pope was everywhere in Cypress Gardens. He knew everything and everyone. He had and he needed the personal touch. Every morning for years he would leave the house he'd built next door to the park and drive around Winter Haven picking up members of his cleaning staff who didn't have other transportation to their jobs. The cleaners appreciated that, and in general people who worked for him appreciated him in all his manic but friendly glory. Cypress Gardens veterans have mixed feelings about his wife, Julie—her very significant contributions to the operation were, it seems, made without perfect interpersonal grace—but the tone of their memories of the man himself is unambiguous: genuine affection spiced with a certain awe. His death in 1987 was felt as a real loss.

The losses, though, began well before then. The Dick Pope of history began disappearing into senility as he and the century approached their eightieth year. Control of his dream passed to his son Dick Jr., a man who could not be expected to, and didn't, care for

Cypress Gardens with the all-consuming passion of his father. Dick Jr. sold the whole shebang to Harcourt Brace Jovanovich in 1985.

Today, although Harcourt Brace has expanded and smartened Cypress Gardens—now you can dine well there if you wish, sip "speciality drinks" and eat designer ice cream, see more shows and buy more souvenirs and walk wider paths among more flowers and birds and animals, more everything—and although the company public relations tone hardly matches the wit and flamboyance of the original owner (the contemporary version of a keep-'em-drooling press kit punch line being "In 1988 Cypress Gardens will continue revitalization development where we feel those additions will further enhance the park for visitor enjoyment"), the place remains essentially as Dick Pope made it.

One part of it isn't, though. If you walk through the turnstiles into the park and go down the hill toward Lake Eloise, then branch right behind the ski show's North Stadium and the scenic cruise's boat docks, then walk through the green mood-music miasma of the densely foliated little old paths nearest the water's edge, you can find the appropriate signs. If you follow them carefully—they don't exactly shout at you, and because this is now a relatively untraveled section of Cypress Gardens, you probably won't have other eager tourists to follow—you will end up at Dick Pope's crowning promotional achievement, that cunning and beautiful Florida-shaped swimming pool.

And there you may be disappointed. From where you stand it doesn't look like much at all. You're at ground level, for one thing, and the color postcards and moving-picture images of this place were always shot from above, from just exactly the right Pope-directed angles—but that's not all that's wrong.

If you step over the mildewed red velvet rope separating you from the Gardens' great old symbol, you'll find the pool itself in sorry shape indeed. Twigs and leaves and algae discolor the water which used to shine so purely blue, and there are sections of broken tile around the rim; if the pool were really Florida seen from your space vehicle, St. Augustine and the Naples area and almost all the Keys would look like earthquake sites. The whole state would seem wild

and uncared for, reclaimed by nature after some disease or apocalypse dropped the curtain on its human Good Life glory days.

You can react however you wish to this neglect. Perhaps you'll
ponder with some regret the passing of the more spontaneous, eccen-
tric, individualistic days of show business, or find it somehow sad that
a Florida-shaped swimming pool is no longer an item thought worthy
of proprietary boasts and public wonder. Personally, I just think that
the HBJ management's neglect is in poor taste. Does Dick Pope's
memory not deserve the minor expense of a new tile job, a daily
cleaning?

Such are my thoughts as I stand a foot away from the ruins of Mr.
Florida's most alluring illusion, listening to the whine of mosquitoes
and the subliminal syrup of some Muzaked melody oozing at me from
the greenery. But you can't have everything, can you, and the symbolic shame of this one little crime is not very significant. From out on
Lake Eloise the bubbling roar of a Mastercraft's 454 Chevy going to
three-quarters throttle and a quick flash of tanned thighs and spangled
swimsuits through the cypresses to my left—*The Aquamaids!!!!*—
remind me quite emphatically that some things at Cypress Gardens
are just as they should be, and better than ever.

It is said that the notion of waterskiing as entertainment at Cypress
Gardens was not the inspiration of Mr. Florida, but of his wife Julie. It
was she who was running things on that day during World War Two
when a group of soldiers showed up at the Gardens expecting to see
people being towed behind boats in the manner depicted by a publicity picture Dick Pope had distributed to promote his power-boat racing shows on Lake Eloise. The picture was old, circulated long before
he went off to contribute to the war effort, but like many of his
exercises in the art of OPM Squared, it was still being published here
and there.

The soldiers were disappointed, then, but not for long. If they
wanted waterskiing, they'd get it. Julie told them to go off and enjoy
themselves in the Gardens for an hour or two, then collected her kids
and some of their friends as they got out of school, put them on skis,
and voilà! One ski show.

It was a hit, a big one. The next weekend eight *hundred* GIs came looking for this novel spectacle, and went away happy. And that was that. Julie ran her family ski shows every weekend for the duration of the war, and then Mr. Florida came home and started giving them his kind of business. The ski show went Big Time. Clear-eyed, muscular young men were recruited and trained and motivated. Fearless stunts, feats no ski-borne person had ever performed before, were staged and publicized. Incredible innovations, new technologies, and ever-higher standards for the summer-vacation skiers of the nation to aspire to were introduced and publicized. World records were attempted and achieved and publicized. Clear-eyed, firm-bodied young women, recruited and trained and motivated on a par with the males, exhibited strength and courage and grace, such grace; their swivel stunts and water ballets were the wonder of the age.

These women, these Aquamaids, were a new breed. As bold as they were beautiful, the soft curves of their fine young swimsuited bodies out there on the water enduring strains few red-blooded males would accept, they were strong and free and unabashed in their competence. Amelia Earhart would have approved of them wholeheartedly; Esther Williams did; so did a whole generation of American women who had learned that the ability to build airplanes and rivet armor plate and support a family just as well as the man across the breakfast table did not in any way detract from their femininity. The Cypress Gardens Aquamaids were living proof that it could all be done with consummate womanly grace.

Goodies for the goose, then, and also for the gander. To the man across the breakfast table the Aquamaids were athletes, but they were also show girls, inheritors of the chorus line's bright erotic menu of almost-matching moving parts, the girl on the flying trapeze's tantalizing gypsy mystery. The Aquamaids may have been wholesome, but they were also very sexy. They were respectable pinups, titillation with taste.

It is no wonder, then, that as Cypress Gardens became the (quite accurately) self-titled "Water Ski Capital of the World," the image of its female skiers shone from daily newspapers and magazine covers and newsreel clips to tell the whole wide 1950s world how fine life could be in the vital, youthful, health-and-life-giving Sunshine State.

No other group ever matched them as advertisements for the best of the Good Life in the planet's supreme, richest, and most joyful Union.

Today, times having changed and American waters having muddied and Dick Pope's publicity mania having expired along with him, the Aquamaids reign no longer as the popularly accepted apotheosis of Floridian-American female allure (Who does? Those two pistol-packin' *mamacitas* on *Miami Vice*? Donna Rice? Jessica Hahn? Roxanne Pulitzer?). In the mainstream consciousness of the world or even the United States, Cypress Gardens' waterwomen are almost, in fact, obscure: incidental attractions included in the gate price of a theme park too far off the beaten superhighway to rank second or even third in Florida's expanding arsenal of major tourist lures.

While the power of the Aquamaids' image has faded, however, their reality hasn't. The thing is, you see, that Cypress Gardens really is the Water Ski Capital of the World, its four-times-daily show really is the Greatest American Ski Show, and the Aquamaids really are the female royalty of the sport. In the ski world they are, in the vernacular of the moment, hot. The hottest.

The power of their immediate impact, what happens to you when you first see them even if you know nothing of the lore and legends and glories they embody, has not faded either. When you sit by the side of Lake Eloise and watch a lovely banner-bearing line of them sweep suddenly across the water in front of you during the first moments of the Greatest American Ski Show, or watch them monkeying up over the shoulders of their male colleagues to proudly stand where very few women have stood before, to crown the show and the Gardens' spectacular four-tiered human pyramid skiing a triumphant circle before your eyes, you're likely to experience the kind of reactions which have been moving Cypress Gardens audiences for over four decades now. You're probably going to realize that no matter what your TV tells you, these women really are the cream, the best modern Florida can do, and then you're going to wonder who they really are.

❂

On a white-hot mid-August morning Cypress Gardens is filling up with its summer people, mostly adults and older children, many of them

Brits and Germans and other Europeans flown into Orlando on pack-age-tour intercontinental shuttles (the Yankees and old folks and little children show up in the winter, when heatstroke threatens less). Aquamaid Lisa Voisard has just given her first performance of the day. Now she is sitting in the bleachers of the empty North Ski Stadium facing the protected circle of Lake Eloise's water in which the Greatest American Ski Show is performed, and talking about the basic facts of the Aquamaid life.

Lisa is no ordinary Aquamaid, if indeed any Aquamaid can be said to be ordinary. A five-year veteran and Florida native who has per-formed every part in the ski show and is married to the show's direc-tor, she is the outcome of my request to the Cypress Gardens public-ity department for an exemplar of the waterwoman species. I wanted their best shot.

She'll do. Lisa is petite, tight, tanned to tasteful near-perfection, and of course spectacularly healthy. She is beautiful in a perky, peppy sort of way: medium-length red-brunette hair pinned up above her neck, alert green eyes set into a rounded face above a straight but still perky nose, and a wide, perfectly sculpted set of flashing snow-white testaments to American oral hygiene. She looks younger than her age, which is twenty-five. She wears a canary-yellow one-piece swim-suit cut high over the hip but otherwise quite modest by the stan-dards of the day. Everything about her appearance sings *Youth! Vim! Vitality!* to an upbeat all-American melody.

She's a pro at the interview game, or at least a person utterly unacquainted with the phenomenon of reticence. She talks up a storm, needs hardly any prompting at all, and so we get the basic Aquamaidly facts covered in moments. There are some twenty full- or part-time Aquamaids here, from all over the country and aged sixteen to forty, but let's get it straight that they're not really "Aquamaids," they're "skiers." They're at varying skill levels, but if they're going to stick around, they all have to learn all the jobs and tricks in the show (which means, among other things, that the work never gets boring). And yes, it is indeed dangerous out there on the water, and they get injured a lot, but they put their all into being extremely fit and safety-conscious to a T, so the accident rate isn't nearly as bad as it could be. Yes, they're a team, and despite little problems and rivalries they work things out and help each other and enjoy themselves. And yes, oh *yes*, they do indeed love the job, they know how lucky they are to have made it to the top of the crest of the water-skiing wave, but no, you can't get rich being a Cypress Gardens skier.

Okay. All this having been communicated efficiently, we move briskly on to more personal, individual information.

It turns out that this officially typical representative is, most untypically, an accidental Aquamaid. Her inclusion in Cypress Gardens' elite fold was the result of a coincidence of time and place. Lisa had in fact never even been on water skis, let alone aspired to the professional pinnacle of the sport, when her future boss and husband-to-be Mark Voisard enrolled in her Winter Haven Jazzercise classes, observed her form (such grace, such athleticism, such a finely tuned sense of balance), thought he saw a ski queen in embryo, and made her a coaching offer she decided not to refuse.

In other ways, though, Lisa really is an exemplar of Aquamaid-American virtues. Born into a good steady three-child middle-class family (young dad a lifetime-career manager for the Publix supermarket chain, young mom an expert and committed mother/housewife) in a good respectable land-o'-plenty upper-middle-class town (Venice, down on Florida's southwest Gulf coast), she was raised in a spirit encouraging security, competence, initiative, and confidence. She would believe implicitly in the ideas such advantaged American homes produce: that competitiveness is a healthy attribute as long as it is softened by compassion and cooperation, that hard work will bear fruit, that nothing is gained if nothing is ventured. She acquired the personality profile of the high achiever.

Her school career matched that profile. She achieved better than average academic grades and star status as an athlete and cheerleader, and at home there was no teenage rift between parents and child. Lisa's father, whose athletic ambitions had been stifled by his own parents, was proud and happy for her, exceptionally supportive, and she in turn helped him combat the effects of encroaching middle age in a sedentary job by taking him jogging with her and monitoring him through a safely progressive regimen of exercise. Later, her father was there for her even though she was following her own lights rather than his vision of her path through life. When she concluded that a career with Publix was not for her (she tried it but hated it), it was he who lent her the money to buy a Jazzercise franchise and establish her own business. Predictably, he had invested wisely. She payed him back as soon as her venture began to turn a profit.

Outstanding, then, a good girl here—no drug problems, teenage pregnancies or runaway attempts or week-long silences, no purple hair or biker boyfriends, not even a speech pattern peppered with "like . . ."s and "y'know . . ."s. Definitely a good girl, perhaps even a goody-goody girl. Well, maybe not; maybe just highly motivated young maturity, a strong streak of perfectionism at work.

Perhaps it was these qualities that made Lisa's first weeks at Cypress Gardens uncomfortable. She had a long way to go before mastering the art and science of show skiing, and she didn't like it one little bit that at the beginning she'd be falling on her face doing tricks the other girls could accomplish in their sleep. Neither did she enjoy the fact that after an athletic and social career of distinction and leadership, she was not just the new girl in school, but the teacher's pet. Mark Voisard was taking more than the usual degree of interest in this novice, and that probably rankled the other skiers; Lisa recalls that they didn't go out of their way to be friendly toward her, and they didn't help her learn her way around the ski rope. Many nights she went home crying, confused and lonely, thinking she'd made a major mistake. She almost quit.

She didn't, though. She was a fast learner. Motivated partly by an I'll-show-'em attitude stronger than her sense of social isolation and partly by the thrill of progressive athletic achievement, she worked overtime, arriving early and leaving late and practicing at every opportunity during the workday, and mastered one trick after another until she wasn't just any old Aquamaid but a Skier One, the highest grade of Cypress Gardens ski performer. She could be given any job in the show, from Corkette the clown to solo Swan, and do it as well as or better than any other girl on the payroll. She got where she needed to be.

She also married the boss. All the time she and Mark spent together over ski instruction and pizza and drinks after work had seemed innocent enough (the fact that she had a longtime boyfriend in Lakeland and Mark had a girlfriend on the ski staff at the Gardens encouraged the illusion), but it wasn't really. Something was sneaking up on them, and one day Mark raised the stakes of their relationship dramatically by venturing the thought that maybe they should go look for a ring.

Lisa had to do a lot of thinking about that. Here was her boss, an older man, successful, with a house of his own and a good salary. Was it these things, power and money and security, to which she was attracted? Also she was now a skier, already beginning to feel a sense of removal from normal-world people, like for instance her boyfriend. Could that be the nature of the bond between them? Or was she, well, in love?

She decided it was okay, she *was* in love, and the other attractions just added to it. She informed her boyfriend and her parents of the imminent wedding plans and weathered the consequent storms, and then she and Mark spoke the vows, and then she moved into his modest but valuable little house on lakefront property in Winter Haven. From their first meeting to Mark's suggestion about the ring, only six weeks had elapsed. Marrying Mark was the most impulsive thing young Lisa Hopkins had ever done.

Mark and Lisa, still living in Mark's little house but planning to build Lisa's dream home on another, larger lakefront lot they already own thanks to the profit-sharing payoffs they received when HBJ bought the Gardens, are parents now. Lisa skied until she began to show at five months (nothing in Cypress Gardens' policy prevents that), and she exercised all the way up to delivery day. She didn't enjoy the last four months at all because she had to work in nonathletic Gardens jobs like selling T-shirts—boy, was *that* a drag; almost as bad as the Publix deli department. And then, like most Aquamaids, who are accustomed to clenching their pelvic muscles as tightly as possible while hanging on to that ski rope, she had a long and hard labor. She had wanted a spinal block when her time came, but they wouldn't give her one, so her predominant memory of her son Jason's birth is one of an agony that made the pains of her previous and subsequent athletic injuries seem like pinpricks. She's not sure she's willing to go through that kind of torment again.

Jason is in preschool now, a bright kid doing very well, and Lisa is a part-time rather than a full-time Aquamaid, facing the challenges of working motherhood. She's getting plenty of chances to allow her perfectionist urge to trouble her life. She wants to be the best skier and the best mother and the best housekeeper too, and it's hard. Sometimes it feels like there's just not enough time in any day; often when she's at the Gardens she finds herself thinking about things she has to do at home, and vice versa. She and Mark are both very busy people; they both give ski lessons in addition to everything else, and Mark also runs a one-man lawn-care service. Lisa does the family bookkeeping; she's good at that, has an organized kind of mind, and thinks of it as training for the as yet undefined kind of accountancy or bookkeeping she will probably take up as a profession when her days as a skier are over. Her life, then, is hectic.

Still, she knows she's blessed. She's gotten to be one of the gang, for one thing, and for another, the whole gang's spirits have improved —for some reason, helpfulness and friendliness among all the skiers has come to be more the norm than it was when she arrived—and so her job has become very pleasant. Working as a Cypress Gardens skier does of course mean *working,* as in punching the clock in the North Stadium and putting in the hours and drawing the paycheck and being responsible, but really, in many ways it's just like being a kid again. You get to do things you really like to do, and you have lots of special friends who really like to do them with you, and on top of all that, people are impressed. The crowds cheer and think you're really neat. You get to travel with the Gardens' road show to exotic places where sheikhs and kings and lords and ladies admire your form and shower you with precious gifts.

There are many ways of stating the basic attractiveness of Lisa's job and explaining the high morale of the skiers. Lynn Novakofski, the Gardens' laconic entertainment director, does it one way in his office —"Oh, sure, the skiers are a pretty happy bunch. These are athletes, you see, and they've got a very healthy job in the open air with a good group of people who are all in great shape, so they *should* be happy" —and as I wander around the North Stadium, I'm treated to a cornucopia of variously articulated employee satisfaction.

The statement I like best, even if it may not be universally true, particularly in the case of older skiers, is the simplest. A nineteen-year-old novice Aquamaid stands tanned and healthy and barefoot and swimsuited in the Florida sun, squinting to watch her friends' form as they practice new ski choreography on Eloise, and says, "You know, they don't really need to pay us to do this. We'd probably pay *them* to let us."

❋

Lisa conducts a tour of the workplace, beginning with the costume room at the south end of the North Stadium. This is where the red-white-and-blue show costumes are dried between shows, and it's all business; the costumes go in wet, they come out dry. To Lisa's mind that's not a lot of fun, and kind of silly too, because before HBJ bought the park the skiers had more costumes than they do now—each girl who worked a star solo spot in the show had at least three unique outfits made especially for her, for instance—so they got to feel pretty more often, and moreover the costumes didn't have to be dried between shows, so management didn't have to pay the salary of a person to organize the drying.

But that's corporate cost-cutting for you, and red-white-and-blue costumes do after all make a lot of sense when you're billing the Greatest *American* Ski Show. It's even okay that the ice show, an HBJ addition, gets all the glitter these days, because unlike the skiers, the poor stiffs working *that* show have to perform ten or more times a day, playing the same role in an entertainment which hasn't changed in over a year now, so they deserve whatever perks they can get. The skiers don't like it much when they have to fill in over at the ice house, which from time to time they do, but at least they have the North Stadium and some excitement to come home to. Despite the greater promotion power HBJ puts into its newer attractions, the skiers are still the royalty of the Gardens' athletes.

From the costume room we move along the corridor which runs the length of the stadium, stopping to view photo portraits of boat drivers and Skiers of the Year ancient and modern (males mostly candid, females all winningly a-ski), and then we visit the crucial spaces. The massage/whirlpool room, home of the very necessary in-house weight-trainer/masseur. The office of hubby-boss Mark Voisard and those of the male and female skiers' other leaders. The ski room, containing many very valuable skis (six hundred dollars and up for a 360-degree swivel job) and miles of carefully cut, lengthened, and maintained ski rope. The supply closet, rich in sunblock. The boat drivers' room. The Ready Room, repository of the vital refrigerator and popcorn machine and microwave and TV/VCR and the even more vital couch and washer/dryer. Being a male/female pair, we visit neither the boys' nor the girls' dressing rooms.

We have now reached the north end of the corridor and are about to emerge into daylight to tour the boat dock and the weight-training spaces under the South Stadium, but Lisa glances at her watch and— "Yikes!"—she has a date with a practice boat. Off she goes.

A couple of items from our tour beckon interestingly. One is a large photo taped to Mark's office door: the only five-tiered human ski pyramid ever accomplished in the history of the world, seventeen people pulled by one boat, the girls alone weighing one thousand and seventy-four pounds. The five-tier will never be a regular feature of the show because it's just too hard, it takes so much longer than a four-tier to build and disassemble again, but my, it's impressive. That's show business you're looking at there, buddy. Dick Pope would have loved it, and perhaps in his honor—certainly in his tradition—they did it right. After the deed was accomplished, they measured and quantified everything (the girls' weight being just the tip of the iceberg) for public consumption: how many feet of rope, how many knots, the works.

The other big attraction is the boat drivers' room. It appeals because while Cypress Gardens skiers come and go, Cypress Gardens boat drivers go on forever. Partly this is because the men behind the wheel don't have to operate at the skiers' level of athleticism (though it helps if they have steel kidneys), and so they don't have to retire as early in life. Mainly, though, it's because experience and consistency in the operation of the show boats is vital to accident-free, correctly timed and judged and executed performances. Management knows this, so it works hard to hold on to veterans and has succeeded quite well. Of the five drivers hauling Lisa and her friends around Lake Eloise, only one has been at his job less than five years, and a couple of them go back to Dick Pope days.

As fortune would have it, the veteran of veterans, Mr. James Campbell, is in the drivers' room when we stop by. So is Mr. Mike Markowitz, the Gardens' longest-serving show announcer. Perhaps these gentlemen will tell us some stories.

Or perhaps not. Jimmy, here since '66, is a nonverbal type, and Mike seems a tad cagey, so the talk has a general-knowledge kind of flavor to it. We learn that Dick Pope was of course very personable and a real smart feller; he brought Walt Disney to Florida, you know, and wasn't it something how those Disney people bought all that land cheap, without ever once letting the cat out of the bag about who they were and what they wanted it for? And sure, Cypress Gardens gets along fine in Disney World's shadow. The Mouse has a much bigger share of the market, naturally, but then the market's a lot bigger than it used to be, so things even out nicely. The Gardens' attendance today is about the same as it's been ever since things really got rolling after World War Two. The only really dramatic fluctuations happen on those occasional days when Disney's parking lot fills up and the turned-away tourists start spilling southward down the line to Sea World, to Boardwalk and Baseball, and finally to the Gardens way down in Winter Haven.

Both Jimmy and Mike seem somewhat awed by the Disney colossus, speaking with wonder of the new hotel, the high-speed train to Orlando International Airport currently under construction, the self-contained nature of the operation (it has its own printing presses, power plants, everything), its incredible cost efficiency, its tax-break arrangements with local government, and finally its future, all those thousands of acres of Disney-owned land awaiting expansion. In that context the little room we're in seems awfully small, remote, and inconsequential, almost a Third World kind of place, and I wonder if the mighty technomouse ever beckons attractively to these men.

I ask. Jimmy, who began his career driving an electric boat in the scenic cruise section of the Gardens, just looks at the floor, shakes his head. "Nope," he says. "Wouldn't even think of it." Mike, an old radio hand who worked his way south from Pennsylvania, job to job, and stopped at the Gardens ten years ago, says that he feels like part of the family here, and Disney isn't like that. He doesn't use the word "ruthless," but it seems to be behind his impressions of the organization, particularly its staff-cutting policies in times of narrowing profit margins. "No, I wouldn't go over there," he says. "Cypress Gardens is a nice place, you know, for everyone, the staff and the visitors too. It's the best-kept secret in Florida, in my opinion."

We change tracks for a while and talk about the ski show. Mike and Jimmy say that it's a more highly produced show than it was in the days when it was all skiing and kite flying, with a guy playing an electric organ and spectators just sitting on the grassy banks leading down to Lake Eloise. The current show, though, has less of a showbiz-glitz feel than the show HBJ put on when they first took over. That one, designed to attract a younger crowd to the Gardens with more stage acrobatics and dialogue than skiing, plus taped rock and roll music, didn't work; the younger crowd never materialized, and neither the skiers nor the existing crowds, predominantly middle-aged and older people, liked it much. That's what led to the introduction of The Greatest American Ski Show, which has lots of skiing and kite flying interrupted by a minimum of other elements; basically, the clown characters Corky and Corkette serve the useful purpose of distracting the audience's attention while the skiers and fliers get set up for their next round of stunts and exhibitions. This balance does well in the ratings. When it was first staged, The Greatest American Ski Show outdrew Sea World's Shamu show—and the crowd-pleasing whale even had a new Baby Shamu at the time.

The ski show has of course changed in ways other than presentation. When Mike Markowitz first arrived at the Gardens in '78, the most spectacular ski jumpers were achieving jumps of a hundred and twenty feet. These days they're breaking two hundred easily. There's also all kinds of new action on the water: swivel ballets of ever-increasing grace and difficulty, off-the-ski-ramp stunts like the spectacular four-man "helicopter," four-tiered pyramids, male and even female barefooting, backward flips. All in all, says Mike, the ski show today is not dull. It's quite a bang for the buck.

I agree with him—the show really is good, even when you've seen it as many times as I have lately—and on this harmonious note I leave the boat drivers' room and go looking for Lisa again. It has occurred to me that I am ignoring the down side of the Cypress Gardens experience, whatever that might be. When I find her, then, I ask her: What *are* the really bad things about being an Aquamaid?

Well, Lisa tells me, that's easy. One word says it all: winter. When folks are sitting in the bleachers of the North and South stadiums in the bright December sunlight, adequately protected from the elements by a medium-weight jacket and perhaps a sweater, they probably don't realize that Lake Eloise is *cold,* and the skiers in their little show costumes are experiencing considerable discomfort.

It is in fact really tough out there, Lisa says. When your muscles are stiff with cold, and the wind is turning the lake's surface into a fair approximation of one of those machines designed to test shock absorbers to their breaking point, just hanging onto the rope is hard enough, let alone performing the feats of strength and skill and outer-limits athleticism the show calls for. In winter aches and pains and real injuries multiply, and morale plummets. Just being wet all the time is a total drag. But winter is prime tourist time, so then more than ever the show must go on come wind, rain, fog, hail, or anything but lightning storms (which, unfortunately for the skiers, don't happen very often in the cool season). Three shows a day, three hundred and sixty-five days a year; that's the program.

Lisa can't stress too strongly how uncomfortable it can get when the Florida winter and what Dick Pope used to call "the best lousy weather in the country" comes around, but she has to think for quite a while when I ask about her other major job-related complaints, and must finally admit that she doesn't have any.

Coming as it does from a woman whose working wardrobe consists of sweatsuits and dancewear and "oh, thirty or forty" swimsuits, I accept that statement without argument.

The skiers are a clubby bunch, united and separated from the outside world by the same factors that drew Mark and Lisa together: the shared values of the athletic approach to life, and the physically intimate relationship of extreme interdependence in which they spend their most important working moments.

In show skiing at the Cypress Gardens level, each performer is quite literally entrusting his or her life to at least two and often as many as two dozen other individuals: the boat driver; the apprentice, whose job it is to "pull the pin" and release the ski rope of falling skiers; every other boat driver on the water and kite flier in the air;

and every other skier involved in an act. All it takes for a pyramid to fall badly is one buckling knee or misjudged step. One ski out of control while four men surge side by side up a ramp at forty or fifty miles an hour and then rotate through a full circle in midair can mean a split-second demonstration of the domino theory in wildly destructive action. So mutual trust comes hard. Each new skier must earn it. Once in place, though, it is absolute, because there is no other way the job can be approached. "You simply can't start questioning the reliability of your teammates, or for that matter yourself," says one skier. "If you do, *you're* going to be the link which breaks the chain, and the bones."

The necessity of great mutual trust determines what kind of person gets hired as a Cypress Gardens skier; introverts, depressives, and other antisocial sorts need not apply. It also affects how the skiers relate to each other once they're on the team. There are formal mechanisms like semiregular group meetings to head off interpersonal disputes and resolve them when they arise, and there is a great deal of spontaneous togetherness. The skiers tend to socialize together, go on vacation together, moonlight together, and date and marry people they work with, all to a greater degree than do most co-workers.

If one were to construct a social-psychological model of the group as a whole, then, the basic building blocks would be high self-esteem and other-reliance, low paranoia, well-developed social and problem-solving skills, levels of perceived job satisfaction climbing off the top end of the graph, and an extreme degree of mostly positive role diffusion. In other words, this is the sophisticated employer's died-and-gone-to-heaven vision of a work force. It is fair to say that these people are worth the $4.50 to $9.00 per hour, with benefits, that HBJ pays them.

It's also fair to say these rates are in firm contact with the rock bottom of the show-business and professional-athletics industries, and so the Aquamaids really *aren't* in it for the money. Other factors must draw them and keep them.

Cheryl Bermeo, an attractive brunette in her mid to late twenties, possesses two very common Aquamaidly characteristics: she is from the Midwest, and as a child she dreamed of becoming a Cypress Gardens skier.

In her case the dream began in the town of Iron Mountain in the state of Michigan, which shares with similarly lake-studded Illinois and Wisconsin the distinction of producing some sixty percent of Cypress Gardens' skiers. A group of professional skiers visited her parents' vacation cottage one day in her seventh year, and she was hooked. She joined her first ski club at the age of thirteen and quickly learned what everybody in the Midwest ski clubs knows about Cypress Gardens: it's the top of the heap. Clubs draw prestige from sending their best skiers to the Gardens much as high schools are honored when their graduates enroll at Harvard or Princeton or Yale. Cheryl set her sights. She'd never seen the Gardens' show; she just knew that the skiers there were really hot.

Hers was not the fast track, straight from the lakes of the frozen North to balmy Eloise, but a logically progressive journey involving applications to ski shows in California and Florida, a connection with Water Ski Shows, Inc. which led to one year's worth of show work in Hollywood, Florida, and two years in Jackson, New Jersey, and then a telephone conversation between her New Jersey boss and Lynn Novakofski that got her to the Gardens. She has been an Aquamaid for four years, and is now an assistant supervisor of the Gardens' female skiers.

"I love it here," she says. "I love to ski, especially swivel, and I really like the people, and I love Florida because I'm a summer person. I play volleyball, Frisbee, things like that, and I eat healthy foods, and I love being outside. I like being an assistant supervisor, too, because I like to have input. So really, I'm very happy."

Cheryl, unmarried, does not date other skiers because she wants to keep thinking of them as brothers and sisters, so most of her socializing with her co-workers involves going out in groups of eight or ten Aquamaids to Bennigan's, or stopping by the Ski One bar at the hotel on the grounds after work. She also participates in the weekly Wednesday night outings with all the athletes in the park, not just the skiers. She finds that when she tells people what she does for a living, they usually regale her with their own skiing exploits rather than asking her more about her work. That's okay, though, she says; it's a good way to start a conversation.

Cheryl doesn't find her work stressful, but she does find it challenging. You're never quite as good as you'd like to be, she says, and there is constant pressure to achieve new heights of performance, to match or surpass the other girls, and, well, to improve yourself. She's been hurt a few times, but nothing major: a couple of back injuries, one minor concussion, a strained neck. Mostly that's because she watches out for herself. She's careful to a fault on the water, she uses the Nautilus machines in the weight room religiously, she plays volleyball, she eats right: "All that stuff. The stronger I am, the safer I am."

Cheryl is pretty certain that she's found her niche in life. She had a year of accountancy in college back in New Jersey, and didn't like it, but lately she's begun to think about what comes after her life as an Aquamaid, and has figured out a more satisfactory educational plan. After another couple more years she's planning to go part-time at the Gardens, use the company benefits package to help her through some business administration courses strong on finance (HBJ pays about eighty percent of its employees' tuition), and thus prepare herself to set up a ski-instruction school. She hasn't got its ideal location pinpointed yet, but she's determined that it'll be somewhere on one of the lakes around Winter Haven, as close to the Gardens as possible. She'll have a house and a dock and a separate building to store equipment and lodge her clients, and that'll be that. She'll be set for life.

"Good plan, huh?" she says. "I grew up on the water, and I always want it to be part of my life, so that's a pretty good way of getting what I want. In the meantime I can keep working here, having a great time, while I'm still young and strong."

Shelley Blum is the only woman in the world who performs front flips off a ski jump. She is also the only Aquamaid with two undergraduate degrees, one in political science and one in psychology. She is at Cypress Gardens instead of being at law school; she was just about to go when, feeling that the Greatest American Ski Show would not be complete without her, Mark Voisard talked her into heading south and having fun instead.

Shelley, the owner of a powerful physique which distinguishes her from the less obviously steel-muscled women in the Gardens' water-borne chorus line, did not realize until relatively late in her skiing career that she was as unique as she is. A ski-club amateur who became a paid summertime performer in Missouri's Lake of the Ozark Water Show at the age of eleven, she simply started "doing all the guys' tricks once I'd done all the girls' tricks." Today she doesn't see herself as an exemplar of Aquamaidly glamour but as "that tough girl who can do both, be graceful with the other girls in the ballet line and then run back into the stadium, change into my wetsuit and gloves and helmet, and go out there transformed into a totally different person. That's a good switch for me." When Shelley is in a bar or someplace, and people ask her what she does for a living, she says something like, "Oh, I work in the entertainment department at Cypress Gardens" instead of saying she's a skier. When she's away from work, she likes to be *away.*

"You see, this isn't what I want to do with my life," she says. "It never was. Law school was always my goal. I never really knew how I'd want to use a law degree, but lately I've been thinking I should be a public defender; women always seem to want to take that side, don't they? But now, I don't know. Since I've been here at the Gardens I've been feeling that maybe I'd like to stay closer to athletics. I read an article in *Omni* magazine about this new profession, sports psychologist/lawyer, and that seemed like something I should check into. Quite a combination, wouldn't you say?"

She has time to think about her choice, because her strategy for now is to stay at the Gardens at least until she's cleared away some past bills and paid for her new car. That way, she'll be able to go to law school with a clean financial slate. Or maybe she'll stay longer at the Gardens, because as she puts it, "the bottom line is that this job is *fun.* I just got back from a knee injury, which everybody around here gets but I get a little more than most, as you'd expect, and when I came back to work, I found myself thinking, 'Every time this happens, I'm getting that much closer to getting a real job.' I didn't like that thought much, you know."

Whatever she does, though, she's not going back up North. She's tasted the Florida Good Life, and those Missouri winters are now in her past, not her future. Whenever the right time comes—when her knees give out, or she just feels the need for a change—she figures that an ex-skier who's now a state attorney in Orlando can help her pick the most suitable Florida law school. "I have lots of options," she says, "so for now I'll just enjoy myself."

For an Aquamaid, Nancy Daley started late. She already had a master's degree from Boston University and had managed a restaurant and bar in upstate New York when, toward the end of a 1978 vacation which began with a friend's wedding in California and ended in Florida, she walked up to Lynn Novakofski and told him, "Today's your lucky day."

After the obvious first question—"Who are *you?*"—Lynn gave her an audition, and she successfully performed maneuvers she'd never tried before in her fifteen years of "better than average recreational skiing." Lynn told her that he had no need of new skiers, and moreover she needed practice, and so practice she did, benefiting from the help and experience of the other skiers (this was before a formal, paid training program existed at the Gardens), until an injury created an opening. Like most Gardens novices, Nancy first performed in the role of Corkette, the non-skiing clown, and worked her way up from there.

Nancy is still an Aquamaid because "I kept getting reasons to stay. It wasn't my plan; it just happened." One of those reasons was her marriage to Russell Daley, a boat driver. Another was the birth of their child. Another was her promotion to an assistant supervisor's job, which she thought would look good on her résumé. Now, although it's hard to balance a job and motherhood, it's not that hard, and as jobs go, Nancy thinks this one's pretty good. It's mostly fun while you're at it, and it's gone by the time you're in your car at quitting time. "I learned the value of *that* while I was pregnant and working as head of the wardrobe department," she says. "That job was fulfilling, but all that stress, all those deadlines . . . I could never get it out of my head. In skiing, you see, the stress is all physical, not mental."

Nancy sees other advantages to her job: "I get to be with my husband a lot, which most working wives don't, and the whole atmosphere here is just like one big family. We all know what's going on in each other's lives, we all know each other's parents, that kind of thing. I know people who've left here and gone other places, even ski places, and they say it's not the same anywhere else. Here it's really interactive."

Like many other skiers, Nancy moonlights, taking on seamstress work for the Gardens and other clients, and thinks about what she's going to do when she can't ski professionally anymore. She might, she says, pick up where she left off before she found herself managing a restaurant. Creative writing and journalism were her areas of concentration in college, and in recent years she's kept her hand in by ghostwriting articles for the Gardens' kite fliers for *Hang Gliding* magazine. The notion of writing a book about the Gardens has occurred to her more than once. That might really be fun, she thinks. "You know, all the stories, all the crazy things we do here, twenty-two world's-first records, people barefooting on their hands. . . . It could be a kind of alligator's eye view of Cypress Gardens."

As to when she might quit being an Aquamaid, Nancy's not at all ambiguous; she'll quit the day her body starts telling her to. As a skier, she says, you owe yourself that much, because the last thing you want to do is injure yourself too badly to continue skiing for fun. She herself doesn't feel that day approaching in her bones yet, so "I'll do it as long as they'll let me. It's a great thing to do. It's a great life."

❂

Lisa and Cheryl and Shelley and Nancy have all described the pleasure they derive from their work quite adequately, and illustrated their competence as athletes and go-getters and women and workers most convincingly, and in so doing they have reflected well on both themselves and the organization that uses and is used by them. Mr. Pope, I believe, would be proud of them. They are fine exemplars of the Good Life in action.

When I think of the man's original vision, though—the gorgeous verdant vital Florida which emerged from his head and beamed sunlight and hope into the darker, harder places of the world, telling the snowbound and the city-crushed and the aged and the ailing of spirit that de Soto's Fountain of Youth was not a myth but a metaphor for the whole great stranger-welcoming, problem-eradicating, bleakness-banishing, Good-Life-giving Sunshine State itself—it is the story of the final Aquamaid I meet at Cypress Gardens that touches me with the greatest force.

Perhaps that is because the Aquamaid in question, Michelle Morris, another boat driver's wife, is like myself an English person converted to the American way, and we share certain perceptions. When Michelle talks in her quiet, composed, very polite and proper way about the unchildish world of her childhood, spent as the only youngster in an adult world—her father's pub on the outskirts of London—I know just exactly what she means when she says that for her, Cypress Gardens and her new life in Florida are gifts she never knew existed until she was given them: a real playground, real playmates, real fun.

Florida, you see, is for me both a natural-world sensorium and a brash bold built-yesterday extremity of a brash bold built-yesterday nation, a place which actually encourages a person to start again in freedom from old glooms—and I am hardly alone in that feeling. The unnourishing roots shared by Michelle and I, the ones tapping into middle-class England's cold gray reservoir of convention and propriety and inhibition, are just one variety among many; other people from other places have other useless roots to cut in the Sunshine State. They have other baggage to shed, and shed it they do.

When you get right down to it, that's the point of modern Florida. And without Dick Pope's Aquamaids, the point might never have been made.

3
The Next Great City

Watch out. Cam Oberting's got her fists bunched tight on her thighs. Her head's thrust forward, cocked straight up in your face. Killer rays are coming off her, big noise is beating against your skull. She's small—tiny in fact, just a squat little tactical mini-nuke in any relative ranking of human explosives—but God, she's loud.

"What do they think? They think we're stupid?" she's saying, the decibels soaring free. "They think they can walk all over us, and we're just gonna lie here?"

Hell no, Cam, never. Not even the commissioners of Hillsborough County could be so unrealistic as to assume that a person like you is just going to lie there. But on the other hand, is that going to stop them walking all over you anyway? Just look at the history you're so hot about, reread all those official transcripts and letters and reports and memorandums you're waving. Don't you sometimes get the feeling that no matter how many kicks and punches you throw in the process, how many decibels you add to the old wham-bam, you'll still be lucky to end up with so much as a "Thank you, Ma'am"?

Plainly Mrs. Oberting feels no such thing. Failure does not exist in her assessment of either her cause-specific chances or her general citizen-housewife-activist future. She's a dynamo, a powerhouse of perpetual positive motion. But all the same, while miracles are indeed possible, even in the politics of Hillsborough County and Tampa, the major metropolis it surrounds—"America's Next Great City," no less —a reading of the history does rather insistently incline the dispassionate observer toward a certain pessimism vis-à-vis Cam's concerns.

The cause-specific history at issue concerns one rather narrow if substantial entity occupying high ground toward the eastern border of Hillsborough County, half a mile from Cam Oberting's personal dream home: a very large, leaky garbage dump known locally as the Taylor Road landfill. The wider history encompasses Hillsborough County's political/environmental record these past few decades, and the issue of growth versus nature in Florida at large.

Both histories are, as one must expect of boomtowns and frontier states, entertaining in an awful kind of way.

The garbage in the Taylor Road landfill came from a metropolis in transition, a place undergoing the first real shock of sudden change.

The Tampa area has never been an insignificant location in Florida's history. Its kindly topography and massive bay sheltered thriving native communities long before the first white conqueror, Hernando de Soto, chose it as his first landfall, and they have supported generations of Floridians since. Until relatively recently, though, the area's population did not expand with today's relentless rapidity. Tampa, which has no real beaches closer than twenty miles from downtown, was never really a participant in the Florida growth dynamic of retirement and tourism, sun and fun. It was, rather, a real town, a small port city with an industrial base centered on shipbuilding, cigar making, and phosphate mining. It grew, but it grew relatively slowly. What was true of its social, economic, and political climate one year was more likely than not to be true five or ten years later; the town retained its basic balance of self-made aristocracy and everybody else, of deep-rooted Florida crackers and just-as-well-established Hispanics, of poor blacks and of migrants moving in and out of its port, its agricultural hinterland, and its military establishments. As late as the mid-1960s or even the early 1970s, then, it was still possible for a substantial citizen of Tampa to know everybody else in town who really mattered.

No longer. Tampa today is a Sunbelt city, maybe even *the* Sunbelt city. The very attributes which caused it to be brushed but lightly by the sun and fun boom cycles of Florida's frivolous past are its prime assets in the economic climate of the nation's present. For since the working population of the United States—not just its ex-workers or nonworkers of one sort or another—is migrating, flowing lemming-like toward the coasts, it follows that a more or less coastal *city*, a place near the water in the sun where jobs of all sorts can be had, is going to be a worker-relocation target of first choice.

Which Tampa is. Today, and every single yesterday and tomorrow, three hundred and fifty people move into the city and its Hillsborough County suburbs and satellites.

The results are what one might expect. Tampa is no longer a city of indigenous crackers and blacks and Hispanics and local nouveaux blue bloods engaged in the physical making of things. Today it's a melting pot of everyone from everywhere, its primary economic activities shifting from manufacturing to white-collar information-age industries and the creation and operation of facilities to service and house the resultant new middle-class population.

That is why, when you drive around Tampa today, dodging speeding Saabs and Audis, the only discernible demographic trend seems to be an explosion of young white quiche-eaters and fast-trackers, the only apparent urban-vista direction an accelerating plague of expensive new homes and intense concentrations of designer ice-cream boutiques, health spas, and planet-sized foreign car dealerships featuring "Motorcars of Distinction." So basically, as long as you stay away from the few older neighborhoods and the city's rather extensive and very troubled pockets of very poor blacks, and you don't happen to have a palm tree in sight (which you probably won't, since local urban planning seems to have involved a blitzkrieg of positively Teutonic efficiency on greenery of all kinds), you could be anywhere moderately affluent in homogenized modern America. Much of Tampa doesn't look or feel like a Southern city anymore. It looks and feels bland, anonymous, familiar: the sort of blurred, built-yesterday environment you see behind the action in any of a hundred made-in-So-Cal TV series.

But perhaps that description is too harsh. Modern Tampa may be a diffuse, slapped-together-any-old-way kind of place, but basically it's not quite as unsightly as many of the communities from which it draws its new blood. And then too, the kind of explosive growth the city has experienced is not just a monster but a powerfully deceptive one. Perhaps, after all, the people who worked so hard to attract the growth beast to Tampa can be forgiven for assuming that since it had powerful magic—since it laid condos of gold and skyscrapers of silver in their laps—it was unlike other creatures in other respects.

Or perhaps those now rich, happy boosters don't deserve forgiveness from the rest of us. When they invited the monster to their party, they should at the very least have considered what it was going to drink, and where it was going to perform its ablutions.

The Taylor Road landfill. What a lovely place, paradise gained for lawyers and carrion birds. Situated atop one of the highest elevations in Hillsborough County, the now-defunct dump was the repository of all supposedly "sanitary" garbage from fast-growing Tampa and its surrounding communities during the years when the city's only incinerator plant was nonoperational by order of the Environmental Protection Administration. During that period Tampa simply trucked its garbage out of town to the small, relatively unaffluent and therefore politically uninfluential community of Seffner, and dumped it into a hole at Taylor Road.

The result, a methane-snorting, leachate-spewing mound most attractive on those nights when its gas burn-off system transforms the local atmosphere into a fair approximation of the more psychedelic scenes of *Apocalypse Now,* crowns a modestly beautiful topography of small rounded hills and pleasant wooded hollows unique to the northeastern corner of the generally flat, wet, low-lying county. If you wanted to be tasteless (and why not, when you're talking about garbage and rot and corruption?), you might say that the dump sits up there like a single horridly infected nipple on an otherwise healthy, quietly comely Mother Earthly mammalian system.

Such an analogy is not entirely spurious. It holds water figuratively (allegedly, the dump is infected by materials—hospital waste, for instance—that meet any criteria for disease), and then of course the whole mess is indeed rotting, decomposing gradually but spiritedly, stewing itself into methane gas and assorted liquids.

The analogy also holds water literally. The area's fifty-plus inches of annual rainfall, the catalyst in the decomposition process, permeate the nipple and then, enriched to the extent one might expect after a slow passage through the assorted leavings of modern man, flow down into Mother's breast and thence into her inner cavities.

The basic arrangement of this process is entirely acceptable in the standard waste disposal scheme of things. To get rid of garbage relatively safely, you either burn it or you put it in a hole somewhere, cover it up, and let it rot in peace. As long as it's not staring you in the face or blowing straight up your nose, who cares? But the bit at the end, the final destination of all that rainwater, that's troublesome. In most places it wouldn't matter—the ground is very big and very deep, the water percolating through even a thousand landfills relatively very small indeed—but in peninsular Florida it's troublesome to the point of being critical, even life-threatening.

This is because, hydrologically speaking, Floridians who live in the lower two thirds of the peninsula are both blessed and cursed: blessed by a water-rich environment, and cursed because they live on a hydrologic island. Their drinking water doesn't come from distant watersheds, borne to them by rivers which may have traveled a thousand miles. It comes from the ground beneath their feet, put there exclusively by rain falling on the peninsula. Good, so-so, or lethal, that water is all peninsular Floridians are going to get.

The main fact of geologic life here is that basically, the ground beneath Floridians' feet is a giant sponge resting on a nonporous slab. The sponge is shot through with billions (and billions and billions) of cavities, some very large and some very small, and it permits the entry and flow of water better than any other large geologic formation on earth. The sponge has a name—it is an aquifer—and it is indeed immense. Underlying the whole state and portions of Georgia and Alabama, in places it is two thousand or more feet thick.

Composed of variously aged limestones layered in the earth over the crystalline bedrock of the Florida Plateau, the sponge is in fact several sponges. The largest of them, the Floridan Aquifer, underlies the entire peninsula but is tilted down into the earth from north-northwest to south-southeast. The smaller aquifers, located around the coasts and in the southern portion of the peninsula (where the Floridan formation is deep beneath the earth), lie above it. Thus at Ocala, in the northwest central part of the peninsula, the limestone of the Floridan Aquifer actually forms the earth surface under the Green Swamp, while at Florida City, way down south of Miami on the Atlantic coast, the upper surface of the Floridan Aquifer sits about six hundred and fifty feet beneath the topsoil; above it are sealing layers of clay and marl known as the Floridan Aquiclude, and above them is the Biscayne Aquifer.

The entire aquifer system is a freshwater processing machine of great efficiency. The rain falls, the limestones absorb what new water they can as quickly as they can, the very substantial remainder runs off as rivers or streams feeding peninsular Florida's uniquely rich and lovely system of bays and estuaries and lakes and swamps, and the water which has been absorbed into the ground moves down-gradient in the aquifers, ultimately to be discharged where the limestone layers emerge off the coasts in the undersea slopes of the Florida Plateau. In places water movement is slow, a very gradual downward seepage through a multitude of tiny cavities. In other places, where large chambers have formed in the limestone, it can be very rapid, an underground river in full flow.

The down-gradient movement of water in the aquifers is the reason why most of the Florida peninsula is a hydrologic island. None of the down gradients in the aquifers move water either south or north across a line between Cedar Key on the West coast and Daytona Beach in the East. No water from north of that line enters the peninsula's system. It all comes from the rain falling on the population's home turf.

Fortunately, a great deal of water falls. Florida's annual rainfall of fifty-plus inches is substantial by any standard. Unfortunately, however, the pattern of its descent from the heavens does not dovetail very neatly with the convenience of the peninsula's human population. For one thing, the rain doesn't fall evenly all year—the months from June to October are very wet indeed, the others rather dry. Thus, for instance, the month of May quite often finds South Floridians burning drought-dead shrubbery one day, and watching the ashes (and perhaps a few other things) go swirling away on rivers of floodwater the next.

Then too, eighty-five percent of the rain does not fall along the coastal strips where eighty-five percent of the people live. Although the drinking and bathing and lawn watering of private citizens in South Florida does not place the largest demand on the aquifer—that comes from agriculture and the phosphate industry—the coastal citizens' needs are in general more substantial than their immediate natural resources, and have been for some time. In the urban coastal areas, the aquifer is not what it used to be. The days are long gone when anyone anywhere along Florida's coastline could sink a two-and-a-half-inch pipe thirty feet into the sandy ground of his or her very own little piece of paradise, attach a pump, and be delivered of fifty to a hundred gallons of potable aquifer water per minute.

Those days are gone because people, such relentlessly increasing numbers and concentrations of them, did precisely that in the early days of Florida development, and then their municipal authorities did it for them on a grander scale: much bigger pipes, much more powerful pumps, and many, many more gallons per minute.

It was fun while it lasted, but it didn't last long at all. In Tampa, all the downtown municipal wells were totally useless by 1929.

What had happened was an inevitability of nature. By causing such large amounts of fresh water to be sucked out of the surface aquifer so close to the coastline, particularly during those dry spells when the all-important lawns began to take sick and die, the city fathers had fallen foul of an alien (and alien-sounding) equation, dating from turn-of-the-century Holland, which in a perfect world would have been nailed to every pump handle and palm tree in town: *one foot of fresh water above mean sea level means forty feet of fresh water below mean sea level.*

So says the Ghyben-Herzberg principle, which defines the problem of saltwater encroachment into low-lying coastal areas, which problem in turn hinges on the density and specific gravity of salt water relative to fresh water (salt water is denser, and of higher specific gravity). In action, it means that if you suck too much fresh water out of the ground near the coast, pretty soon you're going to be sucking salt, and sucking it forever.

The principle's one-to-forty equation is precise and unavoidable, its implications very clear. If the freshwater table beneath your low-lying coastal community stands at four feet above mean sea level, you're okay: there will be four feet times forty, or a hundred and sixty feet, of the good stuff down there before you hit the salt water on which your freshwater, being "lighter," is "floating." But if you keep pumping out the fresh water faster than the aquifer can replenish it, and you end up with a fresh water table only six inches above mean sea level, the salt water is going to move up to only twenty feet below mean sea level. Cut that head of fresh water to three inches, and the salt will rise another ten feet. And then of course, if your fresh water table actually drops to mean sea level, salt water will be all there is. Your community will be out of fresh ground water, and it will be out of it forever. The "lighter" fresh water will never be able to move back in.

This is exactly what happened in Tampa in 1929, and in most other Florida coastal communities at one time or another during their development (nearby Clearwater and St. Petersburg, lower-lying and closer to the Gulf than is Tampa, went saline earlier. Miami, built over the powerful Biscayne Aquifer, lagged behind until truly large-scale draining of the Everglades accomplished what wells alone never could have). Even today, long after the saltwater encroachment problem first became all too evident, the process is continuing. In many places, neglect and history are the significant dynamics. All over coastal Florida, thousands of artesian wells sunk into the Floridan Aquifer back in the good old days, then abandoned when they started producing salt water instead of fresh, are still flowing, spewing out salt-contaminated water which percolates through the topsoil into the shallower surface aquifers, rendering them too unfit for human consumption, irrigation, or anything whatsoever.

But not to worry. Wells are cheap, and so the governing bodies of the Gulf-coastal communities simply did (and do) the obvious thing. They sank new wellfields farther inland, and continued to encourage growth. And that is where most of them, including Tampa, are today: pumping steadily increasing amounts of fresh water out of the aquifer from a steadily growing collection of wells on their steadily inland-receding fringes. The business of getting fresh water these days involves stresses and strains which can at times erupt into outright political warfare—disagreements over fair prices for wellfield lands, competition between city and county authorities and agriculturists and phosphate miners for new or existing water resources, agitations by lawn worshipers faced with increasingly severe and frequent water restrictions—and overall, it's just a mess. The price in saltwater encroachment has been paid, and the price in freshwater delivery costs is rising, but not buying much. Nobody's very happy. Nobody finds it very amusing that most of the cities in a very, very wet state have a water problem.

All the same, the absolute bottom line is that essentially, saltwater encroachment is a regrettable inconvenience rather than an immediately dire threat in a development-oriented economy. Certainly, the flora and fauna of the coastal regions undergo radical changes when salt underlies the surface at shallow depths—plants with deep roots, and other plants and life-forms depending on plants with deep roots, simply die—but subsurface salinity doesn't stop office towers and six-lane highways and condo complexes and Jiffy Lubes and all the other amenities of modern civilization. As long as you can pump your fresh water from some not unreasonably distant wellfield (however contentious the process of acquiring it may be), you can build all you want. And of course the farther inland you build, the closer you get to your water sources.

So no problem, right? Wrong. Your water's still coming from one of only two kinds of places: points where rainwater is actually entering an aquifer through limestone on or very close to the land surface, or points where it's moving through the ground at relatively shallow depths. Therefore, it follows that if you want your turf to maintain its ability to support human life, you'd better be very, very careful about what substances find their way into that water. It would in fact seem somewhat worse than unwise to allow any pollutants at all to enter the aquifers anywhere in peninsular Florida.

All sorts of pollutants do enter the aquifers all over peninsular Florida, though. Just in the area around Tampa Bay encompassing Hillsborough, Manatee, Pasco, and Pinellas counties, the Tampa Bay Regional Planning Council estimates that fully thirty-two percent of all hazardous wastes—dangerous solvents, oils, pesticides, and other fluids—are simply flushed down drains or discarded into pits and landfills.

The impact of such foolishness is officially recognized, and has been for some time. As a 1980 report by the Florida Department of Environmental Regulation put it, most of the state is "in the precarious position of using the same aquifer for waste disposal and a drinking water source. . . . Contaminated waste water plumes from surface impoundments or other disposal means will persist for long periods of time. . . . Florida's drinking water supply is thus in a double jeopardy situation: undetected waste plumes moving rapidly through aquifers containing high quality water while the sources of these waste plumes remain undetected."

In other words, you can't just dump a few hundred or thousand gallons of pollutants into the ground where you are and figure that it's okay, and that you and your immediate neighbors will get your drinking water somewhere else for a while. The poison's going to move in directions which most often are impossible to predict, and somewhere along the plume, wherever subsurface water movements take it, somebody's very probably going to drink it. And you of course are equally likely to find yourself drinking some other uncaring dumper's contaminants.

In which case you may not be dealing with just an offensive taste or smell or visible discoloration, perhaps experiencing a little queasiness now and then. You might well be at risk of becoming a participant in the abnormally high cancer rate which prevails among longtime Florida residents. While air pollution and the release of radioactive radon gas from the earth in phosphate-mining areas are recognized as partially responsible, particularly in inland areas, groundwater contamination throughout the state is a prime suspect in those aberrant statistics.

◉

Cam Oberting is aware of aquifer-borne contaminant plumes. Unlike many other Florida citizens, though, she has a pretty fair idea about exactly where her problem originates. She figures that the black slime now collecting in her dream home's heavy-duty water filtration system—the system she installed following an episode of uncontrollable dizziness and vomiting in her family after her water started looking and smelling bad—flows downhill into her well directly from the aquifer beneath the Taylor Road landfill.

She may be right and she may be wrong. A great deal of effort on the part of various Hillsborough County authorities has gone into arguing the latter possibility. The slime, however, continues to collect in her and her neighbors' water filters, and moreover a considerable body of hydrologic data suggests that her conclusions belong squarely on the rational side of the fear/paranoia axis.

A respectable source of such data is one Dr. Garald Parker, a retired Tampa resident who was chief hydrologist with the Southwest Florida Water Management District at the time the Taylor Road landfill was begun. Among other accomplishments, the rather distinguished Dr. Parker can claim the credit for actually naming the Floridan Aquifer. It was he who made the first definitive study of the South Florida groundwater system as a whole during the course of an investigation of saltwater encroachment into freshwater wells in the Miami area during the 1940s. His saltwater encroachment report, published by the U.S. Department of the Interior under the title *Water Resources of Southeastern Florida,* persists as a standard text in the worlds of hydrology and geology.

Basically stated, Dr. Parker's opinion, which he delivered to the Hillsborough County commissioners when they were trying to decide where to dump their garbage, is that the Taylor Road landfill is in just about the worst place it possibly could be: directly above a limestone dome protruding higher than the aquifer around it.

This alone is bad news, but there is worse. It happens that the top of the limestone dome at issue is sharply crenelated, an affair of plunging pits and vertical outcrops, and that in order to create a level bottom for the bathtub-shaped hole into which Tampa's garbage was to be dumped, the excavators actually had to lop the tops off several limestone outcrops. This little piece of business created the potential for a most unwholesome situation. Should water be allowed to contact those chopped-off limestone outcrops, they would act in the manner of highly efficient storm drains, channeling the water and all its contaminants straight down the fast track into the aquifer.

In theory, and according to the official pronouncements of Hillsborough County officials, this cannot happen, because a layer of impermeable clay was spread between limestone and garbage. According to Dr. Parker and Cam Oberting, however, it can happen, has happened, and will continue to happen. They maintain that if clay was used at all, it was of such poor quality—more sand than clay, they say—that the adjective "impermeable" could be applied to it only after prodigious feats of imagination.

If they're right, that's awful, then, but there's even more. There's also the question of sinkholes around or actually under the dump.

Floridians who have never heard the word "aquifer" know all about sinkholes. They're hard to miss. When a hole appears suddenly in your neighborhood, and whatever's on top of it falls in, your attention is engaged. Sinkholes are easy to understand, too. Invisible underground water movement creates or enlarges cavities in the limestone beneath the topsoil, weakening the ground beneath your feet, and so from time to time, with no predictability whatsoever, the surface of the land simply collapses. Portions of real estate—cow pastures, backyards, roads, even the occasional Burger King or Porsche dealership—topple into the earth.

Usually this is quite an entertaining phenomenon. Mother Earthly swallowings of yupmobiles make a pleasant diversion from the usual Action News parade of serial killers, crack busts, crooked politicians, and "America's Next Great City" pieces. But the prospect of such an occurrence directly beneath several million tons of festering garbage is not funny at all. And that prospect is very real. As Dr. Parker points out, the Seffner area is more sinkhole-prone than any other section of Hillsborough County.

For her part, Cam Oberting simply points: points at one filled sinkhole plainly visible in the center of her own front yard; points at another, more recent and still gaping hungrily, on a neighbor's property a hundred and fifty yards closer to the dump; points up at the garbage mountain looming over her dream home and shrugs. Cam does a lot of pointing in her new vocation.

Cam used to be very, very happy with her home. For one thing, her house and her family were her work and her pride; she used to be a full-time housewife.

Also, the house was such a nice step up and away for Cam and Leo, her engineer husband. They used to live in a low-lying westerly section of Tampa, where, like millions of Floridians past and present, they were plagued by the discomforts associated with a general plentitude of surface water: seasonal floods, riotous vegetable and animal life, mosquito infestation, constant humidity. So when they found their new home in Seffner, they thought they'd entered heaven. Cam's main home-hunting requirements, apart from the usual factors of space and style and the rest, had been highness and dryness, quite literally an ascent from the swamp, and Seffner met those standards perfectly. It exceeded them, in fact, and gave her great joy; there is still wonder in her voice when she extolls the virtues of the area's really quite modest elevation, its gentle water-shedding slopes.

Given such a background and such past happiness, the irony of Cam and Leo's situation now—that here they are again, plagued by water much more dangerous than the stuff in the swamp, invisible in the ground, totally beyond their ability to avoid—is especially sad. It's not hard to understand why they feel compelled to do something about it, why the living room of their house, a carefully maintained fifties bungalow on a large, well-tended lot, is now the action headquarters of the Taylor Road Civic Association and an outpost of several other citizens' organizations.

Today, on a mild beautiful December Monday in Seffner, Cam and Leo are at home and on the job. Cam is pointing at a lurid riot of electric greens and pinks and purples frothing con brio across the screen of her nice big Spanish-style TV console. These are the primary colors of a videotape she and Leo and their neighbor David Brenner made early in 1987 on the crest and flanks of the Taylor Road mound.

"Look at that!" she thunders. "Leachates! Methane gas! Bubbling out of the ground! Look at that hole! That hole's not supposed to be there! That dump's supposed to be covered with impermeable clay, just like it's supposed to be lined with it! Does that look impermeable to you? Does it even look like clay?

"And look at all that vegetation! That's not supposed to be there either! They're supposed to mow it! That's gonna burn like crazy if the gas explodes!

"And there—see? See that red bag? That's hospital waste! See that dirty diaper? See those containers? What's in them? Who knows? Does that look sanitary to you? It certainly doesn't *smell* sanitary, I can tell you! You can't breathe up there!"

On the screen she echoes herself, coughing and wheezing as she points at a bubbling hole, points at an uncovered bag of offal, points at a lime-green leachate pool, points at one pulsing purple pustule after another.

Leo seems to be having a somewhat less uncomfortable time of it than his wife—"Cam breathes through her mouth, so she gets sore throats real easy," he explains—but he too is obviously finding his role as activist/investigator (and trespasser) less than pleasant.

Fortunately, stench doesn't communicate through videotape, but most other things about the expedition do: ugliness, danger, outrage, fear. Watching the tape, I feel for Cam and Leo, and for David Brenner behind the video camera. The sense of peril and pestilence conveyed by their record of the event is such that I find myself waiting for them to pass out, watching their leachate-spattered lower legs for the first signs of ambulatory decomposition, feeling real anger that good honest people such as they should have to be anywhere within miles of that scandalous dump, let alone *walking* on it. Then I begin to wonder about the condition of their lungs and white blood cells and genes, and I wonder if they wonder too (I don't ask). Eventually and predictably I get selfish, find myself wanting to get the hell away from Taylor Road, Seffner, Tampa, Hillsborough County, and maybe even Florida at large before the viruses and toxins turn me into a ten-fingered toad.

Perhaps I'm overreacting. Maybe so. Dr. Parker points out that among its other properties, Florida's aquifer system is a wonderful water purifier. Heavier-than-water impurities adhere to its limestones rather than continuing to be borne along by the water flow, and in its oxygenless environment, organic contaminants—viruses and the like —eventually die. So while a desire to vacate the immediate vicinity of Taylor Road might in fact be thoroughly appropriate, thoughts of evacuating Tampa twenty miles away, down the aquifer gradient to the east, could be simply paranoid.

But then again, one wonders, what if there's one of those fast-flowing underground rivers near the dump (which there just might be; there are powerful underground springs bubbling up from the far depths of the aquifer in western Hillsborough County)? That would whip those poisons along in Tampa's direction quite nicely, wouldn't it?

And then too, what about other sites in the area where pollutants are entering the aquifer? What about the grim little fact that sponge-sitting Florida ranks high on the EPA's list of states with the highest number of toxic waste cleanup sites? What about all those retention ponds full of radioactive phosphate-mining waste? All those aquifer recharge areas where farmers' fertilizers and pest control agents are filtering into the drinking water? All those leaking septic tanks, all those big and little sewage treatment plants and sludge disposal sites either unlined or lined with the kind of clay(?) they used at Taylor Road? Is the aquifer capable of purifying the accumulated total of all *that?* And if it is now, will it still be five years from now, when it will have to support the kind of increased population density that's going to result from Hillsborough County's current average daily *(daily!)* intake of three hundred and fifty new souls?

Nobody knows. The question is so big that even if you really, really wanted the answer, you'd have to commit such enormous statewide resources to finding it that—well, you'd have to get legislation passed, you'd have to capture a portion of the state budget that would actually be significant. Just for that one answer, you'd very probably have to spend at least as much as the pittance the state currently allots to the whole environmental shebang: water, air, wildlife, fisheries, the works. And ultimately, once you'd spent all that money, the odds figure out at around ten to one that if acted on, your answer would most likely raise the cost of new development to the point where the concrete-spewing, condo-laying monster currently keeping the wolf from the door of Florida's economy would get up and go somewhere else. And *then* where would you be?

That home truth might go some way toward explaining why the commissioners of Hillsborough County took no action when Cam Oberting presented them with still photographs of gas bubbles and leachate streams and the like eighteen months after the Taylor Road dump had been closed, covered, and supposedly sealed—and why, therefore, she and Leo and David Brenner had to go back with a video camera one year later and show them moving pictures of bubbles actually bubbling and leachates actually leaching before their questions were addressed with any seriousness.

On the other hand, forces less purely religious than the holy flame of subdivision worship may have been at work, for the stew of human factors comprising the political history of the Taylor Road landfill is as variously ingrediented as the concoction currently simmering out in Seffner.

There may for instance be some pride in there, some defensive self-deception. The simple unwillingness to admit an honest mistake —the gruesome choice of the Taylor Road site in the first place— might be responsible for the commission's long, tenacious, and very costly denial of Cam Oberting's problems. Might pride alone not explain the commissioners' willingness to engage in a riot of open-ended spending on problem-denying attorneys and consultants rather than simply shelling out the onetime cost of connecting Cam and her neighbors to the municipal water supply, which is all she really wanted when she first started making noise (and which, after years of driving up the cost of the fight just by hanging in there, she's finally about to get anyway)?

There might also be some guilt, the kind of emotion associated with actions somewhat more reprehensible than honest mistakes. The commission did after all decide to go ahead and dump Tampa's garbage into the Taylor Road hole despite having heard Dr. Parker, in his official capacity as chief geologist of the Southwest Florida Water Management District, deliver a thoroughly detailed and unambiguous assessment of the site's supreme unsuitability.

That decision, like many others made then and still made today, most likely also reflected an understandable affection for cheap, politically expedient short-term solutions to expensive long-term problems. The county already owned the site, and the site already had a hole in it, and garbage could be trucked to that hole a fair bit more cheaply than to another hole at the Sydney Mine site near the town of Brandon, and anyway, although the Sydney Mine site was bigger and better in every way—infinitely more secure vis-à-vis the aquifer, for instance—it was a problem, because the dump-resisting citizens of Brandon happened to be somewhat better heeled than those of Seffner, and they were putting the heat on the county commissioner for their district, who happened to be a heavyweight nobody else on the board wanted to cross.

Then too, less seemly speculations suggest themselves when you go a little further back in the history.

They concern the reason why the hole at Taylor Road, and others close by, happened to be there in the first place. They were "borrow pits" from which both municipal and private contractors had removed the area's sandy clays and limestones for use as very high-quality fill dirt, the essential stuff of roadbeds and swampland dredge-and-fill projects and shopping malls and office blocks and subdivisions by the hundred. Dr. Parker notes that the fill dirt in the Seffner area is "almost worth its weight in gold," and he and others including Cam Oberting suggest that an investigation of where the profits ended up after all was permitted and borrowed might be rewarding. Less than entirely ethical connections between private borrowers and public-official permitters could conceivably be revealed. Given the typically colorful and often outright criminal tone of Hillsborough County's political past, the possibility does not seem entirely remote.

There are also other guilt-provoking questions concerning the establishment and operation of the landfill after the decision to install it was made: whether the hole really was lined (and with what); whether health and environmental regulations on what could be dumped into it were observed; whether mandatory monitoring procedures ever happened.

Cam Oberting maintains that the record in these areas is one of abuse and deception on the part of both the county and Waste Management, Inc., the operators of the dump. Among other things, for instance, she says that the headless corpse of an elephant is rotting somewhere in there.

Conceivably, then, there might be skeletons in some closets of the Hillsborough County courthouse, just as there might be in the dump itself, and it is possible that a hint of fear might at times have motivated the county's strenuous defense of its virtue vis-à-vis Taylor Road. But whatever the lie of the land in this area, it is almost certain that overall, a feeling of anxiety must pervade the county commissioners' dump-related musings.

Anxiety would after all be a thoroughly appropriate emotion, for what would happen if the county were to declare, in public, that the Taylor Road landfill is a danger to its neighbors? And that its own decision-making process was responsible for that danger? Might such an admission not open a Pandora's box of other sites and other neighbors, other fights and other costs? And lawsuits, and judgments? The forcing of solution after solution after solution to problem after problem after problem? The cleaning up of who knows how many past messes, the finding of who knows how much money to do it with?

Ultimately, of course, there might appear the most frightening prospect of all: the arrangement of a future in which problems like the Taylor Road landfill would not be permitted to happen in the first place. Such a future would demand nothing short of an all-encompassing, intelligent, and successful compromise between the unstoppable forces of development and the immovable limits of the natural world, a plan infinitely more realistic than that which guides Hillsborough County's growth management today. And that compromise would cost.

It would cost in every way you can imagine—effort, popularity, conflict, and money, lots and lots and lots of money. To even attempt it would mean the end of convenience, the final death of business as usual; a step into a new, unfamiliar, almost unimaginably difficult world.

●

Three hundred and fifty new people per day. Even in Florida, that's impressive, and there may really be a dynamic kernel of truth in

Tampa's self-conferred title. It may in fact be America's next great city, the dynamic hub of a Hillsborough County megalopolis. Situated at the north end of the enormous tidal inlet known as Tampa Bay, with the densely populated Pinellas County peninsula shielding it from the Gulf of Mexico to the west, Tampa is surrounded by a great broad arc of Hillsborough County land stretching from the landlocked north all the way around the eastern shores of the bay. Unlike Los Angeles, which could in many ways be its prototype, the area is not hemmed in by mountains. For the most part it consists of a flat or attractively contoured patchwork of decreasingly profitable citrus grove and farmland, and virgin Florida scrub and swamp.

Over all this great verdant crescent of land the superb shifting coastal Florida skies tell you, with one upward glance, that you are in an earthly heaven of sorts. You are in a place a great many people would like to share. You are in a developer's wet dream.

If you live here already, you cannot avoid moving with the tides and spoutings of the dream. You are already in a place of mirage and illusion, a kind of magic all the more disorienting because it is so material, so literally concrete. You turn a bend in a road somewhere you've been before—last year, last month, last week—and suddenly you're somewhere new. You look in vain for the old peeling Florida cracker bungalow with its wraparound veranda and two blood-red rocking chairs where sometimes people whose lives you could ponder in a month's worth of idle moments sat laughing or dozing or watching you back. Gone is the engineless '54 Chevy pickup rusting in their yard beneath a spectacularly mature citrus tree bowed by oranges long past their picking time, and the stand of cypress back across a hundred yards of scrub oak and palmetto which used to hide . . . what? . . . reptiles, certainly; lizards of all kinds, and green snakes and rattlers, maybe a sleeping cottonmouth if there were water on the ground . . . and field mice too, and most likely armadillos; perhaps even a wild sow and her shoats foraging for acorns, invisible and untroubled by the noise of your exhaust beating across the tops of the palmetto fronds. All this has just vanished.

Now not even the road turns the way you remember. It widens suddenly and angles to the right, not the left, inviting your entry into the parking lot of a peach-colored Spanish-style strip mall—video stores, a Hallmark Card Center, a Larry's Ice Cream—which fronts similarly themed homes layered along lanes curved back into the land, the more commodious and expensive houses farthest from the sudden new highway.

You adjust relatively quickly (this is not a novel experience) and note the star of the new geography, the Larry's Ice Cream store, on your mental map. But even while you do this you know it's futile. This new community is very like another down another road nearby, and another twenty miles away on the other side of town, and still another across the bay in Clearwater, and moreover you know with absolute certainty that the next time you see it, it will have changed, or rather undergone a diffusion. It will still be identifiable, more or less, but the markers by which you fix it in one place as opposed to another—a particular sequence of highway stop signs, a specific span and density of condominiums strung along your route of approach— will have been erased, replaced or obscured or swallowed by even newer sights and structures. So will the markers of all the other places it resembles.

With this one new place, then, you have just this one moment. When it's gone, it will join all the others where on some future day you will wander confusedly, looking for an ice-cream cone or birthday card you're never quite sure you'll find, asking yourself the most basic question: Am I really where I mean to be, or where I only think I am?

And so if you live in Hillsborough County today, the very nature of your traveling imagination changes. Where in other times and places you might be able to ponder the color and complexity of your surroundings more or less at leisure—*Who are those people? What rules a swamp?*—here and now in the land around America's Next Great City you must pay attention. You must be attuned to operational data. You must be programming new information in order to manage the most mundane movements and decisions of everyday life. And gradually but surely you begin to acquire a defensive reflex. You begin to lose touch with the ideas of continuity and stasis. You stop seeing places as they are or how they must have been, and start seeing their future, all the ways in which they will be transformed.

You become an expert. When you travel a country road, you estimate how long before it's choked, it's got to be four-laned. When you see cattle in a pasture, you wonder how the rancher's doing, when he's planning to sell out, how good his attorneys are. When you see a tumbledown old cracker house on five acres near an interstate, you think millions, you think retirement in Maui; you feel jealous.

Eventually the inevitable happens. You start looking at swamps with lust in your heart, wondering how to find a few cheap thousand, risk them, and watch them multiply. The loss of nature, and of the places of your personal history, may still disturb you, but unconsciously you have become a hustler in a hustler's paradise. You have crossed into the realm of Development Thinking.

Development Thinking is seductive. It's a gold rush, it's a crapshoot, it's outrageous, it's a trip. It's the fast lane, boy, the big time. You play in this game, you're *living*.

Look at Buddy Buildit in his office, home of the action. Here he is, one sharp bright young man in a going-places company. His outfit's scattershooting mansions and condos all over the Hillsborough County map, gobbling up the greenbacks and the greenery, transforming not just hundreds but thousands of acres, and he's right there in the center of it, a prime mover. In his mid-thirties, fast-tracking furiously up the big-boy ladder, he's getting things done—done and done *right!*—and God, he's loving it. He's growing, he's expanding, getting richer and richer and better and better and more and more important; he matters.

"I'm on top of the fucking world!" he says, loosened up after an hour of development talk to the point where, unable to contain himself, he's just about doing the tango around his office. "This shit is *great!*"

Maybe Buddy, who isn't really Buddy but someone else who doesn't want his name mentioned, wouldn't be letting his hair down like this if he were talking on the record. Maybe then he'd have to be concentrating on his dignity, his social conservatism, his civic responsibility, his environmental sensitivity, all that stuff your New Age/Old Boy development professionals feel compelled to accentuate in public, while in private, among their own kind, they romp around like princes in a planet-sized sandbox.

These rules of public decorum are of relatively recent vintage. In Florida's previous Golden Ages of Building, a dredge-and-fill king was actually admired for holding a flamboyant court, proclaiming and testifying to the high-rolling carnival-barker instincts which made him tick. No more, though. Since the anti-fat-cat revolution of the Sanctimonious Sixties and the sunshine-law initiatives of the Cynical Seventies, the big boys have found it wise to hide their hoodoo lights under thick gray bushels of banker bluster and corporatespeak: *Just a servant of the community, Ma'am, accommodating the desires of the populace as expressed by your fine upstanding elected officials and your just-as-important self; ears open to everyone, eyes on the letter of the law, wouldn't sucker-punch a cypress swamp if it reared up and bit me in the BVD's.*

Quite naturally, this kind of mealymouthed public posturing, and the builder-baiting sociopolitical atmosphere which makes it necessary, get a bit wearing after a while, and so for the first few minutes of our candid chat with Buddy Buildit, we have to listen to him whine.

"How come *we're* the ogres?" he protests. *"We're* not the ones attracting three hundred and fifty people a day to Hillsborough County. *We're* not the ones who won't come up with even a halfway intelligent plan for handling them. We're the ones who are trying to give them shelter, give people one of the basic necessities of life!

"So really, why *are* we the villains? Why does the public think we're just hell-bent on uncontrolled, unconscionable growth no matter what? Why do they think we're out there raping and pillaging the environment, that all we want is wall-to-wall concrete? Don't they realize it's not in our interests to do that? And all these civic groups, these so-called 'environmentalists.' Why is it that when we lobby government for what we want, we're 'developers,' but they're 'citizens'? How come a single rezoning petitioner representing a company trying to house ten thousand people is 'a rezoning petitioner,' but a single activist is 'a citizen' speaking for 'the people'? Who are these 'people'? How many of them are there? Why are *we* their enemies?"

You can think up quite a few snappy counters to the basic "poor-us" tone of Buddy's speech, the most apropos of which concerns who actually makes the profit from concreting a significant portion of the environment and should therefore be prepared to endure a few sticks and stones along their path to the bank, but as to the issues of substance—well, snappy comebacks don't quite suffice. Buddy has a few points which demand elucidation at least.

One of his last points first: the identity of the people kicking against the developers. On this issue Buddy can get downright annoyed.

"Look, I don't have any problem about not developing an area where there are red-cockaded woodpeckers or certain kinds of endangered turtles or something like that," he says, "but most of the time, is that what's really going on when some private citizen starts screaming about how we're going to destroy the environment?

"Bullshit, it is. Usually what it's all about is that here you have some doctor or lawyer or college professor who's sold his house in Chicago or Long Island for some ungodly amount of money, and moved down here. So here he is in his $170,000 house on its nice big lot out there on the fringe of town someplace, and he's just heard about a plan to put high-density, low-income housing on the undeveloped land out back, and—bam!—he wakes up the next morning, he's an environmentalist! All of a sudden there are wetlands to be protected, indigenous flora and fauna the developers want to destroy; whatever excuse he can come up with.

"Now really, and I have to say this again, I'm one hundred percent with the people who are against the destruction of wetlands and wildlife habitats—but this guy? All *he's* against is a bunch of local yokels living next door! And that's just hypocrisy, big-time."

In this scenario, which has been known to happen in locations other than Buddy's rhetoric, we have the bones of a meaty subject. Rather obviously, the kind of development which wins awards from civic groups and planning commissions, and which causes the least ravagement of virgin land, is the most expensive kind: big single-family homes on big lots, with plenty of preserved or re-created wetlands and wildlife habitats, and plenty of open space between one development and another. So if you were building only that kind of development, subdivisions with homes beginning around $150,000 and going right on up, no problem; you'd be eating up God's green earth, all right, but both your private and state-sponsored environmentalists would be thinking you were a swell bunch of fellows.

But that's not the real world. A regional economy can't survive on fat cats and queen bees alone. It needs drones and workers. It needs the salt of the earth, and unfortunately salt kills. You want seventy-thousand-dollar homes, they have to be small, and you have to put lots of them on an acre, and you have to think hard about whether you can really afford that damn tree's root system, whether you might just be able to wangle or threaten your way around the various statutes protecting that useless swamp in the middle of nowhere which happens to be the only affordable land left.

According to Buddy, that's when you get into trouble. The moment you propose any high-density, low-income project in Hillsborough County, he says, the guardians of your grandchildren's quality of life —activists with the media's ear, bureaucrats with sanctions that'll cost you a fortune—come howling after you like bassets on a bear. The only folks on *your* side are a bunch of unorganized, inarticulate working stiffs looking for any old home they can afford, be it ever so environmentally compromising.

The questions of social and environmental conscience get rather nastily tangled in this arena, then, but the end result is simple: the working stiffs pay through the nose for their homes. In Hillsborough County, the term "affordable housing" is a joke. Certainly, people get to live under those beautiful skies with a palm tree or two somewhere in sight, but on the square-footage and neighbor-proximity fronts they're up the creek.

Two factors drive up the price. First is the basic, constantly rising cost of land in a rapidly developing region; a dynamic exacerbated by the limits placed on land use, and therefore land availability, by environmental laws. That's a given, an inevitability. You can't do anything about it but repeal a lot of statutes a lot of very loud people are very attached to.

Second is something else again: the price added onto the cost of land by government in exchange for services and amenities such as roads, sewers, and water.

That's not inevitable at all. It's going to cost, of course, but how much it costs depends on how well, or badly, the system supplying the services does its job. And right there you have a situation which causes the fuses of Buddy Buildit to snap, crackle, and pop.

Buddy's contention is that in Hillsborough County the authorities quite literally do not have their shit together. Sure, the roads are a pretty gruesome problem, and the freshwater supply isn't something a sane person should have to think about for too long, but the fluid-waste disposal situation in America's Next Great City is—well, Buddy will tell you.

"Here's a little statistic for you," he says. "Here's one I'll bet you didn't know. You know how much every single public utilities customer pays each year just to cover the fines the county has incurred for violating waste treatment and disposal laws? I'll tell you: twenty-six dollars. Just for the *fines,* man!

"I mean, it's ridiculous. The county's utility system has gotten itself so badly overextended and so badly in debt that their waste disposal plants just can't handle the amount of waste generated yesterday, let alone tomorrow. It's a mess. Everything about it's a mess. A colleague of mine went out to one of the waste treatment plants a few months ago on business, and found the place empty. There weren't any operators there! Raw sludge was overflowing a weir built to contain it because the grates were clogged; nobody had cleaned them. So he got out there and scraped the shit off himself.

"That's a little thing, sure, but it's typical. They're trying to play catch-up, you see, but there's no way. That's why they've had something like eleven directors in the past nine years. The new guy comes in thinking he's gonna solve the problems, looks around, realizes what he's up against, and loses it. Nobody can take that kind of heat."

The heat Buddy's talking about comes from all sides. Developers trying to get their spanking-new subdivision's sewer lines hooked up to the new waste treatment plant they were promised become enraged when they're told the plant isn't capable of handling as much waste as it was supposed to, so we're sorry, sir, no hookup; your houses may be ready, but nobody can live in them. Other developers, ready to start the permit-getting process after being lured to Hillsborough County by those three hundred and fifty daily new customers and Florida's highly attractive tax breaks, are understandably upset when they discover the terms of the waste disposal deal: sure, we'll give you a "dry line" permit—go right ahead and build your sewers—but sorry, we can't guarantee when or even whether we'll let them get wet. Those developers leave to consult with their attorneys—ha, a respite!—but no sooner have they left than here comes a new citation from the state's Department of Environmental Regulation or the Southwest Florida Water Management District or the county's Environmental Protection Commission, and now your poor utilities manager is dealing with even less waste treatment capacity than he could offer ten minutes ago, and in walks another builder to whom that margin was promised by whichever former utilities manager had this headache back in '85.

The manager can always duck this stuff, of course—hide in the bathroom, read the *Tampa Tribune*—but he'd better stay away from the editorial pages. Likely as not, they're going to contain all kinds of opinions—rage from the Builders Association of Greater Tampa, bemused thanks from antigrowth environmental groups, soul-destroying sarcasm from all and sundry—about the moratorium on new sewer hookups to county plants which is the end result of the history he's trying to avoid.

Buddy Buildit isn't a vindictive person, so you don't doubt him at all when he says, "I feel for those guys, I really do. They've got a *horrible* job. You go by their offices any day of the week, and it's like someone's running a cockfight in the middle of a lawyers' convention. And the shame of it is that the managers aren't the ones responsible for their problems. It's the county commissioners who got them into this mess."

The story Buddy relates is a sad and silly one. Briefly retold, it goes like so. In 1983 the local Environmental Protection Commission came down hard on the Next Great City's overextended liquid-waste disposal system, imposing a moratorium on new sewer hookups into one of the larger plants serving a prime development area. This displeased the development community mightily, and so they strove to get something done about it. They wanted that moratorium lifted, and both they and the regulatory agencies wanted some sort of plan: how, pray, was the area's liquid-waste disposal system going to be expanded so that it could handle not just current but future demand?

The developers got the moratorium lifted, but only for a short while. Then it was reimposed, and other moratoriums on almost all the county's other plants came into effect, and then the utility authority conceded the day to the EPC by placing the onus for the treatment of new developments' liquid waste onto the developers themselves. The developers would have to build and operate septic tanks or "interim waste water treatment facilities" at their own expense, and continue to do so until such time as new municipal facilities became operational.

This solution was not exactly pleasing to the developers—their cost per lot went up by an average of one thousand dollars, and they still had to pay impact fees despite the fact that they weren't getting sewer service in return—but at least now they could build.

The second response spoke to developers, regulators, commissioners, and everybody else on the utility authority's back. It was a plan: a commitment to building X number of new facilities over Y number of years, to be capable of handling Z million gallons of additional sewage. It was drawn up, and it was accepted by the county commissioners, and its existence was comforting.

Unfortunately, says Buddy, it was a terrible plan. It hinged on the utility authority's assignment of credibility to one particular, very conservative population growth projection offered by the University of South Florida. Other, higher projections were offered by USF, but—well, the low one was chosen. The number of millions of gallons of future sewage was based on it, and the number and capacity and location of future treatment plants was based on that. And of course, that population growth projection wasn't credible at all. It wasn't even close. Doubtless it sugared the pill somewhat (increasing daily capacity by thirty million gallons doesn't cost nearly as much as increasing it by a hundred and thirty), but as Buddy puts it, "right there and then, as soon as I saw those figures, I knew we were fucked."

Buddy can talk for quite a while on this subject. He'll tell you about new municipal plants being booked to capacity as soon as they form on the drawing board; about what a pain it is to have to build your own facility and get it licensed; about how stupid it is that that and all the other environmental permitting processes for your basic new subdivision require more time and effort than is involved in actually building the damn thing; about how *that's* what puts an $80,000 home on the market at $90,000. Then, if you ask him, he can broaden the scope of his complaints to address such problems in the whole state of Florida. He can bitch for hours about the fate of the state's development infrastructure law, designed to prevent exactly the kind of mess Hillsborough County's gotten itself into. That law prevents local governments from permitting new development without first ensuring that monies are available and plans in place for adequate roads and sewers and the like, and in theory it's great. In reality, though, it's a white elephant. The funds earmarked for it were to come from Governor Bob Martinez's statewide service tax on professional and freelance persons (which the development community backed after much reluctant soul-searching). Now, though, the service tax is defunct, repealed in a very nasty political free-for-all. So there are no funds.

Which means, essentially, that local elected officials are back to taking the heat square in the chest. Unsheltered by the primary virtue of the state legislation and its accompanying tax—the fact that it removed the onus for funding development infrastructure from local government—they must grapple once again with the worst kind of decisions: whether to raise impact fees on developers, who then pass them along to new residents, or to raise property taxes on the people already voting for them. Either way they lose, and so for the most part they choose to avoid making such choices.

This is why, when all's said and done, Buddy's central point remains simple. It's the same as that hammered home time after time by his foe Cam Oberting: the commissioners of Hillsborough County, who are ultimately responsible for balancing the forces of the local development/environment equation, just can't hack it. That's why Buddy and most of his friends keep trying to find solutions in rearrangements of the local political structure. Recently they tried, but failed, to get the county utility authority privatized. Now they're shooting for the installation of an elected county mayor over the heads of the Board of County Commissioners. Such an individual, provided of course that he or she were a person of mettle with the right kind of sympathies, could surely do what a whole gaggle of variously courageous, variously accessible county commissioners can't. So yes, the Strong-Man-to-Drain-the-Marshes-and-Make-the-Trains-Run-on-Time approach might just work. . . .

But well, enough of this. Enough bitching and scheming. When you get right down to it, Buddy's an optimist, and basically he's feeling good. Somehow or other things are going to work out okay. If you doubt that, all you need to do is watch as he swivels in his desk chair to contemplate and explain the large, multicolored, special-purpose map he has on the wall behind him.

It's a lovely map of a wonderful future, starring one of the greatest building bonanzas the Sunbelt has ever seen: a corridor of undeveloped land, thirty-five miles long as the crow flies, around the I-75 Interstate highway running from the border of Pasco County in the north, circling Tampa to the east, and plunging southward all the way to the border of Manatee County. *All* that land, all those cow pastures and strawberry fields and citrus groves and stretches of palmetto scrub, is slated for development.

Buddy has a little trouble containing himself when he talks about the I-75 corridor. "It's unbelievable," he laughs. "It's almost scary. Just look at one section of it, what's on the books already in that one little section from the Pasco County line down Route 581 to just north of the University of South Florida . . ."

There ensues a lilting litany of numbingly contemporary subdivisional place names—East and West Meadows, New Community, Williamsburg, Tampa Palms—accompanied by figures of multiples of thousands spoken with happy pride. A thousand acres and twenty-five hundred lots are projected here. Thirty-five hundred units on twenty-eight hundred acres are planned over there. South of that, thirteen and a half thousand units are "already real, man; they're actually *in the ground!*"

Buddy can't stop. His arm goes stabbing southward down the map, illuminating the high spots which are going to make international financiers and pan-Sunbelt developers and individual property owners and cartels of local farmers filthy stinking beautiful rich. Not to mention young hotshots like himself.

He beams. "It's *amazing,*" he says. "I still can't quite believe it. And man, the amount of money going around is just ridiculous. The wage scales in the building industry in this town are incredible! I mean, God bless those three hundred and fifty people a day."

A week or so after Buddy says these words, the euphoria of the development community is demonstrated in another way, at an enormous Christmas party his company holds. The festivities occur in a slightly shabby area—not quite the kind of place a real fast tracker, let alone a social lion, would wish to call home—and so the party paints that part of town some unusually rich colors that night. There's a lot of silver on the streets, sheening off mink and the paintwork of motorcars of distinction, and of course there is gold galore, everywhere. And then too there's a certain atmosphere in the air, a certain attitude.

As the party breaks up in mid-evening, the guests can be seen strolling casually to the cars they have parked willy-nilly throughout the neighborhood. They're laughing and joking among themselves as they stroll along the pavement, and they're taking their time. They can do that because a few of their dominant males have stationed themselves at strategic intersections and are halting local traffic.

The traffic backs up. The small fry just have to wait while the lions and fast-trackers act as if they own the place.

Buddy speaks harsh words about the Hillsborough County commissioners and their staff, but he can certainly see their side of things.

He knows that in a state whose refusal to impose a personal income tax on its residents is written in stone, where public monies must be raised by sales and property taxes and county bond issues and whatever other more creative instruments elected officials and their consultants can dream up, the task of paying for sewers and the like is daunting indeed.

Buddy knows too that it must be extraordinarily difficult for politicians raised in the good-ole-boys-behind-closed-doors tradition of public service to operate in the light of the state's relatively newfangled sunshine laws. He acknowledges that this requirement alone is capable of immobilizing even the most committed elected effectuator.

Also, of course, he admits that were he in local government, his own mind would simply fuse, his balls wither and freeze, when he came face to face with the unholy mess of past mistakes, administrative mediocrity, financial shortfall, legal stricture, and every-which-way public pressure which confronts the county's governing body at every step of its effort to cope with the runaway horses of growth. He has the greatest sincere sympathy for individuals who would even think of taking such a job.

Furthermore, his view of the specific people in those specific posts is benevolent; well, he admits, they sure do try. They really do. They're not at all asleep at the wheel; they *are* doing their best. And in the final analysis, when you really get down to brass tacks, Buddy really can't think of those people as his adversaries. He knows that most of the hard-pressed county commissioners genuinely want to help him, and he subscribes to the basic attitude of the development community: *they've got an awful tough row to hoe out there in the activist-infested badlands, and God bless 'em, they're doing what they can for us.*

This is why Buddy has requested anonymity. Although he doesn't mind a lot of the things he says ending up on the record, he doesn't want his final judgment—that ultimately, the commissioners simply can't hack it—attributed to him personally. He has to live with those folks down at the county courthouse, and he knows that when they're backed into corners in public by the big noise and vitriol of Cam Oberting and her colleagues, they really don't need to be reading about how even Cam's enemies think they can't cut the mustard.

No. What they need is friends. They need private visits from soothing people, respectful high-tone folks with answers rather than questions, good relaxed professional sorts with the facts and figures at their fingertips; fellows who may push a little in their own interest but, being men of the world, can always find a dignified way clear of the messes over lunch or a sail in the bay or a round on the links. What they need, in short, is what they get: lobbyists.

They get a lot of them, and they get them frequently. Between February and July of 1987, for example, eight development-interest lobbyists met with county commissioners a hundred and eighteen times. And while the tangible results of these visits don't amount to much—you can't retire on the cash value of framed photographs or Seiko desk clocks or carved wooden ducks or helicopter rides and bouquets of roses—the worth of the feeling behind those trinkets and courtesies is inestimable. The feeling can often amount to real friendship.

The basic picture comes into focus pretty quickly when, waiting in the reception area of the commissioners' offices for your appointment with one or another of them, you get to watch the casual comings and goings of the developers' smoothies, hear the friendly laughter, catch that easy body language as they're escorted to the door. Sometimes of course it's a slow day, so you have to seek other sources of entertainment. You cast around for something to read—Hmmm, what *do* the commissioners of Hillsborough County wish their visitors to know?—and there it is again. Only two items are available: a few copies of the county employees' internal newsletter and a much larger stack of *The Building Barometer,* a professionally produced, articulate, and persuasive organ through which the Builders' Association of Greater Tampa promotes its various accomplishments, arguments, and ambitions. So while you await your county commissioners' pleasure, you can discover in detail just why impact fees discriminate against pioneer spirits, environmental agencies are un-American, and sewer moratoriums suck.

And yes, this stuff gets to you. If you personally have any doubts whatsoever about the blinding beauty and utter righteousness of endless subdivisions marching out proud and purty across that broad sunlit horizon of West-Central Florida's fabulous future, you can't really read *The Building Barometer* without beginning to feel mean spirited, uptight, unadventurous. You're a party pooper, aren't you? You're a bloody-minded goody-goody who just can't stand to see a bunch of nice ole boys and gals doing the right thing for everybody, making money and having fun.

Well, as they say, go for it. You feel like this, you might as well *really* feel like this. Go visit with the person the good ole boys have marked as the starchiest starchy-pants and prissiest party pooper of them all, the one Hillsborough County commissioner whose whole political career has been spent lobbing ice cubes into the happy hot tub of their sweet long condo-spouting wet dream. Oh, yes, she's chilly all right. Her very name is cold, flat, antitumescent: Jan Platt.

In person, and in her social as opposed to her political reputation, Ms. Platt is not at all mean. She seems in fact quite warm and gracious, even sweet. But yes, she is definitely different. Her conversation is careful, tentative, economical, and quiet; a hardy-har-har or a quick shifty shuffle or an odyssey of obfuscation, the usual tricks of the conversational trade around the Hillsborough County courthouse, would seem as out of character from Ms. Platt as would antlers on a barn owl (that bird being, in fact, a creature our lady of lonely resistance somewhat resembles). Ms. Platt, in short, is about as far from being a good ole gal as it is possible for a Florida politician to be.

Her sense of separateness, both self-perceived and obvious to anybody with eyes and ears, is immediately apparent when, after appropriate thought, she answers the first question: why do Florida politicians, as a rule, support developers no matter what?

"I've often wondered that myself," she says slowly, "and I think that if there were old money in the state, there might be people of stature who would speak out against what is occurring as it relates to growth and the environment. Such people would have a broader perspective. But the way it is, there is no old money. There is no hierarchy of individuals who play the role of elder statesmen. The people of stature, the key people in the state, are *participants* in the growth game."

And, although a high-tone person such as herself is not about to cast stones any more substantial than "the source of a politician's campaign funds can often tell you a lot," the fact is that her fellow commissioners are substantial beneficiaries of development-participatory largess. Not she, though: the $2,000 total of contributions to her last campaign for office, in 1984, included not a dime from development interests. Among other things, this fact makes her policy of refusing private meetings with development lobbyists less awkward than it might be for her colleagues if they ever tried it.

It also excludes her from another popular activity. She can't dream the dream of many others in the Hillsborough County courthouse (or for that matter most other parts of the nation and levels of government). Her vision is unlighted by what is often the single bright ray of hope on the gloomy, storm-plagued landscape of public service work. Should she decide to retire from public office, it is unlikely that developers around town will be lining up to bid on *her* services as a "consultant."

Such an option is very real in Hillsborough County, where the average assembly of development lobbyists could quite easily be mistaken for an annual reunion of courthouse and environmental-agency hotshots. And no wonder, really, because as a career track the option functions very well indeed, its ultimate virtue being that where you start out doesn't matter. This track doesn't require a law or engineering or political science degree, or even prior acquaintance with the people who matter; it just requires that somehow or other you get yourself elected. And that just requires some smarts and some money. And *that* just requires singing the right song when you hold out your hand to the developers. Any ambitious realtor or schoolteacher or Jiffy Lube franchisee, any retiring cop or bought-out strawberry farmer, can connect *those* dots.

The heart of the matter is right there in black and white in the public record. In the county elections of 1984, development interest sources accounted for twenty-one percent of Commissioner James Selvey's $33,488 in declared campaign contributions; thirty-two percent of Commissioner Pam Iorio's $51,957; thirty-six percent of Commissioner Haven Poe's $84,050; thirty-nine percent of Commissioner Rodney Colson's $29,750; forty-three percent of Commission Chairman Rubin Padgett's $60,067; and fifty percent of Commissioner Pick Talley's $91,195.

The confluence of interests represented by these figures, if unfortunate for interest groups such as Cam Oberting's CAST (Civic Associations Sticking Together), is entirely legal in an exquisitely calculated, very-fine-shades-of-gray kind of way dependent on factors like how many individual checks make up an interest bloc's total campaign contribution to an individual candidate, and so nobody on the Board of County Commissioners needs to be looking over his or her shoulder in this particular area.

Then too, the word around Hillsborough County political circles is that neither are the commissioners at great risk on the corruption-in-office front. These are not, it is said, people in search of envelopes full of small-denomination bills, folks who'll wangle you a quick quiet minor rezoning for the price of a long weekend in Bimini, free rein on a cypress swamp for a kid's college education. That approach to public service work, it is said, ceased to be an option in Hillsborough County after three of the seven commissioners who preceded the current crop exercised it extensively and stupidly enough to get caught, thereby initiating a scandal which dropped the chop on two or three dozen other courthouse insiders, bolstered the confidence of the area's federal prosecutors, scared the bejesus out of all the good ole boys and gals who somehow escaped with only their reputations tarnished, and made it abundantly clear that in future, influence peddling had better be done right or not done at all. So the kind of low-tone wrongdoing revealed in the '83–'85 scandals—some half-wit who'd somehow gotten himself a county commissioner's chair putting the rezoning screws to an unmistakably hostile do-gooder for a quick five hundred dollars, that sort of thing—just won't wash anymore.

Even so, Ms. Platt's point, that the source of a politician's campaign funds can tell you a lot, is well taken in Hillsborough County. The consensus in local political circles is that most of the county commissioners continue to serve their sponsors in the development community however they legally can. And so, nourishing her dream that one day, candidates will arise from the ranks of the local civic associations and actually make it through the elective process and sit in the chairs around her (Why not? It's already happened in California local government, and what happens in California quite often happens in Florida a decade or so later), Ms. Platt smiles her long-suffering smile and keeps up her lonely fight.

She campaigns for the registration of lobbyists visiting her colleagues; not just the annual "I am a lobbyist" declarations her colleagues suggest but a detailed record of who visits whom when and where, what is discussed, and what is spent. So far, though, she has crashed and burned on the issue. She also wants Hillsborough County to copy the state law which prohibits government personnel from lobbying government on behalf of outside interests for two years after they've left office or government employment. So far, no go on that one either, and the consensus is that it'll snow for a week in Tampa in August before such a restriction acquires the force of law. All the same, she just keeps chipping away, registering her single No vote on issue after issue when she perceives the long-term health and welfare of her constituents to be threatened by the profits of the developers and the short-term political interests of her fellow commissioners.

It's that short-term business which really gets to her. Although she

speaks as circumspectly as always, the look of long-suffering pain so
familiar to witnesses of the county commission's weekly public meetings conveys her feelings quite clearly as she notes that "Yes, one of
the problems with a high-growth state *is* a tendency for people to
prefer the shortcut solution to one which has a chance of lasting.
Long-term solutions cost more money, you see, and it's my observation that there's a push to do things as quickly and as cheaply as
possible, to stretch the tax dollar as far as it will go."

She refers for example to the issue of the installation of viral filters
on the county's wastewater treatment plants, a very hot potato in the
latter half of 1987. Kicked off by reports of viral meningitis allegedly
attributable to treated sewer water sprayed on various lands in the
county, the county commissioners' see-sawing on the issue pivoted
not on whether viral filters might be a good idea but whether good
money should be spent on them.

Ms. Platt just sees red on this point. "That shouldn't even have
been a question!" she exclaims. "I mean, *really*. There are some
things government just *has* to afford."

She calms down again, pauses, and resumes her usual circumspection. "It's my observation that probably, some of the resistance to the
viral filters has been because spending money on them would take
money away from building more sewer lines to new developments,
and from building new sewage treatment plants," she ventures. "That
wouldn't aid and abet the developers at all."

She sighs; a weary, frustrated sound. "I don't know. It's hard for
me to understand. If we're building a metropolitan area that's going to
have any substance, it ought to be done right the first time. But the
fast money . . . you see, a lot of the development money, which
comes from California and Texas and other places—they're national
companies, international companies—is in and out of here quickly.
But those of us who make this place our home are still going to be
here long after that money's gone, living with the negative impact of
all those shortcuts."

She sighs again, and explains what she means about the shortcuts.

"What happens, you see, is that when a developer petitions the
planning board for an ammendment to the land use plan to allow
greater density or intensity, which happens all the time, I consistently

bring up infrastructure costs: roads, sewers, all the other things. That's what ought to be taken into account when you ammend a land use plan for higher densities and intensities. I always ask, 'If we can't pay for what's currently on the map, how are we going to fund more?'

"The response I usually get is 'Well, that's something we'll deal with at zoning time.' So zoning time comes around, and zoning says, 'Well, you can use septic tanks,' or 'You can use an interim wastewater treatment plant,' or 'You can drill your own water wells.'

"That's just fine for the developers, but what about the rest of us? What good is your planning doing when the planning decisions are being made at the zoning level, and what's happening there is that you're deciding to allow more septic tanks, interim plants, and private wells? Do you know that Hillsborough County is one of the top four counties nationally for total number of septic tanks? That the county has more than thirty thousand private wells? That everywhere you look, there are interim wastewater treatment plants that are only monitored on weekdays, when very obviously their maximum usage and worst violations are occurring on weekends, when people are at home? Recently I questioned that particular policy, and do you know what the answer was? It was 'Well, inspecting on weekends would cost too much.' "

Unstated by Ms. Platt, but obviously relevant, is the point that a change in the interim plant inspection policy, like a lot of other good ideas circulating in Hillsborough County, would end up costing more than employee overtime. A few fines might result, and some disagreements. A few uncomfortable realities about the integrity of all those privately operated plants might surface. The whole issue of why they're there in the first place would have to be hauled out from the county's monster closet. Somebody might have to face up to the terrifying notion that in the waste treatment arena, growth costs two things: better government, and a bigger county budget.

There is, too, an even worse nightmare lurking out there: the queasy question of how long America's Next Great City can sustain its boom on an economic diet composed primarily of development money. The way things are now, Tampa has a characteristic in common with the sharks which prowl the waters of its bay. It must keep moving, or die.

Ms. Platt addresses this question. "Our major industries in Florida were always agriculture and tourism," she explains, "but now you don't hear very much about those. The emphasis has shifted to building. The construction industry is now the major force. As I was growing up, for instance, Tampa was considered an industrial community with a very conservative economy; things were *made* here. But now that's all changed, and the economy is out of balance. Certainly, Time Inc. and Citicorp have come to town, but those have been the only major companies that have moved in in recent years—and I just wonder what's going to happen down the line if all the financial interests in the area are geared towards this building thing. What happens when there are so many skyscrapers and subdivisions that people have no reason to move here?

"But still there's this push for increased density, increased intensity, which of course serves the interests of the developers, because for some reason, we've got to keep up with Texas and California and everywhere else to bring the high-tech industry down here, we've got to be on the cutting edge of—oh, something.

"For instance, I attended a meeting on mass transit the other day, where it was said that in order to get mass transit, we have to have high-density areas. The planners had gone to Toronto to look at how the mass transit system works there, you see, and that's the conclusion they'd reached: we need high density.

"I listened to that and realized how absurd it was. Aren't the people who move down here wanting to get *away* from the Torontos of this world? Don't they want to live a traditional Florida style of life, on a lot, with palm trees?"

Maybe they do and maybe they don't. Maybe they really want to pay whatever they have to for a thousand square feet of half-assed high-density housing with a blue sky somewhere up above, no matter what kind of crap they have to drink or what kind of taxes or impact fees they have to pay so they don't have to drink crap. Maybe they really want to suck exhaust fumes everywhere they go, and get to the beach via multibillion-dollar public transportation systems. But what if potential migrants won't accept that kind of life? What if the Tampa and Hillsborough County governments don't somehow provide the kind of low-cost infrastructure that will attract enough industry to ensure a continued migrant flow no matter how degraded the area's living conditions become? Then, you're looking at a disaster. You're not talking Los Angeles without mountains; you're talking Houston without oil. You're talking empty office towers, deserted subdivisions, plummeting land values; a lot of very unhappy good-byes.

Jan Platt is not alone in her misgivings about Tampa's future, and the frightening thing about the people who share her pessimism is that they aren't all environmental activists or change-hating natives.

Consider, for instance, the opinion of Buddy Buildit, a building booster speaking straight from the mouth of the development horse.

"Right now, we're doing just great—wonderful, incredible, there's money *everywhere*—because we're buffered from the effects of the national economy by those three hundred and fifty new people a day," he says. "But that can't last. There's just no way, no matter what happens. Those people just aren't going to keep coming to Hillsborough County. So you want the truth? I'll tell you. In ten years, it's going to be all over. The building money's going to pull out, and this town is gonna *die*."

Even if America's Next Great City dies, though, life will still go on in and around it. Very large numbers of people will still breathe its air and use its roads and drink its water and flush its toilets. And so the basic question remains: *can* Tampa and Hillsborough County get their organic human waste together?

Roger Stewart has to think about a lot more than organic human waste product. As administrator of the Hillsborough County Environmental Protection Commission, he has to deal with air pollution, water pollution, wetlands destruction, toxic waste dumping, radon poisoning, solid waste disposal; everything, in short, that is a threat to Hillsborough County's ability to support relatively healthy human habitation. So he and his agency have quite a catholic agenda on their hands.

All the same, though, shit is the key to it. It was the most outrageous of the county's environmental problems when Stewart first entered the arena in 1968, it's been the most contentious issue he's dealt with throughout the years since, and quite possibly it will end up doing him in. Mr. Stewart's long, bitter campaign against Tampa and Hillsborough County's gruesome approach to sewage treatment may just end in utter defeat. For likely as not, America's Next Great City *will* get its organic human waste together, and then it will dump it into Tampa Bay.

The bay is where it all started, where in the mid-1960s Roger Stewart found himself assessing the effects of decades of uncontrolled pollution—intentional wholesale dumping of everything you can imagine, from radioactive phosphate waste to industrial petrochemicals to semitreated sewage—for a federal study. At that point in time, he remembers with great clarity, the upper bay close to Tampa (Hillsborough Bay) was a cesspool. The water was either acidic or highly organic, the sea grass and marine life were dead or dying, the bottom was either a crust of phosphate waste and industrial chemicals or an oozing sludge of human offal. Slicks of oil and chemicals and sewage fanned out across the surface of the bay from all manner of private and municipal facilities, moving wherever wind and tide took them.

It was too much for the people who lived around the bay. To the campaign against air pollution already begun by hacking, vomiting residents of upscale Davis Islands was added a new initiative by residents of upscale Bayshore Boulevard, people wearied by the constant stench of human waste pervading their otherwise gracious lifestyles. And since these were citizens who mattered, something got done. The Environmental Protection Commission was created by an act of the state legislature in the fall of 1967, and by the spring of 1968 it was in action. Roger Stewart, a high school dropout equipped with a brand-new degree from the University of South Florida after a twenty-one-year career as an Air Force pilot (starting in World War II P-40 fighters, ending in the Strategic Air Command's midair-refueling jets), was right there in the center of the storm as a staff biologist.

It was Citation City in those days, akin to combat. Major employers and taxpayers, unaccustomed to petty government functionaries with real power in their pens, tended to regard the EPC's inspection and citation activities as a nuisance which could be eliminated by the locking of gates, the telephoning of friends in high places, the issuing of personal threats, or, in cases of unusual persistence, the judicious wielding of blunt instruments.

They learned better quite quickly, for the EPC had teeth. Backed by the state and the Feds and the stench-sick local hoi polloi, and cheered on by a general citizenry motivated by a rabidly enthusiastic press, Stewart and his colleagues kicked ass and took names. And soon even the most powerful local industrialists were forced to recognize that in Hillsborough County it was becoming unwise to fool too brazenly with Mother Nature. By the mid-1970s it was a foregone conclusion that in order to get rid of your waste, whatever it might be, you simply had to do something other than flush it into Tampa Bay, and whatever you did had to meet the EPC's requirements. Otherwise ol' Roger, now in the pilot's seat of the agency with the courts and public opinion as his crew, would harry you quite mercilessly. He'd be fair and open and legal, and he'd work tirelessly with you to minimize the pain of legal compliance, but if you tried to squirrel away from him on the bottom line, you'd get strafed; he could and would swoop down and nail you, stop you dead. This was a man in a job with real power, and unfortunately for the transgressors, he just happened to be a blunt-talking, square-dealing, bottom-line kind of guy.

Which is putting it mildly, for in a world of often-befuddled bureaucrats and frequently hysterical activists and too-loquacious lobbyists and elected representatives who seem to expend most of their energy ducking issues and covering their tracks, Roger Stewart's way with a question of substance is nothing short of shocking. Five minutes after you penetrate *his* office in search of illumination on Hillsborough County's environmental state of health, you feel like maybe you've stumbled in on the Duke after a hard day hanging Apaches and slugging tequila.

Which is quite refreshing. Very quickly you arrive at the purely instinctive conclusion that here, really, is an honest-to-God straight shooter. A man with Command Presence, Balls of Iron, and Real Old-fashioned Common Sense.

On the Taylor Road landfill issue, for instance, his stance is practical. Sure, he says, the dump is mislocated in the worst way. He's always held that opinion, right from the beginning. Like Dr. Parker, he recommended quite emphatically that the county truck its garbage to the infinitely more suitable Sydney Mine site. On the other hand, Stewart believes that many of Cam Oberting's criticisms are naive. "Garbage dumps aren't *pretty,*" he says. "They're what they are: garbage. Any garbage dump is a goddamn mess. You get a stink, you get leachates to a certain degree, you get methane gas you have to vent somehow. And when you talk about covering up a dump, you're not talking about some nice, even, fresh-mown lawn up there; you're talking dirt bulldozed over trash. It's gonna settle, the rain's gonna fall on it, and all sorts of stuff is gonna stick out here and there through the top. So given all of that, which is all perfectly legal and acceptable, I think the county's done an okay job out there. Even now, the contractors are always out there. They're *always* working on it."

On the issue of groundwater contamination from the dump, he is more ambivalent. On the one hand, he says, he thinks that Cam is off the beam about the dump's being to all intents and purposes unlined. He notes that there has been very little hard evidence of groundwater pollution (with the exception of one plume moving south from an older, unlined section of the dump, to which the county reacted correctly by connecting the affected homes with the city water supply). But he also thinks that the county's failure to ring the dump with first-alert monitoring wells was stupid, and so was their decision to save a little money by not connecting all the homes near the dump to city water. "It's worth something to have your taxpayers able to sleep nights," he says, "and as experience has proven, providing good water would certainly have been a great deal cheaper in the long run."

All this speaks to the central premises of Roger Stewart's approach to environmental protection. As he explains, "I'm not an activist. I don't just jump on the bandwagon whenever some group or individual starts screaming. I'll look at what they're concerned about, and I'll get interested if they have a legitimate case, but I'm sure as hell not going to spend the resources of this agency just because somebody wants me to.

"Then too, I'm not a preservationist. I have no problem at all with doing everything possible to keep the Grand Canyon and places like that the way they are, but where you have a society already entrenched, as we do here, pure preservationism is pure fantasy. You can't go tearing down people's homes to restore coastal mangroves that were dredged and filled thirty years ago; you can't turn Tampa Bay back into what it was before people lived on it. There's not enough money in the whole world to pay for a job like that, even if it *could* be done.

"The bottom line, you see, is that sure, you want to keep the environment from just getting raped—but you can't stop development, and really, you shouldn't want to. In human society, the environment is not necessarily the most important thing."

Well tut-tut. When Roger Stewart says things like that in public, which he does quite often, certain very vocal elements of the Tampa Bay area population see bright flaming bloody scarlet. Aesthetes and elitists howl when he opines that so long as not a single wetland is destroyed or a legally protected critter directly done away with or any other environmental law transgressed, he's completely at ease with the idea of not just tiny pockets but endless tracts of ugly, nasty, low-income housing eating up Hillsborough County real estate. Then too, sportsfisherpersons and everyone else who can't live with the effects of humanity on Tampa Bay itself haul out their lynching ropes when he just flat refuses to listen to their demands that public monies be spent on the daunting task of planting new sea grasses in the bay bed. They can't stand it when he tells them, and gives hard-number proof from the EPC's rigorous baywide monitoring system, that thanks to the steady improvement of bay water quality brought about almost solely by his work, Mother Nature is seeing to the regeneration of sea grasses all by herself, very efficiently and for free.

Stewart is aware of the reactions that his positions elicit, and he finds them ironic. "The problem is, you see, that activists need a cause," he rumbles, "but what have they got when they look at the bay? It's improving very demonstrably—we've quit bullying it, so now Mother Nature's bouncing back, that's how it's done, for God's sake!—so the activists have to say it's not improving fast enough. And then too they need enemies. Since there aren't any big bad polluters to fill that role anymore, they've made *me* the enemy."

Which may be true. The shining heroes of the environmental crusade back in the David-and-Goliath days, Roger Stewart and his agency are now quite often the targets of choice for frustrated

preservationists, *Tampa Tribune* editorialists, and all the other activist factions whose trolls and nightmares the EPC's efforts have
rendered a good deal less readily definable than they used to be.

For Stewart that is bad news. Having set the bay back on track and
forced developers to respect the wetlands and done all he can on air
pollution, having muscled his agency into a position of quite extraordi-
nary influence (there isn't another county-level environmental agency
in Florida or perhaps even the nation quite as effective or innovative
as the EPC), he needs public support to expand his activities. He
wants all sorts of new weapons for the wars he's waging already—a
mechanism, for instance, for inflicting penalties on the unscrupulous
private-sector engineers who approve plans for interim wastewater
treatment plants which don't work once they're built. It is time, he
says, for a really thorough investigation into what *are* the key factors
in the marine biology of Tampa Bay; time to expand the local air
pollution battle beyond the boundaries of inadequate federal laws; it is
time, God help us, to begin piecing together an accurate picture of
exactly how the aquifers under Florida work, and to come to grips
with the means and the costs of protecting them effectively.

Roger Stewart has the history, the expertise, and the courage to
begin such initiatives, but there's a question now where there wasn't
before. Does he have the power, otherwise known as public support?

The question emerges from one very large, crucial, and complex
battle. And that battle, unsurprisingly, is over sewage. It's all about
shit and what to do with it.

The history behind the battle is to be found in the huge godawful
mess of the local utility authority's catch-up game, that long-running
circus of dry-line permits and interim wastewater treatment plants
and sewer moratoriums and thumb-in-the-dike planners and pissed-off
developers, but its flash point is an issue concerning teeny tiny little
things of only recent notoriety: viruses, and whether or not they can
be lived with.

The majority opinion—the very emphatic, outraged, utterly black-
and-white majority opinion—is a resounding "NO!!!!! NO VIRUSES
ANYWHERE, EVER!!" When it was speculated that the county's
long-established practice of irrigating golf courses and other lands
with treated sewage could conceivably be implicated in the local epi-

demiology of viral diseases, the outcry was such that you'd have thought the county commissioners had been caught loitering in school yards, selling AIDS-infected nuclear hand grenades to five-year-olds. The utility authority's response was that the treated sewage at issue contained fewer viruses than are present in water in which the Environmental Protection Agency, the Centers for Disease Control, and virtually every other authority in the nation consider it safe for five-year-olds to swim; but that information made no impression. The sleeping giant of Hillsborough County public opinion, hitherto approximately as attuned to issues of local sewage disposal as to questions of fast-food preference among Eskimos, bestirred itself. Commissioner Platt's basic stance on the issue—How could anyone even consider *not* installing viral filters on all major sewage plants right now, immediately, whatever the cost?—was the message, and it was communicated loudly.

Roger Stewart heard it, but his view of the general alarm was that it originated in paranoid, simple-minded piffle. According to him, the twentieth-century urban sophisticate's fear of environmental viruses shares an empirically scientific basis with medieval medicine's faith in the curative power of bloodletting leeches.

"Human beings *need* a reasonable level of exposure to pathogens, or they lose their resistance," Stewart says. "Look what happens to populations suddenly exposed to viruses they've never encountered before—the Indians in Florida when the white men arrived, for instance. They get decimated! They die off like flies! So having a few viruses loose in the environment isn't really the terrible idea the public seems to think it is.

"Just look at the facts. Since time immemorial we and all the animals, back to the dinosaurs, have been crapping on the land, and we're still here, aren't we? All that crap hasn't contaminated the ground water. It takes months if not years for contaminated surface water to travel laterally as well as vertically until it finally reaches the ground water, and along the way the soil and the crops and the subsurface organisms absorb the crap; the waste material of the person or the cow or the dinosaur or the beetle or the bird is the food of the grass or the tree or the other green plants, plus a whole ecosystem of organisms below the first three inches of soil. All those organisms are literally eating the waste materials of these big, inefficient organisms like cows and people."

As far as Roger Stewart is concerned, then, there is nothing to fear and everything to gain from the current practice of getting rid of treated sewage by putting it into the land.

"What do you do with your treated effluent?" he asks. "Simple. You disperse it, in an intelligent and controlled manner, in the swamps, which right now are drying up and dying out there because we've diverted their natural water supply through development. Your cypress swamp, you see, is nothing more nor less than a free, highly efficient wastewater treatment plant built by Mother Nature. That's why we go to such lengths to preserve them from development in the first place, for God's sake!"

He's right. The Florida swamps really are quite wonderful, natural waste treatment plants. Rain washes the land's organic waste into them, and their hungry cypress trees soak it up, turning it ultimately into oxygen while containing it in an environment in which it breeds teeming life of all sorts. So as long as the load of organic materials flowing into any given swamp does not exceed the capacity of the cypress trees to absorb it (in which case you get a stinking mess), the end result is a strong, healthy, and rather beautiful place which regenerates the land in much the same way coastal wetlands support the life cycles of the sea.

Roger Stewart's logic, then, is to use Mother Nature as she indeed set herself up to be used in the waste disposal business, rather than struggling against her. That is why his twenty-plus years of work in this area have been governed by one overriding principle: you take your sewage uphill to the swamps where it's going to help, and you do everything in your power to stop it from running downhill into open waters where it's going to hurt. In this scheme of things you can have many small, uncomplicated, inexpensive sewage treatment facilities rather than a few of the massive and extremely costly plants needed for turning sewage into effluent of 5:5:3:1 purity (five parts per million of biochemical oxygen demand, five parts per million of particulates, three parts per million of nitrogen, and one part per million of phosphorus). The small installations can be located exactly where they're most needed, in the areas where the protected swamps are being suffocated very slowly but very surely by the artificial environments of the subdivisions built around them.

In the virus-haunted public climate of Hillsborough County, however, such wisdom has little impact. And so, the trend is for sewage to travel in the opposite direction from the swamps. These days the ca-ca is headed for the bay.

Roger Stewart is not amused by this trend, and he has a lot to say about it. Much of his comments have to do with a piece of legislation, known as the Grizzle-Figg Bill, passed by the state legislature in 1987. This well-intentioned legislation, Stewart says, has unwittingly undone almost everything he has accomplished in twenty years of trying to protect Tampa Bay.

The problem, he says, is that Grizzle-Figg changed the relationship between two environmental-law bottom lines concerning treated sewage effluent disposal in Hillsborough County.

The first bottom line governs the specific nature of treated sewage effluent, setting standards it must meet before it is allowed to be discharged from an Advanced Waste Water Treatment facility. If effluent doesn't meet the 5:5:3:1 standard, it doesn't meet the legal definition of Advanced Waste Product (AWP) and may not be discharged from a plant into an open body of water.

The second bottom line, known as a Waste Load Allocation, governs quantity as opposed to quality of treated effluent. For each sewage treatment plant, says state law, there will be a specific figure limiting how much effluent that plant may discharge within a given time period. A plant may not discharge any more than its limit, which means it also cannot take in any more raw sewage than the amount which translates into that specified quantity of effluent.

Until Grizzle-Figg, it was the rigid enforcement of Waste Load Allocations by the EPC which fired the intermittent explosion of sewer wars in Hillsborough County, controlling how many new subdivisions could hook into the municipal systems at any given point in time. Waste Load Allocation numbers were the triggers of de facto sewer moratoriums; if you tripped them, the EPC could and would let loose that all too familiar hell of interim measures, outraged developers, suddenly unloquacious lobbyists, and legal recourse.

Now, though, Waste Load Allocations are no longer the key factor.

The definition of AWP is. Because of its wording, the Grizzle-Figg Bill has created a situation in which sewage treatment plants are able to discharge as much effluent as they wish—and discharge it straight into Tampa Bay—just as long as they can demonstrate that the effluent meets that 5:5:3:1 standard of purity.

You should see the evil cloud which descends on Roger Stewart's brows, hear the hard bitter gnash of teeth when he has to think about the implications of this little bit of business.

"It's a goddam disaster!" he growls. "Grizzle and Figg meant well, I guess. What they wanted to do was broaden the law on AWP so that all the counties releasing effluent into the bay, not just Hillsborough County, would have to meet the 5:5:3:1 standard. That they did—but by making the AWP requirement the only standard, they've pulled the rug out from under me. I'm sitting here right now with a desk full of new permit applications from treatment plants all over Hillsborough County. Every goddam one of them wants to start releasing their effluent into the bay, and because of this bill, there's not a thing I can do to stop them!"

But why, one wonders, should that be a problem? What's wrong with the logic argued by Grizzle-Figg's supporters? Since that new regional law on advanced-treated sewage effluent calls for a level of purity higher than that of water presently circulating in Tampa Bay, does it not follow that only good things will happen to the bay if large quantities of such effluent are mixed into it? Is it not true that the more treated effluent you pump out there, the better? Will the marine biology of Tampa Bay not respond to all that pure new water with a great flowering of vigorous new life?

Stewart snorts when notions like that are presented to him. "I don't buy those kinds of grand ideas. I don't like neat, idealized models," he says. "I want reality. I want evidence. When somebody tells me that Advanced Waste Product is going to restore Tampa Bay, I say, 'How do you know that? Are you a shrimp, or a mullet? Can you say for certain that if you were, you wouldn't know that water for what it is—treated human shit—and stay away from it?'

"That water, you see, is different from the water in the bay in many very concrete, specific ways, but nowhere in the Grizzle-Figg Bill is there any requirement for a demonstration of its effect on the water body. So nobody knows what'll happen, and nobody's trying to find out. They'll only know when it's too late to change anything. I can't believe so many of the 'Save the Bay' people around here bought that crap!"

Furthermore, he says, the whole question of that "pure" water's effect is moot anyway. Sure, he says, the 5:5:3:1 product is squeaky-clean—clean enough to drink, as former utilities chief Dale Twatchman demonstrated by downing a whole glass full of the stuff on the six o'clock news when he opened Tampa's huge new Advanced Waste Water Treatment Facility a few years back—but Roger Stewart is certain that the 5:5:3:1 product is not going to be all that flows into the bay.

"Look at the facts. Look at the history. Certainly the City of Tampa plant is an exceptionally modern, well-run, well-designed facility—really, it's outstanding—but it doesn't work the way it's supposed to all the time. From time to time something goes wrong, and bad stuff gets away from it. And the city plant is the best of them, by far. *It* just doesn't work *some* of the time. Most of the county plants don't work *most* of the time. All too many of them are in trouble with us every day of the goddam week!

"So I tell that to the county commissioners, and what do they tell me? They say, 'Well, yes, but things will improve.'

"I don't know. I just don't know what to say. I'd love to believe that, but there's no way. How can I accept a statement like that? It's like when the Board of County Commissioners asked me, 'Don't you think that Hillsborough County, with its new sewer plant proposals and all the new bond money, is going to do better in the future?' I thought for a moment, and then I had to tell them that in all honesty I simply couldn't have any faith in anything like that. Time after time after time in the past, you see, they've put up a new system, and the goddam thing didn't work.

"In fact, the head of the county utility system was in the audience at that hearing, and when I asked him, not even *he* could think of a single county plant that was operating consistent with its permit at that moment. That's quite a tale, right there: that every goddam system the county operates fails to comply with its permit!

"So I just had to tell 'em, 'No way. I'll believe it when I see it, but until then I can't have any faith at all in the future you're describing.' "

The politicians chose not to accept Roger Stewart's misgivings about liquid waste disposal, just as years ago their predecessors chose to ignore the testimony of Dr. Parker on a similar question about where the Next Great City's solid party trash should be dumped. It is not impossible that their decision was prompted by the same brew as that which moved them to create the nightmare at Taylor Road: Short-term convenience and a hint of motives even less noble.

The short-term convenience aspect of the Grizzle-Figg solution reveals itself when you consider one of the problems it solves: what to do with liquid waste from the monstrous new Tampa Palms development and all those other northern-fringe enclaves listed with such fervor by Buddy Buildit.

Until Grizzle-Figg, the problem was that the builders could not do the obvious thing: hook their new developments straight into the great big high-volume sewer main that the city had run out to that part of the world when all those new homes and shopping malls were just a glimmer in the eyes of a visionary few. Roger Stewart stood in their way, enforcing the law which said that the City of Tampa treatment facility on the receiving end of that all-important sewer main could not operate beyond its already-spoken-for Waste Load Allocation of sixteen million gallons per day, period. So all those builders had a real mess on their hands.

Now, though, after Grizzle-Figg, it seems that the City of Tampa plant *can* handle more than sixteen million gallons a day. If need be, it can double its capacity. So voilà! End of problem.

"I didn't see that coming," Roger Stewart admits ruefully. "Before this bill, the State of Florida was under a legal mandate to perform a Waste Load Allocation on the city plant, but for the last three years they hadn't done it. The state consistently failed, or refused, or was unable—we don't know which—to release a definitive Waste Load Allocation for that plant.

"Now, obviously, we at the EPC have been very concerned about that, and we've been pushing the state. At first, the information we were getting back from the staff working on it was 'Hey, look, the figures we're getting say they'll never be allowed to go beyond their present sixteen million gallons a day.' We thought that was okay. We thought we didn't need to do anything but keep pushing them."

Taking that position turned out to be a mistake, though, because the political sands shifted. Now, most of the staff people who were predicting no change in the state's position "aren't there anymore, and the new people are telling us, 'Hey, we don't know if we're going to come out with this or not, but all the information we're getting today says that you need to put more and more AWP in the bay, because it makes the water quality better.'

"So what can I say to that? I can't argue, because I have no evidence. I've been waiting for the goddam state to put out their Waste Load Allocation! And now, now that they have utterly and miserably failed to do that, and the Grizzle-Figg Bill is law, I don't have a legal leg to stand on. I can't oppose this obvious out."

Stewart is reluctant to attribute the state's change of personnel and attitude to the ascension of Bob Martinez from the Tampa mayor's office to the Florida governor's chair. "I can't draw any conclusion about that," he says, "and neither can I say how the state arrived at the position they're taking. I just think that before the City of Tampa is allowed to literally double their waste load over the next few years in serving Tampa Palms and all that development up there, somebody, whether the law says they have to or not, *must* demonstrate that that will not cause a reversal of the improvements in the bay I've been measuring in the last four or five years. I would really like that assurance."

He's not going to get it, though, because his is a lonely voice. A few of the local environmental activists are in his corner, notably the Mannasota 88 group, but the majority are either silent on the issue or actively supportive of Grizzle-Figg.

Roger Stewart says that that puzzles him; that he has difficulty accepting the positions of people who ought, he thinks, to know better, people with whom he has had common cause in the past on many environmental issues. He wonders why those people are now adamant that treated sewage should be released into the bay, rather than distributed over the land.

"I really have a lot of trouble with their arguments," Stewart says.

"You have to understand here, you see, that years ago, when we were trying to get the sewage out of the bay, they were the key people helping us. This idea of releasing reasonably treated sewage onto the land isn't new to them.

"So again, why are they saying what they're saying now? I guess it's possible that they have a legitimate paranoid feeling that somebody's going to get sick, but if so, what's their reasoning? Nobody has ever demonstrated that those viruses are getting to anywhere where they're going to hurt somebody. If surface fecal material contaminated the groundwater, we would all have been dead centuries ago. Millennia ago. They know as well as I do that water dumped into the ground doesn't just go *whoosh!* into the aquifer."

Why, then, one wonders, *have* Stewart's old allies, particularly those with ties to the University of South Florida, come to the conclusion that treated sewage is unsafe in the swamps, but perfectly acceptable in the bay?

Stewart treads lightly at first. "Just what is pushing them to further all this is a mystery to me; I have certain concerns which cross my mind, but I hate to express them, because frankly I don't like to think about them." Then, though, he decides to jump in headfirst. "I can't help but think about a piece which appeared in the *St. Petersburg Times* a little while ago," he says. "It was quite a thorough piece, and what it did was link the interests of the big developers in the Tampa Palms area, the City of Tampa, and the University of South Florida. The university stands to benefit directly from all that development around it, you see."

He shakes his head, looks quite depressed. "I don't know," he says. "Maybe I'm wrong. I hope so. I've been wrong about a few things lately. Like when I called Grizzle-Figg the 'City of Tampa Relief Bill' because the city had just annexed all that property up there, and would have been in bad shape if it couldn't pipe the sewage to its Advanced Waste Treatment plant—I was wrong about that. This thing's bigger than that. It doesn't cover just the City of Tampa plant, you see; it covers *all* the damned things! I didn't realize that the county staff as well as the city people were up there in Tallahassee lobbying for it, falling all over themselves because so many of *their* problems can be solved by simply running big pipes to the nearest open body of water. One simple little law, and the whole messed-up system gets off the hook!"

Roger Stewart sits there with his desk full of new bay-dumping permit applications, and ponders the implications of Grizzle-Figg. "It's like a railroad roundhouse, where you put a locomotive on a big turntable, and turn it around to go the other way. That's what's happening here. It's going to take years for the full effect of the law to make itself felt, but from now on, every locomotive coming out of the chute —every new plant in the system—is going to be running downhill into the bay."

That, he fears, means that Tampa Bay is screwed. A daily influx of tens of million gallons of Advanced Waste Product, spiced with cruder stuff whenever a plant malfunctions or otherwise transgresses the law on AWP purity, is much more likely than not to compromise its self-regeneration and hasten the onset of larger freshwater crises. Every day that Hillsborough County's effluent flows downhill, the sludge of life-choking nutrients will thicken on the bed of Tampa Bay, the swamps of Hillsborough County will wither a little more, and ultimately the aquifers will suffer further. More and more development will place greater and greater demand on their water, accompanied by less and less return as increasing quantities are thrown away into the bay.

In the final analysis, then, Grizzle-Figg is—well, disastrous is probably not too strong a word. Initiating a major escalation in regional water problems is not a very responsible way for a metropolis to deal with growth.

Thinking about the future of America's Next Great City in this context is not a pleasant pastime. One can of course hope that in another decade or so, another great environmental hard man will contemplate the mess around him, and begin again the fight to turn Hillsborough County's waste water back uphill. But even if that happens, you have to wonder whether, with an enlarged population straining the resources of government in a local economy likely to be undergoing the very opposite of a boom, such a task will be possible.

❂

Near the end of my research on this story I went to two very different places which ended up feeling the same.

The first was the Hillsborough County courthouse, where I attended the weekly public meeting of the Board of County Commissioners. It was as entertaining as usual—watching those folks tread lightly is always fun—but it was also relevant to my job. One topic of discussion was a motion to spend six million dollars of county funds to buy a parcel of land on the Sidney Mine site for use as a sludge disposal facility, a place to dump the bad stuff removed from raw sewage by various county wastewater treatment plants.

The Sidney Mine site, you may recall, is the place where Roger Stewart and Dr. Parker and many another credentialed individuals, considering its exceptionally secure position in relation to the aquifer, its distance from people's homes, and its abundant supplies of both high-quality lining clays and covering sands, thought the garbage that ended up at Taylor Road should have gone in the first place. In theory the same attributes which qualified it so well as a location for solid waste back then make it an ideal site for sludge disposal today. If you dump the stuff into Sidney Mine, quite possibly it won't go anywhere you don't want it to.

At the commission meeting the site's probable suitability was not an issue. The issue, raised by Jan Platt, was why it was so important to spend six million dollars for that particular land at that particular time. Noting that the site was not yet permitted for sludge disposal by the Florida Department of Environmental Regulation (as it would surely, unavoidably have to be), and that furthermore no engineering study of the location had yet been performed, Ms. Platt opined that the public's money might better be spent when and if these essential steps achieved reality. She ended her comments by proposing an amendment making the purchase contingent on receipt of a D.E.R. permit at the very least.

The other commissioners heard her out, and then one of them suggested that the motion as originally forwarded go to a vote.

Well, no deal. Now Ms. Platt wanted to know if six million dollars was really the sum at issue. Was this expenditure, she asked, not just the first irrevocable move in a longer-term plan to buy other, much more expensive lands adjacent to the six million site?

The other commissioners listened again, and then, quick as a wink, it was done. A vote was called and the purchase was approved on the commission's all too familiar six-to-one say-so, Commissioner Platt voting No.

Figuring that some of the subtleties of the transaction had escaped me, I went looking for illumination from a courthouse veteran, and found Cam Oberting in the cafeteria. As usual, Cam was more than willing to comment. She set about the Sidney Mine subject like a mongoose loosed in a nest of vipers, and there among the steam tables the snake meat flew.

What she described was your basic boondoggle: the channeling of inflated amounts of public money into the pockets of friends of the public's servants, to the eventual benefit of the servants themselves. Two items emerged as most relevant in Cam's story. First, she said, the commissioners had just decided to spend six million on land that had been offered to the county for less than a million less than a year previously. She thought I should look into that. Second, she said, the purchase *was* the first step in a plan to buy a much larger parcel of land, and I should look into that too. "I'll give you a hint," she said, mongoose vibes electrifying the air between us. "I'll tell you who owns the land they're planning to buy . . ."

Cam then spoke a corporate name which I can't publish today for fear of legal retribution because on that day in the courthouse cafeteria I'd had enough. I had no desire to spend my time documenting or disproving the allegations she had made, the way investigative newspersons and United States attorneys are supposed to; frankly, I'd rather have spent my next few weeks dining on flying cockroaches, modern Hillsborough County's most abundant natural resource. So I just said, "Thanks, Cam," and left her in her snake pit. I went home, collected my stuff, and got away.

The next day's dawn found me in a place of peace and wonder. A mile or so into the woods from the nearest dirt road, I sat in the gathering light just below the crest of a little rounded ridge, with a wide panorama of terrain and vegetation revealing itself slowly to me through the early morning mist. In this place, one of Mother Nature's minor crossroads, coniferous trees met deciduous, pines gave way to hardwoods, and sandy hillsides anchored by scrub oak and palmetto ran gently downward toward tight tall stands of cypress trees growing from the swamp bottoms of the lowest land.

Such places are ideal locations in which it is possible to meet Mr. Pig or Bambi's brother in the half-light as he makes his way back to deep daytime cover from his nocturnal feeding forays—from open, acorn-rich scrub oak turf toward swamp or hardwood thicket, for instance—and so for the first hour or so of that day, I sat dead still and waited.

No large tasty animal came my way in that first all-important hour, and so the world around me brightened and stirred into the rhythms of its full morning without the sudden environmental adrenaline blast of a gunshot.

I too shifted gears. I cleared the chamber and closed the scope covers on my old Savage 99, laid it to rest across my lap, lit a cigarette (bye-bye, Bambi), and let my attention wander where it would.

One of the places it took me was my work, for as I studied the topography and vegetation of the panorama before me, I realized—suddenly and with great force—that the lovely place in which I found myself was an aquifer recharge area. It was a high spot on the map of the West Central Florida peninsula with limestone just a few feet, maybe only inches, beneath the sandy topsoil of the slopes. In this place I could see exactly how light rain would soak straight through the sand on which I was sitting, how a late-afternoon summer downpour would clean the land, sluicing organics straight into that little cypress swamp seventy-five yards downhill to my right, that much bigger one half a mile away in the lee of another semicircle of small rounded hills.

The power of that sudden direct understanding of land and water was exciting. I wanted more, and so, putting aside the pursuit of whatever superior meat might still be at large in the neighborhood, I spent the rest of the morning and part of the afternoon simply wandering from scene to scene in the woods, stopping wherever the fancy took me to watch and listen and feel and learn.

I didn't learn a great deal because, being almost entirely ignorant in this kind of setting, I didn't know how to interpret what I was seeing. That was okay, though, because what I really found was a new curiosity, new questions about flora and fauna and rain and wind and fire and flood and balance and change.

Those few hours were a very special kind of free time, illuminated by a notion which struck me during the first of them: that just for the joy of it, not for art or money or anyone else but myself, I could slowly, comfortably find the answers to a few of those natural-world questions during the remainder of my time on this earth. I could talk to some good ole boys who've done just that all their lives, read some books, wander again in this and other Florida places to look again with more insight and find more questions.

But that quiet thrill didn't last very long, because something else happened. I didn't like it then, and moreover I don't like making it the next part of my story now. It feels too convenient, too neat a tie-off to the whole smelly package I've been wrapping these past many weeks. But I can't help that. It happened.

The "it" in question first revealed itself as an anomaly in the horizon of the woods, a lateral slash of paleness several hundred yards long behind the far trees a mile from where I stood. My first impression was that it might be a high sandy riverbank, or perhaps a disused railroad cut, neither feature an uncommon sight in the Central and North Florida woods. I changed the direction of my slow ramble and started toward it.

From two hundred yards away it was obvious that the feature in question was indeed a sandy mound of some sort, and with a sick, unwilling instinct I was beginning to suspect what sort that might be. For the last half mile or so, the woods had been changing in progressively more obvious ways: a thinning of the ground vegetation, an unhealthy, stunted look to the larger plants, here and there a withered skeleton standing among the tallest trees; and although the wind was at my back, there was a certain something in the air, a kind of bitter-sweet, acidic-organic edge. The woods were beginning to smell like the parking lot of a battery shop where the workers aren't too picky about restroom sanitation.

My instinct had been correct. Ten minutes later, I found myself standing on the access road of a large municipal garbage dump, staring up at a sandy piecrust patterned by bulldozer tracks, pierced here and there by its filling, and stained by the release of its juices. Looking up into the sky, I watched the purposeful circling of carrion birds and the erratic flutter of empty garbage bags on their way to join others already snared by the branches of the dead trees which were all that remained of the woods this close to the dump. Looking down at the ground, I traced the intricate delta cut by the fluid poison which had killed the woods on its way downhill toward swamp and limestone.

Well, lucky me. Here was another live-in-person experience of how the rains and the topography and the aquifer and local government (in this case Hernando County) cooperate in west-central peninsular Florida.

So there I stood, crashing from my bucolic high and burning in Hernando's party trash. And now my Savage, at dawn a meat getter but afterward just dead weight, felt newly right. Now it felt thoroughly appropriate to be standing in this place with a weapon, dressed in camouflage to kill from cover, for here all around me were the signs of war in a wooded environment: the stink of decay and chemicals, the random detritus of uncaring occupation, the blasted tree line offering thoughtfully enhanced fields of defensive fire. And here too, most essentially, was a clear cold understanding. This place could take years off my life.

4

The Sage of Fish-Eating Creek

Another magic place, this. Probably *the* magic place, in fact, its beauty indescribable in any way that really does it justice. Let's just say that at half an hour past a springtime dawn on the dense cypress bank of a wide, curving, mist-covered Florida creek in the wild green heart of the southern peninsula, it's gorgeous. It's your ultimate prizewinning Friends of the Earth pinup poster, Mystic Southern Swamp Division: ethereal, mysterious, Old-South Arthurian-romantic. The Lady of the Lake should thrust Excalibur through those vapors, she really should.

It's rich in life, almost absurdly so. Here's a lovely delicate white ibis spearing crawfish. There's a magnificent great blue heron competing for fishing rights with two or three less spectacular species. Far off across a quiet wet swirl of snakes and eels and bass and catfish, a turtle plops suddenly into the creek and a turkey gobbles somewhere back in the woods. Much closer, in the water only feet away from the feral hog rootings which form our poster's vantage point, the cold yellow eyes of a ten-foot alligator stare appraisingly straight into our lens. What a place: Fisheating Creek.

Indians gave it its quite adequately poetic name. Fisheating Creek was one of their very favorite places, and it served them well; for centuries they flourished here in some numbers, enjoying its looks and using its gifts with enthusiasm. But now, predictably, the Indians are all gone, the beauty of their home having ensured their eviction the moment European eyes first beheld it. These days, no more than a dozen humans roam their old country at any given time.

Today I am one of those fortunate souls, and I am doing what we lucky ones do. I am hunting on fourteen thousand acres of unspoiled, professionally managed, and abundantly game-rich private land in one of the most beautiful environments I have ever seen, and really, it's wonderful. Certainly I'm humbled, and of course I appreciate the irony of my situation and experience the occasional stab of racial guilt, but mostly I feel exactly like what my good fortune makes me: a prince, a pasha, a potentate, the temporary but fully blessed and officially sanctioned lord and master of this heaven on earth. Searching stealthily through the magnificence of flora and fauna for my particular objective, some sweetly meated feral hog in the fifty- to hundred-and-fifty-pound weight class, I'm very happy to be here.

❂

Lovett Williams and David Austin are familiar with location-related happiness. They see it in the eyes of many of their customers, and of course when their customers aren't around, in those moments when it's just either of them roaming the land with gun or rod or camera, they feel it powerfully themselves.

Both men, old friends, have known and loved Fisheating Creek for a long time, twenty-plus years apiece. Introduced to it as junior game wardens working for the Florida Game and Fresh Water Fish Commission, they penetrated further into its secrets as they evolved into managers and game-biology researchers (becoming, among other things, world authorities on the ways of the wild turkey). Now, divorced from the state but still wedded to this particular jewel in its crown, they are getting to know the demands and rewards of the land in increasingly intimate ways. Having leased it from its owners, the

Lykes Brothers agribusiness giant, they are making their way in the world by running a commercial hunting camp on it; attracting a small number of customers, accepting their not-inconsiderable payments, feeding and housing them, and transporting them to certain spots where the prospect of sighting deer, hogs, turkeys, bobcats, and a whole wilderness's complement of equally interesting wildlife is a great deal more likely than elsewhere in Florida, Georgia, California, New York, Illinois, or most other locations in the United States.

Which means, among other things, that unlike the great majority of other tenants or landlords in Florida's past or present, Lovett and David have a profit incentive served in ways that quite categorically do not involve draining, leveling, contouring, paving, or otherwise radically altering the natural environment of the peninsula. What they are attempting is in fact a reversal of the entire tide of Florida history: they're trying to achieve increased economic productivity without the burden of increased population. At the end of each of Lovett and David's transactions, the Yankees go home and the land stays as sweet as it is.

So far, three years into this endeavor, they're doing okay; business is brisk, and their revenues are as high as they expected. But God only knows what the future holds, and the partners themselves can only guess at the intentions of the potent forces ranked against them. Whether they will fare better than the Indians remains to be seen.

Let's be specific about what kind of wilderness we're talking about here, just exactly what it is and what kinds of life it sustains; what will cease to exist if Fisheating Creek goes the way of most other Florida beauty spots.

The creek itself is the only natural stream remaining in South Florida, the only one of the southern peninsula's few significant watercourses which has not been dammed, channelized, or actually created to serve agriculture, industry, urban growth, navigation, or some other economic imperative. Originating in the sandy hills south of Lake Placid, some sixty miles northwest of Lovett and David's lease, Fisheating Creek describes a meandering arc southward and eastward through the sparsely populated rangeland and wilderness of the interior until it discharges into Lake Okeechobee, whence its water becomes part of the slow, steady flow which spills over the lake's southern banks to create the huge freshwater marsh known as the Everglades.

Fed exclusively by rainwater runoff rather than by springs, the creek experiences frequent minor flow fluctuations and a broad seasonal pattern; generally, but by no means predictably (for South Florida rainfall is a phenomenon subject to unusually dramatic incidences of climatic whimsy), its water begins to flow in earnest sometime during the month of June, continues at high volume through the summer, decreases in October or November, and then maintains a moderate level until dropping dramatically in the spring drought.

Thus the creek is contracting and expanding continually, as are the streams feeding it, and this means that almost its entire length is bordered by cypress swamps which have established themselves as far out from its banks as its waters reach during maximum flow. So the creek bank is a shady, stately, primevally attractive, and abundantly life-supportive environment—a wide cool rich dark-green ribbon twisting through a south-central Florida landscape of various aspect: scrub and cattle range country for the most part, burned and bleached to grays and duns and yellow-greens by the relentless South Florida summer sun, with here and there the gentle military precision of citrus groves and the more casual geometry of cracker towns and migrant worker settlements and trailer parks undergoing gradual replacement by planned blue-collar senior communities and the occasional attempt at a high-walled upscale Living Environment, the density of settlement decreasing from north to south. West of all this is something else, the Gulf-coastal belt of rich resorts and retirement towns, either long-established or built yesterday—Sarasota, Venice, Charlotte, Punta Gorda, Cape Coral, Ft. Myers, Sanibel Island, Gasparilla Island, Marco Island—and then the smugglers' country called the Thousand Islands, the wild mangrove tangles defending the peninsula's southern coastline from sea, wind, and the Drug Enforcement Administration. To the east is Lake Okeechobee, Fisheating Creek's destination, with sugarcane country and the teeming concrete Gold Coast beyond. Directly south, beyond more cattle ranges and settlements, are the Everglades, the trackless swamp.

Much of this geography has its own unique and not inconsiderable appeal: the rich, tasteful, gentle-breezy pastel ease of Venice and Sanibel and Boca Grande; the hard-bitten romance of Everglades City, the Thousand Islands' outlaw town; the enormous, almost alien monotony of the saw grass swamp; even the sun-beaten silence of the wide dry cattle ranges. But for sheer physical presence, for human sensual-stimulation power, the cool green life-vibrant ribbon of Fisheating Creek has no equal.

It is in the heart of the sweet lush sanctuary, on the sharp bend of a cypress-shaded stream flowing into Fisheating Creek itself, that Lovett Williams and David Austin built their hunting lodge. In that lovely spot, on an April afternoon midway into the accelerating springtime decline of the creek's water, we find Lovett, the more loquacious of the two, explaining the scope of his guardianship.

He's a tidy-looking little man, every inch of him well defined and energetic in a supremely unfussy kind of way—"crisp" is the word for Lovett, whose features suggest a younger, more compact, impossibly alert Ronald Reagan—and his speech is as purposeful as his looks.

Making a good hard conscientious attempt to list at least the more interesting life-forms he has under his temporary care, he begins with what we can actually see from the deck of the lodge, a simple but sturdy affair overhanging the abrupt drop of the highest and therefore most flood-resistant stream bank in the immediate area. The opposite bank is only the slightest of inclinations into a cypress swamp.

"Okay," he says, "right across the stream there, you've got your cypress trees, of course, and their knees, those knobby things sticking up from their roots—people say they're for breathing, but we don't know that for a fact—and the ash trees, which are very water-tolerant—that's what we call pop ash right there—and cabbage palms of course, which are the state tree—that's where you get the hearts of palm people put in their salads around this part of the world—and then there's laurel oak, and red maple. . . . And well, let's see, that's about all the *trees* we can see from here, except this big live oak on our bank here; the live oaks are less water-tolerant, so they grow in higher places, same as saw palmetto and a lot of other plants adapted to drier ground. . . . And then there's all the different kinds of ferns, and the air plants on the trees: pineapple air plant, Spanish moss, the cardinal air plant, all the others; the resurrection fern, which a lot of people like because it looks completely dead and dried out until it gets a little water, and then it's lush and green again just like that. . . . And the grass on this bank is maiden cane, a real strong grass that looks like lawn grass, the St. Augustine you've probably got on your lawn, but isn't really related very closely except that it's a grass. . . ."

He pauses and looks around for a moment, concludes that no more plants but a few kinds of irises and orchids are in immediate evidence, and begins describing plant life beyond the stream. Out there on the land beyond the reach of the creek or its streams, he says, are drought-tolerant oaks (scrub oaks, Chapman oaks, myrtle oaks, live oaks, and the waist-high runner oaks with their stems buried in the earth so that fires simply burn off their tops). There's wire grass; the saw palmetto, where turkeys make their nests; various varieties of pine; and encroachments of fireproof Melaleuca trees from Australia.

There have to be more than these varieties, says Lovett—though perhaps not many more, since his lease's fourteen thousand acres are part of a typical peninsular ecology in which the rule is a smallish number of relatively exotic species rather than the riotous multiplicity typical of larger tropical landmasses—but he can't remember them right now.

On to insects, then: mosquitoes, dragonflies, ants by the billion, red paper wasps and the smaller guinea wasps, bald-face hornets, praying mantises, grasshoppers (a principal summertime turkey food), black widow spiders, wolf spiders, garden spiders, the jumping or fighting spiders that look just like tiny tarantulas; scorpions, ticks, millipedes, centipedes, diving beetles, giant water bugs, dozens of different species of moths and butterflies and caterpillars . . .

And snails and lizards and snakes: the now-endangered tree snails, whose lustrous shells grace many a Florida mantelpiece, living inexplicably far north of their usual habitats; the Carolina anole, which local people call chameleons, plus sand skinks and swift, or fence, lizards and two or three species of gecko brought to Florida by banana boats; coral snakes and indigo snakes and pine snakes and black racers and coachwhips and diamondback rattlers on land, brown water snakes and bandy water snakes and cottonmouth moccasins where it's good and wet. And all the other critters close to the ground: rabbits, rice rats, cotton rats, mice, armadillos, gophers, skunks, coons, opossums, pig frogs and grass, or pickerel, frogs and common toads; box turtles and endangered gopher turtles where it's dry; soft-shell turtles and snapping turtles and sliders and otters—otters everywhere, thousands and thousands and *thousands* of them—by the water. And then in the water itself you have, again, not many varieties of fish but plenty of them: game fish like bass and a few varieties of catfish (speckled cat, channel cat, yellow bullhead, blue cat, etc., one as tasty as the other); panfish such as bluegill or brim, shellcracker or red-headed sunfish, stumpknocker or spotted sunfish, speckled perch or black or white crappie, and warmouth perch; rough fish like spotted gar, mudfish or bowfin (or whatever they're called where you live), grass carp, and the walking catfish which leave their homes when the water levels drop and go randomly in search of spots where the species can survive, the same way seeds blow randomly off trees. And of course in the water, and near it, you also have your alligators, lots of them. The banks of Fisheating Creek are no place for poodles.

The skies above the land are likewise populous, the domain of some three hundred species of birds. Some are on the endangered species list: the caracara or Mexican eagle, the bald eagle, the sandhill crane, the wood stork, the burrowing owl, and the red-cockaded woodpecker. Others are threatened, unique to this part of the world, historically rare, or simply very nice to look at: the pine sparrow and the swallowtail kite, and beautiful indigenous or visiting water birds like the blue and great blue and yellow-crowned night herons, the snowy egret and the great egret, the white ibis, the water turkey, and the roseate spoonbill. Hawks and owls abound too, more numerous than the eagles, and so do black and turkey vultures. Ducks and doves and tits and jays and sparrows and robins are everywhere, living year-round off the land or moving through from season to season.

Man also goes about his business in the skies over Fisheating Creek, honing his predatory capabilities at five hundred knots above the treetops in pairs of Air Force F-16s or proceeding less rapidly but no less threateningly in drug-heavy Cessnas, but the birds don't seem to mind; on Lovett and David's lease there remains a variety of avian life, and a catalog of truly exotic species, unavailable to professional ornithologists and recreational bird-watchers on any other fourteen thousand acres in North America.

Finally there are the species of most interest to those of Lovett and David's customers who do not belong to the specialized, fanatic brotherhood of America's wild turkey hunters: the large tasty mammals. Fisheating Creek's white-tailed deer population is respectable by the most exacting of standards, and growing larger and more robust each year, and its wild pig count is spectacular. Until twenty years ago this was domestic free-range hog country (just as today it serves as rangeland for Lykes Brothers cattle), and the descendants of those animals, now fully feral, have multiplied to the point where energetic pruning by bullet and arrow is a necessity if the whole damn place isn't going to get rooted and wrecked to the point where it resembles the Somme in 1918 more than South Florida in 1989. Man is aided in the task of hog pruning by a healthy number of indigenous bobcats and alligators, and even, from time to time, one of Florida's surviving panthers passing through the fourteen thousand acres on its daily seventy-mile stroll. Black bears, also feared by hogs, are present a few miles to the north, but not on the lease itself.

That, then—a riotously active food chain beginning with the action of sun and rain on water algae and soil nutrients and ending with the predations of the alligator, the eagle, the panther, and *Homo sapiens* —is the basic arrangement which gives Fisheating Creek its great beauty, and creates its unique and powerful appeal to hunters, fishermen, botanists, ornithologists, game biologists, and other practitioners of the earth sciences.

By rights, that same combination of flora and fauna should inspire a similar degree of enthusiasm among Florida's numerous associations of preservationists and environmental activists, a segment of the population which, though long accustomed to frustration and defeat on every front, fights a good and highly visible fight throughout the state. But it doesn't. Lovett Williams and David Austin are the only people fighting for Fisheating Creek.

Lovett finds that annoying. Perched on his deck above the cool green heart of all that unique life and beauty, he starts to steam at the very mention of the people who should be his allies. One moment he's discussing the extraordinarily energetic mating of his otters and the protein requirement of his endangered shorttail hogs with benign enthusiasm, the next he's a scrappy angry little Napoleon strapping on his fool-killer sword, summoning his personal bodyguard of science and reason, spurring his hobbyhorse, and charging hell-for-leather at the mighty mass of the misinformed.

"It's like the image people have of the Everglades—you know, a Florida wonderland of swamp and cypress trees which must be saved for future generations at all costs," he says. "Well, that's not the Everglades. The Everglades aren't beautiful, they aren't rich in wildlife, and they aren't rich in the variety of their wildlife. They're just a big, monotonous, not very interesting saw grass marsh, and anyone who knows what the hell they're talking about *knows* that.

"So why do most people think otherwise? Simple. When the news media and the tourist board and the conservationists show pictures of the Everglades, what they're really showing are places like the Fakahatchee Strand, or this place right here. They come out here with their cameras and take a photograph of Fisheating Creek—I've been here when they've done it—and the damn picture ends up on a 'Save Our Glades' poster!

"I suppose that makes sense, because if you took a picture of the real Everglades, all you'd get is a bunch of saw grass and sky, maybe a few vultures, and that's not the sort of thing that gets most people excited. But really, it's ridiculous. It's disgusting. Truth doesn't matter. Congress will appropriate the money to buy the rest of the Everglades because they've been misrepresented to the damn public, and the truth in the pictures, the *real* beauty of South Florida, will go down the drain. There are more rare, interesting species on fourteen thousand acres of Fisheating Creek than there are in the whole damn Everglades National Park, but nobody gives a damn. Reality just doesn't matter."

Once the fool killer's in his hand, Lovett finds it hard to stop slashing. "People think that because certain places are national parks, by definition they're our most valuable and beautiful natural assets, and all the rest of the land is just stuff tying those places together," he says. "But that's just not true. Usually national parks are either land nobody really wanted in the first place, because they couldn't mine it or farm it or build cities on it or whatever—swamps and mountains mostly—or they're forests the government can use to subsidize the timber industry.

"I mean, what's the Ocala National Forest up there in the center of the state? It's mile after mile after mile of planted pine trees that get cut and sold for one tenth of their market value by congressional act! Just one giant damn boondoggle, in other words. We'd all be better off if the government just gave our money outright to the timber industry and left us with some natural forests! And what are the Everglades? Saw grass! You think the Everglades would exist today if somebody had figured out an economical way of draining them? Not on your damn life!

"Ah, God, it drives me crazy. The conservationists are just so damned ignorant; just another bunch of people who need a cause. I wish they'd all go work for the March of Dimes, where they might really do some good.

"But they don't, so here we sit in the most beautiful piece of land in South Florida, and it's owned by a private company that doesn't have even the slightest interest in it or the wildlife it supports. If some developer wanted to tear this place up and fill it with roads and subdivisions and gas stations, none of those damn so-called friends of the earth would bat an eye. It's pathetic."

But life goes on at Fisheating Creek today. It's a full life, a long day.

For Lovett Williams it begins just before dawn, when he rises from his bunk bed in the house trailer he and David Austin share when staying at the camp, then briskly performs his ablutions, dresses for the day, and prepares a breakfast of coffee, eggs, grits, and bacon. His movements are characteristically precise and economical—crisp— and so are his wardrobe and general appearance. No two-day stubble on this man's face, no mussy hair or escalating body odor, no crumpled GI fatigues or bloodstained jungle-camo paratrooper pants bulging here and there and everywhere with Sharper Image survival tools, no knee-high custom snake boots; nothing whatsoever that shouts *Warrior of the Woods!* to a wife or secretary or fellow worker carried in the mind. No. That's the customers. The host faces the wilderness in a neat light-blue short-sleeved shirt, tailored dark brown cavalry twill trousers secured by a sturdy leather belt, and comfortable low-heeled cowboy boots. When it matters out there, Lovett avoids snake bites by not stepping on snakes, and he evades the attention of game animals by eschewing sudden movement. His clothes don't snag on the vegetation, and if he needs to cut something, he uses the three-inch folding penknife in his trouser pocket.

Thus equipped, he begins his work, which today consists of two main tasks that dovetail nicely: scouting turkey activity for a party of Georgians due to arrive tonight, and showing me around his heaven on earth. We mount one of the camp's four-wheel-drive pickup trucks and move out, heading north and east toward the generally higher, drier sections of the fourteen thousand acres.

The turkey activity we see—mostly jakes, young males strutting out and about while the hens and the older males stay prudently under cover—is respectable, really quite encouraging given last year's miserable acorn crop, and Lovett seems satisfied. The turkeys aren't exactly bountiful this spring, but there are enough of them to ensure that those Georgia boys will at least hear a gobbler or see a jake even if they don't get a shot. This year's new growth of acorns looks to be in fine shape, so next spring there should be plenty of turkeys, provided of course that factors like the predation of coons on the eggs now hatching can be skewed a touch in the turkeys' favor.

Lovett realizes that this last point needs attention and resolves to lay out some traps this very night. He also suggests that should my evening's hog-seeking ramble happen to coincide with the path of a coon or two, I do my share of the pruning. This is not something he'd ask a paying customer, of course (shooting at anything but one's primary objective being one way of ensuring said objective's immediate departure from the area), but I'm in sort of a gray area here, working and hunting too, so it's okay. And anyway, I don't have to worry; the damn hogs are all over the place, and the younger ones I'm interested in aren't nearly as easily frightened as the big old boars by gunshots and other human phenomena. Fisheating Creek's hog population hasn't yet reached the point where fear of man is inbred rather than learned from experience, so, as Lovett puts it, "some of them still think we're just another kind of hog; they don't know we're really a kind of panther."

But panthers we are, and panther-like we roam, going where we please when we please. We bump along rough dirt roads through hundreds of acres of saw palmetto, watching hawks thermaling and snakes slithering and armadillos lumbering, but having to imagine the turkey hens nesting safely below the dense waist-high cover. We pull to a halt at the edge of a palmetto prairie, and Lovett demonstrates how you figure out when the last major fire swept across the land, by examining the patterns of new growth on a wiry little scrub oak. Then we move downgrade through a sudden dense stand of assorted hardwoods and pass through a flooded hollow where the receding waters of the spring drought have concentrated so many fish that it would seem a man could walk on silver. We pause in an eerie stand of Melaleuca trees, a place so cool and dark and uncharacteristically devoid of other vegetation—the life-giving light of even the noonday sun above us is snuffed out—that it is graphically obvious why these exotics pose such a threat to Florida's indigenous flora.

Lovett, being who he is, has given serious thought to the Melaleuca problem. He peels a long, four-inch-thick strip of ultra-lightweight bark from a handy tree trunk, explains that the stuff is both fireproof and insect-repellant, and ventures the thought that there exists a way for Florida to get stripped of these pests in a hurry. Some bright spark, he thinks, could market Melaleuca home insulation. It's natural fiberglass, organic Styrofoam, and moreover it would have both Australian-image oompah and Buy-American consumer appeal. Yes . . . Lovett might have something there. Yuppie homeowners would probably pay a premium for a product like that.

Lovett seems excited by this notion for a while—it's his kind of tonic, a good workable solution in which everybody wins, nobody loses—but an all too familiar gloom descends quickly. He starts thinking about the self-interest of the fiberglass and Styrofoam industries, all those lobbyists, all that money changing hands in Washington come product-approval time, and he begins to see how this novel notion, like all too many entirely sensible win/win ideas, should probably be cast as a prey species in the predatory drama of life. Which (bucking up a little here, his expression lightening a shade or two) doesn't mean someone shouldn't *try* it at least. . . . Perhaps the Styrofoam producers themselves, yes? But then, why would they bother? Styrofoam sales are doing just fine as things are. . . .

This speculation gets pretty tiresome, so we drop it and move on. We see otters at work, watch a column of vultures marking the final resting place of some large mammal, recognize by a few straight lines of citrus trees in the random woods that we are passing through all that remains of some pioneer cracker's homesite. Finally, before heading back to the camp, we stop at Lovett's favorite fishing hole. I stand ready with my rifle at this spot, rather than fishing, because Lovett says he found the biggest hog turd he's ever seen right here on this creek bank.

"If I'd had something to carry it in, I'd have brought it back to the camp, used it as an ashtray or something," he says. "Wouldn't that have been a nice conversation piece? I'd like to have seen that hog, though, I really would . . . probably this tiny little hog with this great big asshole."

He laughs happily, then gets down to business. He catches bait on his first cast, then hauls in a catfish dinner for four in six or seven minutes, wham-bam thank you ma'am.

This is Lovett's kind of fishing: small outlay, big return. He's not the type to approach fishing, or hunting, as a game in which the point is to win despite having imposed severe handicaps on one's superior predatory self. You won't find this gentleman stalking a two-hundred-and-fifty-pound boar with a handgun or a bow, or going after big game fish with ultra-light tackle; the very last thing he wants is a prodigious expenditure of skill and effort ending in a broken fishing line and a fought-to-death fish, or the escape of a mortally wounded but not immobilized creature. For him the point is to eat, and so he's as direct as possible about finding it, killing it, and cooking it.

Which in no way means that Lovett is a hun. He's just experienced, he just knows what's what, he doesn't want to play unnecessary games. And neither does his pragmatism imply that he is not a romantic. The better scientists and investigators in many fields, including game biology, quite often cherish a wondrous and at times poetic appreciation of natural phenomena—the more they learn, the more sensitive they become to the mysteries and marvels of the natural order which confronts them—and Lovett is not unusual in that regard. He is moved by the inexplicable. When for instance he speaks of the mating, breeding, and learning habits of the extraordinarily long-living sandhill crane, a bird which has been known to reach an age of twenty-five years or more, and when he then dwells on the sheer density and interdependence of the other life chains which make such a creature possible, he is enthused and energized. He is not awed, though, because he understands the forces and the logic at work in such a phenomenon.

What he doesn't understand, and what does awe him sometimes, is the special nature of *Homo sapiens,* the mystery of what happens in the imagination of men when they confront questions such as the sandhill crane's life span: the very process of human understanding. Lovett really gets a kick out of thinking about how, alone among the creatures of the earth, man is able to use his powers of deductive reasoning to fill in whole pictures from a single observation. Such and such an animal must behave exactly *so,* and this plant over here must have *that* capability, because if neither of those deductions were true, it would not be possible for this second (or nth) animal to be doing what it has been observed to be doing.

Lovett enjoys musing on the place of *Homo sapiens* in the natural world, and today he gets a good opportunity. Bumping along in his pickup past a place where last year he found panther tracks, the subject of large feline predators suggests an instance of humanity in nature which for some reason really got home to him.

It was a photograph in *National Geographic* or *Natural History,* one of those magazines, of some villagers in northern India paddling a canoe down a river at dusk, each man wearing a beautiful stylized mask of a human face on the back of his head. The caption explained that the masks were not decorative or symbolic but utterly practical. The men were wearing faces on the back of their heads to confuse tigers, who typically attack humans from behind. With no "behind" in sight, the tigers might not attack. And being human, the men had made their masks beautiful.

"Isn't that wonderful?" Lovett asks. "I mean, doesn't that just say it all: man living in nature, surviving against superior predators by using his intelligence, and at the same time creating art. That's man at his best, isn't it?"

He chuckles about that for a while, then comes back to the here and now, and a less idyllic approach to the subject of men and big cats in environmental proximity.

"I don't know, though," he says. "We get all pissed off today about how the Florida crackers used to shoot panthers on sight—more than that, they went out hunting them—but you see, those people were just trying to survive by free-ranging hogs or cattle, and the damn cats kept eating up their livestock. And those people in India . . . I read in the paper the other day where a tiger had killed, oh, twenty-six people in one village in one day. And that shit happens all the time over there! Something like three or four hundred people a year get killed by tigers.

"Now, isn't that just ridiculous? I don't understand it. Why don't they just get organized, go out and *eradicate* the fuckin' tigers? *I* would.

"I dunno. All this sensitivity in this country these days toward cats and bears and gators and all the other dangerous animals . . . it's a luxury, isn't it?

"You see, we're safe. A goddam panther isn't going to quit hiding in the swamps, sneak across five miles of concrete, and bite your head off while you're watching TV, now is it? So the only reason we can afford to worry about protecting them is that we've boxed them in and wiped them out to the point where we don't have to be scared of them anymore. There aren't enough of them left to get *us*. That's funny, isn't it?"

We bump back to the hunting camp. C'est la vie.

○

There is something of the military man about Lovett Williams: his personal neatness, the order in his movements, his straight back and high chin, his casual profanity, a certain air of authority. And then too, at times there's the fighter's gleam in his eye, the kick-ass spirit.

To the outsider, these qualities might seem inappropriate in a wild-life biologist. Is that not a profession for ex-hippie peacenik loners, a job at the far end of the sociophilosophical spectrum from the armed services' intimate, rigidly structured brotherhood? Such however is not the case in reality. Lovett, remember, entered the profession under the auspices of the Florida Game and Fresh Water Fish Commission, a rank-conscious civil service organization in which (during his first years, at least) he worked as a game warden. He was in fact a cop, a man with a badge and a gun and the power of the law behind him.

So yes, Mr. Williams is quite familiar with the business of kicking ass and taking names. And, like most American males his age, he is also a military veteran. Before he got started with the state, he served his hitch in the Coast Guard. He got his college education on the GI Bill.

At lunch in Palmdale, a settlement near the hunting camp which looks impressive on the map but in reality is just a diner and a general-store-cum-gas station stranded on Route 27, Lovett talks with his usual mixture of humor and intolerance about his service in the Coast Guard. To this day, he says, he keeps meeting people who heard about him back then—so *he* was that guy, the one who ran the cutter this-a-way and that-a-way after interesting seabirds, burning Uncle Sam's fuel oil in bizarre inshore maneuvers—and yes, even in those days he'd find the fool killer appearing in his hand. He remembers, for instance, being just appalled by the ineptitude of the powers-that-were who shipped plainly marked crates of U.S. Army ammunition on open flatcars to the port of New Orleans in preparation for the supposedly clandestine Bay of Pigs invasion. Neither did he enjoy standing guard with an unloaded gun while the ammo was transferred to sugar freighters for the one-way trip to Cuba. What would he have done, he wonders, upon the appearance of the enemy? Insult them to death? Lovett figures he pretty much blew his chances of further promotion when he didn't keep his thoughts to himself about *that* little piece of business. . . .

The conversation continues in this vein until events conspire to banish the rebel and bring forth the cop in Mr. Williams. What happens is that a young game warden, well known to the local men at the tables adjacent to ours, stops in for a pack of smokes and a cup of coffee to go, and while he waits at the counter, some of the younger ole boys take the opportunity, by passing remarks among themselves in slightly louder than normal conversational tones about how many out-of-season deer and privately owned hogs they've poached so far this year, to let him know where he stands in their regard.

The young warden doesn't rise to the bait. He keeps his back turned while he waits, and on his way out he just nods to them, says, "Hi, boys" in a nice flat neutral voice.

Lovett thinks that was all right, a whole hell of a lot better than getting into any kind of conversation, but admits that it's not the way he personally would have handled the situation. He personally would have ignored those boys while he did his business, just like the young warden, but on the way out, "I'd have had a word with them. I'd have let them know real plainly what would happen to them if *I* caught them taking game that wasn't theirs."

Really, he says, those boys are just trash, strictly amateurs. In all probability, they came to that point of decision faced by young outlaws all over rural South Florida, and backed away from biting the big bullet: they opted not to follow their fathers or brothers or friends into the big money and big risks of the drug business ("A few timely funerals around here helped a lot in that regard," Lovett notes). So now they're sitting around diners, needling low-level nature cops.

We leave them to it. As we drive back to the camp, Lovett says that while most of the people who live near the fourteen thousand acres are decent folk, those boys back there are the product of households in which there persists a conviction that the taking of game from big landowners' property is a perfectly proper, justifiable activity.

He understands that attitude, but he doesn't agree with it. As he points out, "Those people never did own that game, and they don't own it now, and they never will own it unless they pay the money and buy the goddam land. But for some reason, probably because they're descended from a bunch of poachers who got kicked out of Europe, they imagine they've got the God-given right to just go steal it, and they're all pissed off because these days it's getting harder and harder for them to do that.

"Well, tough shit; there ain't no free lunch, you know. There really isn't."

Lovett adds that growth and progress, so pervasive in Florida, have had their effect on poaching, too. "Poaching isn't nearly as serious a business as it used to be around here," he says. "The young guys watch TV like everyone else, you see, so they know there's a world out there, and most of them get up and leave before they learn enough to be a real problem. That's the difference between them and their pappies; a generation ago, being a real shit-ass was about the best thing a boy around here could aspire to."

❂

Eleven baby gators and their mother on the cypress creek bank. . . . Solitary and spotted woodpeckers. . . . A jake called to within shotgun range by Lovett's expert imitation of a horny turkey hen. . . . Riotous rootings where hogs have dug after the tubers on pennywort roots. . . . The little shady meadow where three or four years ago a hunter killed Fisheating Creek's record boar, a three-hundred-and-sixty-pounder. . . . An adult little blue heron fishing in company with a young white ibis, the one by binocular vision and the other by feel. . . . A beautiful stand of big old live oaks that wouldn't have been here a century ago; government agents would have taken them for the curved stems and keels of Navy ships. . . . A University of South Florida Cessna buzzing us, letting us know that somewhere on the lease there roams a radio-transmitter-carrying panther. . . . A red-tailed hawk, an indigo snake, white-tailed deer, otters, turtles, armadillos. . . .

This is our afternoon along the creek. We travel either with an imposing rumble by swamp buggy, a massive black-boilerplated pig of a vehicle cushioned and elevated by huge tough balloon tires—the wildlife flees from us in this monster—or we go quietly dismounted, shuffling our feet, avoiding the sudden snap of even the smallest twig. At around four o'clock, with the power of the sun just beginning to wane, we find ourselves at a lovely curve in the creek where the fast constricted flow of cool, deep, tannin-stained water has created a tiny white-sand beach among the oaks and palms and cypresses, and here we are stunned gently into peace.

"It's beautiful, isn't it?" says Lovett after a while. "When you come in here after a day out banding turkeys in the sun, and you're tired and hot and sweaty and dirty, and you're worrying about this or that or the other thing, it's just like taking a tranquilizer."

I've stood in places very like this one before—one in particular, at a bend in the Alafaia River near Tampa, tranquilized me so powerfully that I moved my life two thousand miles to have it near me—but I've never been able to examine their beauty with too fine a focus. Someone before me has always left a calling card: anything from a used diaper or a pile of beer cans to mountains of garbage or heaps of fish killed by agricultural/industrial effluent.

This section of Fisheating Creek is different. It's pristine. After five years in Florida, I've finally found an unsullied place.

I shot a hog this evening, so I'm feeling the way I felt the last (and first) time I did it: elated, revolted, confused.

The hog was a small one, even smaller than I thought when I first drew down on him, fifty or sixty pounds rather than the seventy or eighty pounds I'd estimated. Therefore he reacted in ways both good and bad to the big heavy soft-point .308 bullet which entered an inch to the left of his lower spine as he started to run from me.

On the bright side, he just dropped in his tracks and flailed through a few seconds of the usual death spasms, and that was that: confirmation of the theory that a hunter should always be overgunned rather than undergunned. When I walked up on him and rolled him over, though, his belly revealed the negative side of the power-to-spare approach. A large bloody hole between his front legs, oozing a thick brown sludge of partially digested nutrients, made it immediately apparent that those one hundred and eighty grains of copper-jacketed lead traveling at twenty-four hundred feet per second had literally exploded his intestines, and God only knew what else, on their way clean through his body.

This was not good. If you're hunting to eat, the last thing you want is meat contaminated by digestive and glandular fluids and fecal matter. Never shoot 'em in the guts, in other words—and that, apparently, is what my overgunned spine shot had accomplished. A lesser bullet might have expanded shortly after penetration, delivering great shock and coming to a halt in bone or muscle before it reached the creature's innards. But then again, a lesser bullet might not have had the power to drop a bigger hog, especially if the hog were going on the offensive; the sheer momentum of two or three hundred pounds of hard-charging muscle and armor plate, wielding four hatchets on the end of his legs and a pair of razors on his lower jaw, is about as impressive as you'd think it would be. So in the quite possible worst-case scenario of insufficient bullet power, I could end up decorating the scenery with bright red arterial blood and wishing, in my final moments, that I'd brought along a gun that shoots steel-tipped telephone poles.

The essential points of this debate, while lurid enough for most tastes, are, essentially, pragmatic. Not so the components of the other confrontations within me as I sit with Lovett back at his camp: pride butting against nausea, fear struggling with elation, the guilt of the killer spoiling the thrill of the kill. Lovett, though, is a cool comfort. He tells me that the pragmatic issue is simple: if I want to hunt, I should keep my .308 but use lighter bullets traveling faster. Increased velocity plus decreased mass equals greater shock, less penetration, and shock's what it's all about. And as to the other stuff . . .

"I know what you're talking about," he says. "I've been hunting all my life, so you'd think that nothing about it would bother me. But as I get older, I'm getting more and more sensitive. It's weird. I don't hunt near as much as I used to."

There is something here, between the trauma frequently experienced by the novice hunter and the vague unease often intruding between an older woodsman and the hunting that has been a mainspring of his whole life, that unites the men and the boys, and quite obviously separates them both from the beasts. The subject interests Lovett because, like the instance of those tiger-deceiving Indians, it bears on the question which occupies much of his philosophical energy: what kind of animals are we?

On the one hand, there's a professional hobbyhorse Lovett rides hard and frequently. In his opinion, the past thousand or so years of man's most profound thinking, the whole train of intellectual effort running from theology to social psychology, has been a self-deceiving and basically paranoid series of attempts to distract man's attention from the biological imperatives which by rights should be the starting point of any investigation of human nature.

"We deny what we really are," he says. "We relegate all kinds of things about ourselves to the category of the disgusting and the unmentionable. Like shit. We don't want to know about it, even though we all do it. The Queen of England does it. She shits—great big turds! "Now, a damn tumblebug, *he* doesn't think shit's disgusting. He takes little piles of it and rolls it around and lays his eggs in the middle of it, and he thinks it's the most wonderful thing there is!

"It's the same with how we're scared of blood and uptight about sex, and how we wear clothes even in places so hot that wearing clothes doesn't make any sense; all those things. I mean, you know what I'm getting at. We humans are just so damned *arbitrary*. We're the only animal that refuses to believe whole areas of what its senses tell it."

Lovett laughs when he says this, but professionally the issue annoys him. He finds it very irritating that even today (to employ an inorganic but nonetheless appropriate naval analogy), man spends his energy trying to understand the meaning of the instruments in the wheelhouse without referring to what's happening in the engine room; that biologists are confined belowdecks like some inferior breed of mechanic, free to investigate the 'lower' forms of life— animals, plants, insects—but verboten in the spaces on high, the very precepts of their science an affront to the dignity and uniqueness of the men conferring on the bridge. "I mean, that's understandable, certainly," quoth the fool killer, "but it's *stupid,* isn't it? Vain."

On the other hand, Lovett's just like everyone else. He can't help but find it endlessly fascinating, for instance, that alone among the predators on earth, man feels guilty about killing to eat. Whence comes this oddity, this uniqueness?

Unsurprisingly, then, Lovett and I spend the next couple of hours talking about higher powers and cosmic orders and spiritual notions of our separate wholly inadequate understandings, Lovett making frequent trips to his refrigerator for another of the beers which opened his door to this kind of discussion in the first place.

Eventually, though, biological necessity intrudes. The turkey hunters arrive from Georgia, moving like rag dolls in molasses after a spectacularly alcoholic eight-hour drive—two or three of them are so drunk they can't even talk—and both they and we must be fed forthwith.

The meat we eat for dinner is pork: acorn-fed, free-ranging feral hog, amazing stuff. So delicious, you'd kill for it.

○

Dinner slows Lovett down, but not by much. There are more horses waiting for his ride, and the world is full of fools.

We get started quietly, though, with some reminiscences of a native son. They're fun, really fascinating, for in Florida a native in his fifties can reach back and tell you about a place very different from the one you see around you today. So for that matter can a thirty-year-old, or even a Yankee transplant who's been in the sunshine nine or ten years; a decade means a lot in a state whose population has grown from two million to twelve million since World War Two.

In Lovett's young boyhood, though, rapid change was a phenomenon of the immediate future rather than the common past. The real boom hadn't quite begun, and the community into which he was born was still a relatively stable affair featuring technological growth but little in the way of radical social change; Florida was still populated for the most part by crackers and blacks descended from the outcasts and adventurers who disposed of its aboriginal inhabitants, and the settlers who followed in their path. Except in the few coastal port/industrial and resort communities, and in the central peninsula's phosphate mining areas, Floridians lived off the land or the sea: they were foresters, citrus and vegetable growers, sugarcane cutters, cowboys, hunters and trappers, or fishermen. They made their homes in the woods or in little towns which hadn't changed significantly for a hundred years, and a newcomer to their communities was a rarity.

In those days a tangible sense of separateness was common in much of Florida; not the awareness of media glamour and sunbelt-boom good fortune and spectacular lawlessness which lends a certain unique élan to a Sunshine State address today, but a real feeling of isolation from the greater United States, a forgotten-country, poor-relation kind of atmosphere all the more powerful for the knowledge that the state was after all the place at the end of the line, an extreme appendage geographically, historically, and in every other way. Until the interstate highway system and cheap air travel put it squarely in the center of vacationers' and retirees' sights, Florida was a place which just didn't matter much. And whether they liked it or not, Floridians knew that.

Lovett liked it; liked the wild woods and coastlines, liked the untraveled landscape and the extended-kinship social dynamics of his obscure North Florida home, never felt much of a desire to travel to the sources of the civilization shown on TV. In fact, as a fifth-generation North Floridian, the proud descendant of industrious and independent small landholders—Florida crackers—he never even much wanted to mingle with the people immediately north or south of his home turf. The Alabamians and Georgians to the north were largely perceived as an inferior bunch, either inbred and ignorant sharecroppers or inbred and arrogant plantation pseudoaristocracy, and the folks bred down South, the Conchs, were mostly outlaws, poachers, hermits, half-breeds, and other varieties of miscreant and riffraff.

Where Lovett grew up, then, near the Georgia line in Gadsen County, the term "cracker" was a subtle appellation. If you were a North Floridian of long, honest lineage, you could of course claim the title with pride—shout it from the pine tops if you wished, include your friends and family too—but let that word come your way from the lips of some other type of person, some snooty Mobilian or Jacksonville Yankee or Tampa Hispanic, and that person had a problem on his hands. The hardest fight of Lovett's boyhood was with some stuck-up citified little sonofabitch who made the mistake of equating "cracker" with "trash." (Being just as undersized and overaggressive as Lovett, the kid gave as good as he got, teaching our man to think long and hard before picking on people his own size.)

Oddly enough, most of the world in which Lovett grew up still exists. The really radical change, the massive population growth, has happened along the eastern and southwestern coasts of the state and in the central strip running from Tampa through Orlando to Cape Canaveral. Most of the upper Gulf coast, and the piney hills of the northern peninsula and the Panhandle, are still in the hands of the indigenous crackers. In a way, Lovett finds it amusing that the places generating the most common outsider's images of the state—scenes of graceful palm trees flurried by sea breezes, of little pastel stucco bungalows shaded by citrus trees, of lovely cypress swamps and mangrove tangles and coral reefs and places where a low flat semitropical landscape meets a gentle aqua sea—have been submerged under the population pressure of millions of Yankees and Midwesterners, leaving intact only those sections of Florida which never resembled the images in the first place. That, sadly ironic as it is, does of course make sense, for what relocating New Yorker or Chicagoan would be attracted to a place which looks like southern Georgia and is full of unwelcoming back-country rednecks who act as if they own the place?

Lovett can still go home to his obscure Florida, then, and find his culture still alive. He doesn't do so very often—his work's down South at Fisheating Creek, and he lives in Ocala, a central peninsular town not quite far enough from the I-4 theme-park belt or the I-75 corridor to resist gradually escalating development—but he doesn't really have to. He remembers his home well enough, and he knows he's a cracker through and through. Lovett cherishes the clannish, deeply rooted sense of difference and independence he gained as an accident of birth, and he feels quite comfortable with the way his raising engendered a low tolerance for foolishness and false premises. He remembers very clearly, for instance, how he used to read in his grade-school textbooks that robins arrived in your yard in the spring and in winter it snowed, and how his cracker spirit interpreted those black-and-white statements (written of course by Yankees, though he had no way of knowing that at the time). Since any fool knew that robins *left* your yard in the springtime, and it *never* snowed, where were you supposed to place your trust?

Certainly not in the pronouncements of those in authority. "I got a jump on most people," Lovett laughs today. "I learned the value of cynicism very early in life. It's a curse, but now and again it comes in real handy."

Tonight it comes in very handy indeed. After the memory lane segment of Lovett's monologue, we get a veritable orgy of pissed-off cracker grit and cynical analysis.

A lot of it concerns the chain of events which landed Lovett in this house trailer on these fourteen thousand acres, aligning Fisheating Creek's natural resources with his ambitions as a private businessman. For according to Lovett, it was the venality, incompetence, disloyalty, predatory competitiveness, and other truly rotten qualities of his fellow humans which ended his career as a big man with the state.

His and David's noble preservationist experiment is, sad to say, the eventual outcome of an involuntary process.

As Lovett explains it, five years ago he was riding high in the Florida Game and Fresh Water Fish Commission. After a career of almost thirty years, he was head of the department's field research division, running what he says was an exceptionally tight and efficient ship which under his captaincy had grown in importance and explored an ever-widening range of the state's natural-resource issues. His outfit, he claims, was the most dynamic of the commission's operations, and also the most important in any rational analysis of the commission's primary function: without the real-life data provided by field research, he asks, how can informed natural-resource management decisions possibly be made?

Lovett, in short, is of the opinion that he was getting a crucial job done well. Other, less partisan observers share that opinion; Mr. Williams had the reputation of being an unusually clear thinker and excellent administrator, though not much of a diplomat.

Lovett's problem, he says, arose when his boss decided that it made more sense for the chief of field research to work in an office in the state capitol than in the field. Following this line of reasoning, Lovett would have to move himself and his family from Ocala to Tallahassee, give up his personal involvement in research, and ride a desk like all the other division heads.

Lovett didn't like that idea at all—he didn't want to leave the field or enter the political arena of Tallahassee—and he suggested an alternative wherein someone else who actually wanted a desk job could be promoted to direct field research, while he could take on a new role as liaison between Research and the commission's other divisions. The liaison function, he says, was sorely needed. Without it, too much work was being wasted, too many purposes were getting crossed.

Things didn't turn out the way Lovett wanted. Someone else was indeed promoted to the post Lovett had refused, but no new post was created. And so Lovett took what he felt to be his only remaining option. He resigned.

The way Lovett characterizes the affair, he just got shafted: dealt with in bad faith by bosses who had agreed in principle to the new position, betrayed by colleagues who had encouraged him to push for the new post but wouldn't support him when the going got tough, and maneuvered out of the power structure.

"I'd been an important person in the organization for a long time," he says, "and I guess a lot of people must have gotten tired of kissing my ass. That's natural, I think, but when I think back on it, I sometimes still can't believe the way some of those sons of bitches lied to me. It really amazed me, how people I worked with didn't give a damn about anyone or anything but themselves. You see, a lot of those guys, all they saw was the slot ahead of them opening up when I was gone. That's what it was really all about."

Lovett's feelings about the affair have not mellowed with time, and he still burns whenever he lets himself think that the creation of the liaison function, which was a way for the Florida Game and Fresh Water Fish Commission to better serve Florida wildlife and thus Florida people, was apparently not an issue as far as his colleagues were concerned. It also annoys him that he himself, a hoary veteran of bureaucratic politics and a supposedly cynical old cracker to boot, could have been "so fuckin' naive."

In the end, though, his anger with himself is but a mote in the blistering convection of his contempt for other individuals in the specific, and the self-serving imperatives of bureaucrats and politicians in general.

Heat rises in the house trailer. The color of the epithets intensifies. The fool killer leaps to his hand, and flashes and scythes. The indictments mount into a dossier of impressive heft and lurid detail. The questions, all those basic lines of broad and narrow inquiry a real public servant should in Lovett's opinion be pursuing, multiply geometrically. . . . Why are Florida's public service agencies all run by professional politicians rather than by people who have at least a passing acquaintance with the field they're supposed to be managing? . . . What's the use of a law that encourages landowners wanting development permits to simply do away with any protected flora and fauna before they make an application? . . . What the hell is the point of a regulation, which state game officers spend all kinds of time enforcing, that says a hunter can't go out in the woods with a shotgun capable of holding more than three shells? . . . It goes on and on until Lovett grows weary and feels the need to sum it all up somehow.

"None of this crap makes any sense," he says. "It's all just archaic bullshit, old ways of doing things that don't work anymore or dumb ways of doing things which never worked in the first place, but do you think anyone's going to throw it out and do something rational for a change? Not on your fuckin' life! Just about everybody with the power to start making sense in this state has got one eye open for an ass to kiss, and the other on a big fuckin' sign that says DON'T MAKE WAVES!"

That statement seems to satisfy Lovett for the present, and he chuckles his way to the refrigerator for another beer. Then he jumps tracks toward the semipositive.

"It's funny, because growth is the main problem in the state," he says, "but I guess the only real hope is how Florida is changing. All those new people coming in from all over the country, all over the world; they're more sophisticated than the folks around here, they've seen ways of doing things that work in other places. Right now, you see, the state's pretty much still run by a bunch of good ole boys who don't give a shit as long as the cash is rolling in, but I don't know how long all these new citizens are going to tolerate that kind of stuff. Probably not much longer, don't you think?"

What I think doesn't really matter here (for the record, it varies, its optimism content more a function of factors like recent or too-long-ago feeding than cerebral analysis), so I tell Lovett that, and he seems to understand. He moves forward. He's on to something here.

"You know what would be fun? You know what would really shake things up?" he asks excitedly. "I'll tell you. You could *use* the screwed-up system we have in this state. You could find yourself some real fireball, someone who's real strong on environmental issues and doesn't give a damn about getting in tight with the good ole boys, and run him for Secretary of State! You don't have to have any qualifications to get that job, you see—it's always just some goddam politician who has it, and usually he never does anything with it—so it's wide open. And someone could really do things if they got in!

"And you know, I bet you could pull that off. I bet people would come out and vote, and I bet that guy could get elected. I bet if I were serious about it, *I* could get elected. Wouldn't that be something? Can you *imagine?*"

Oh, yes. A rational order to last a thousand years, government truly in the service of the people . . . the salvation of natural Florida and a shining beacon in the state-governmental night . . . or an orgy of ass kicking and name taking, the slaughter of dozens of fools in high places before the surviving few hundred hired a hit man. . . .

Lovett's idea isn't really a serious one, though, or at least it doesn't really seem to be. It's hard to tell. Whatever, the fact that he's talking about it does indicate that he's not entirely resigned to his role as a hunting camp owner in the private sector.

And maybe he never really was. For one thing, his original plan for the lease on Fisheating Creek included not just hunting but also family camping and organized nature tours through the fourteen thousand acres' magnificence of abundant and endangered life. This made sense to Lovett both on economic grounds and as a way of really tapping the land's full potential for human pleasure, but apparently it didn't make sense to Lykes. Lovett says that the company balked at the nature-tours idea and refused permission for their land to be used in such a manner.

Lovett can see the point behind what he suspects to be the company's rationale: why allow a steadily multiplying number of relatively well-heeled, quite possibly quite influential citizens to fall in love with land you want ultimately to sell as a job lot to some concrete-spewer? With regret, he also accepts his powerlessness over the issue. He has not, however, abandoned the hunting/camping/nature-tours package concept. Currently he's looking into other parcels of South Florida land which might be suitable for such use. And then too, he's still thinking about Fisheating Creek, thinking about destruction and preservation and public service and politics. Thinking about staying in the game. Thinking about playing hardball.

Here we are, then. Lovett's not at all whimsical or impassioned or unrealistic now; no daydreams or philosophical rambles in *this* moment. He just leans back in his chair and says it quite calmly, matter-of-factly: "I could make a *real* good case for the state buying this land, turning it into a state park. In fact, I can't think of another parcel of land in the whole of Florida which is better qualified."

So why, I ask, doesn't he just do it? Make a move, begin a process, and preserve all this life and beauty for the people forever?

"Well, there's a conflict with every person like myself or David, every wildlife person," he says. "You see, all of the years David and I have been around this land, we've had this tremendous opportunity to utilize aspects of the place that even the owners don't care about. Hell, they don't even *know* about them!

"Really, you see, all this land has been ours. That place we fished today, Gopher Gulley, those sandhill cranes we saw—nobody but us can take advantage of those things, and we can do it just the way we want, by ourselves. We drove eight miles out today and eight miles back, and we didn't see a single human being.

"Think about that. What do you think would happen if this place were made into a state park? I'll tell you. What we have now would be gone, that's what! It would end. It wouldn't be possible anymore.

"So it's like Florida itself, isn't it? It's that same old Catch-22 again: what appeals to people about the place is destroyed by the people coming here to appreciate it."

This is all too painfully true, and the point reverberates, echoes everywhere in Florida. You can't spend time with any people who grew up in the state without at some point hearing about personal magic places—a hidden mangrove inlet in which they learned the secrets of the wily snook; a cool deep swimming hole hidden by stands of riverbank hardwoods; a field full of doves or a wood full of childhood adventure—where now those same people buy gas or rent movies or sit in traffic jams watching the malls and condos and Jiffy Lubes grow.

It's sad, and that's not all it is, either. Sitting in his house trailer in the heart of his particular magic place, Lovett asks a final question. "You know what's valuable about this land, and why David and I are able to do what we're doing? Why we can even *be* here?"

Then he answers it. "It's because wild Florida's going down the drain, and this is one of the only places left," he says.

"Now, speaking in grand terms, I don't know how *Homo sapiens* is going to fare in a world where he can't hunt or fish, or even have any relationship at all with wild nature. I don't know what the emotional repercussions are going to be when the species is separated from his origins as an animal. I don't think anybody knows that; it's something we're only going to find out when it's too late to do anything about it. But I *do* know that if it weren't for the destruction of nature in this part of the world, David and I couldn't be doing what we're doing here. If Fisheating Creek were in Arkansas, or Kentucky, or any other beautiful place with a very low human population, we couldn't charge people money to see it. So really, the worse off Florida gets, the more hopeful our enterprise becomes.

"That's too bad, isn't it?"

5
Gators The Hard Way

As we glide across the last few yards of night-black water separating us from Karen's boat, we still can't see the gator she needs our help with.

We can however perceive the dimensions of her problem. The two fellas with her, the gig man and the light man, are having to strain hard to keep ahold of the snare lines going down to the creature's neck and tail beneath the surface of the water, and the lines are pretty far apart, and the little johnboat's listing sharply under the weight.

"That there's a big gator," says Don—"a *biiiiiiig* gator."

Karen confirms it. She and the two men and the gator have been in their standoff for a while now, she says; they got the gigs into him and bang-sticked him twice in the head with .44 Magnums and got the electrical tape around his jaws more than an hour ago, but that's all they've been able to do. Can't haul him up for love or money; he's heavier than all three people in the boat put together. Probably a lot heavier, in fact, because he's about the same length as the boat, which is thirteen feet.

Don, who's our gig man, takes charge, first things first. Well now, he asks, is he dead?

Karen isn't willing to bet on it. It wasn't too long ago, she says, that he was smashing his tail against the boat, still trying to reverse the predator/prey relationship, get the humans in the water with him.

So just how long ago was that? Don asks.

'Bout ten minutes, says Karen.

Well then, Don concludes, he's right likely dead, isn't he? Otherwise he'd have come up for air already. Or he'll be coming up any minute now.

There's a pause now, quite a lengthy one, which seems to involve more than the rationally procedural act of waiting and seeing. We've all shifted into neutral somehow, sort of disappeared from the situation. All seven of us are standing or sitting around in the two boats, not talking, gazing at stuff which seems suddenly very interesting: the lights of the other boats working Lake Hancock's mosquito-infested shoreline, the gear lying around in our own boats, the glow of Lakeland's city lights in the sky to the north, the stars above, each other; more or less anything which isn't the narrow slice of water between the boats.

"Well . . ." says Karen.

"That gator's dead," says Don. "Let's get 'im up."

Whether or not anyone, Don included, has any faith in the accuracy of his first sentence, there's no longer any point in trying to deny the relevance of his second. Unless we want to try dragging the gator along the lake bottom to the shore (almost certainly ruining the value of his hide, quite probably burning out an engine, possibly swamping the boat, and most likely losing the beast entirely along the way), we're just going to have to haul him up out of the water by brute force, and then we're going to have to lay our tasty little hands on him and pull him into Karen's boat whatever his condition: genuinely dead, just stunned and temporarily incapacitated, or wide-awake and awaiting his next chance to kill us. Those are the rules in this game; that's how it has to happen. It's the law.

❂

There are a lot of laws about alligators in Florida, and therefore there are a lot of alligators. Since 1962, when the state banned gator hunting and the federal government banned interstate commerce in Florida alligator products, the beasts have multiplied most wonderfully.

Nobody really knows the true figures, but any Verne, Martha, or Fido who's been near fresh water lately has no problem accepting the Florida Game and Fresh Water Fish Commission's admission that its estimate of one million alligators in the state, or one gator for every ten people, is very conservative; the real number could be fifty percent greater, or even double that. When Verne and Martha go looking for gators in Florida, they find them. When Fido goes where gators are, they find him.

Basically, the beasts are everywhere in the state, occupying any place offering a combination of fresh water, nesting grounds, and adequate food. You do not have to venture into the hinterlands to encounter them, either, for the fact of the matter is that a gator has no natural fear of humans and will coexist quite happily with the people who are encroaching on his habitat in ever-increasing numbers. Your friendly international subdivision developer can pave and civilize all he wants, but unless he eliminates fresh water from his landscaping plans entirely (which of course would be foolish, waterfront property being so appealing to the buyer), the indigenous gators are not going to get up and leave. In Florida, then, there are plenty of gators in what's left of the wild lakes, rivers, and swamps, but they are also thick in the water of canals, abandoned phosphate pits, and the thousands of natural and artificial bodies of fresh water that soothe the souls of the citizenry from the Panhandle to the Keys. Gators go about their business in these places just as they do in the wilderness, but with the added element of humans to pique their instinctive curiosity.

Contact is therefore inevitable, and commonplace. When you visit someone's parents in their retirement home on a lake or bayou someplace, you hear about "their" gator, the one that takes his ease under their boat dock during the day. When you take a summertime canoe trip on a river, you see gators. In one spot on the Withlacoochee just outside the suburbs of Tampa, you can't paddle fifty yards without watching a ten-footer slide off the high bank into the water with you. There is familiarity here; gators are part of the scenery.

Humans react variously, as one might expect, with everything from country respect to the most abject urban ignorance. A newspaper photograph of a big gator scaling an eight-foot chain-link fence to get at a poodle in the suburban Miami garden on the other side is very cute, very funny—the gator just looks so goofy, a real-life cartoon—despite the fact that this is proof of totally determined predation in action. And although you aren't quite stupid enough to actually go swimming in the Withlacoochee or any other gator-infested body of water during the summer months, and the voice of reason is telling you that a big gator could easily flip you out of your canoe if it wanted to, isn't it a fact that the beasts' mere presence adds a certain appeal to your trip? That they attract you rather than repel you?

A lot of urban/suburban Floridians play around with gators in these and other ways despite the fact that the media acquaint them with the possible consequences of such games on a relatively regular basis. As I write, for instance, I remember very clearly a recent flurry of local press on the excruciating death of a six-year-old girl who had taken to feeding a golf course gator with marshmallows. I also remember a lesson a lot closer to home. For the last few months, we in our house have shared the horror lingering in a close friend whose brother went diving in the freshwater springs at Wakula, and didn't come back on schedule. He was found three days later; a group of tourists viewing Wakula's underwater wonders in a glass-bottomed boat were treated to the sight of the alligator that had killed him taking another meal from what remained of his corpse.

In these incidents, and in urban Floridian consciousness at large, the humans are the prey and the gators are the predators. Gators can be amusing, or colorful, or fascinating, but in the most honest places of the urban heart they are beasts of blood and nightmare, horrors of the natural world. In country Florida, though, other perceptions are the rule. Gator meat is good eating, and gator hides bring good money.

The state recognizes this fact, and just as for years it has taken measures to stand between urban populations and the gators in their midst (currently some forty-five licensed individuals are killing some eight hundred urban/suburban "nuisance" gators annually), it has recently adopted a policy of putting country folks and gators back together in the most intimate of relationships. The trading of death and food and money in selected gator habitats is now a highly controlled but entirely legal activity in the Sunshine State.

This odd reversal of the tide of history began several years ago, when Florida Game and Fresh Water Fish Commission biologists began to perceive that the wild alligator populations in the state were reaching an optimum level: that if their numbers continued to multiply, the gators would soon run into food and habitat shortages that would adversely affect (or, officially, "negatively impact") their size, life span, and general health and well-being. The state therefore began a carefully controlled, minutely monitored "experimental harvest program"—that is, it allowed certain local fellas in certain places at certain times to go get themselves gators legally, just as long as they did so exactly according to the rules and let the state's biologist observe the results—and that program revealed that if approximately fifteen percent of the adult gators in a given habitat were to be taken by hunters each year, the net effect on the gator community would be zero. Their numbers would neither grow nor decline, but remain at a constant optimum level. For the gators collectively, then, life would stay as sweet as it was, while for the lucky locals it would get a lot sweeter.

Thus, the first commercial alligator harvest since the early sixties: a great boon, adventure, and media event. The state has announced its intentions well in advance, received between five and six thousand license applications, held a lottery amid much media fanfare, and after putting the winners through mandatory classes and accepting their $250 fees, has issued two hundred and thirty-five individuals with licenses entitling them to take up to fifteen alligators apiece from assigned hunting grounds on specified nights during the month of September.

All in all, the conception and execution of the state's policy is impressive; no flies on the biologists and nature cops and public relations persons of *this* game and fresh water fish commission. The rules and regulations the lucky "trappers" and their "agents" must digest and obey are many and varied, abundant in clause and subclause and footnote and appendix, but they make sense. The total ban on fire-arms in gator boats eliminates the very real potential for accidental close-range shootings or longer-range ricochets off the water into somebody's boat or home or automobile, and it ensures that mortally wounded gators will not escape to die later. The ban on alcohol in boats means one less disadvantage for the humans in their struggles with an extremely dangerous adversary. The stipulation that every gator hide and piece of meat and other "gator product" be individually tagged and sold only to licensed buyers and processors reduces the risk of health problems and makes it very difficult for poachers to slip illegally taken gators onto the market amid the products of the legal harvest; and so on with all the more minor fine-print do's and don'ts. The impression here is of a very carefully, professionally, and intelli-gently considered operation. The Florida Game and Fresh Water Fish Commission seems to be covering all its bases quite nicely.

The operation is in fact so well conceived that one is forced to the somewhat wide-eyed conclusion that the commission actually wants the gator harvest to succeed and continue in future years; that it is not just halfheartedly throwing a bone to a frustrated minority of the state's citizens but attempting to make them genuinely happy. Why, one wonders, would this be?

One asks, and is answered by Mike Jennings, one of the wildlife biologists who designed the harvest program. Jennings begins by say-ing that let's have no mistakes here, the harvest program is *not* a gator-control operation. The state is *not* overrun by hungry predators in need of searching and destroying. Gator-related human fatalities are *not* getting out of hand, and the nuisance-gator program is func-tioning well in areas of potential disaster. What we have in the har-vest program, rather, is just what the state says we have, an enhance-ment of gator well-being and an opportunity for folks to make money.

Jennings hasn't figured out how much money is really involved, but I have. Although the thirty-five hundred beasts to be taken in the harvest will contribute only about twenty percent to the total of alliga-tor hides and other products coming out of Florida (the nuisance program will yield eight hundred or so packages, and commercial farms will produce the rest), their value represents a lot more than small change. If you say that the average alligator taken in the harvest is eight feet long, and the average wholesale price per foot for hide and meat together is ninety bucks, and then you multiply all that by thirty-five hundred (the total number of gators to be taken statewide), you get a total of just over two and a half million dollars. And that's the wholesale total, just the beginning of the harvest's impact on the Florida economy.

That brings us to Mike Jennings's most important point, which emerges from his and his colleagues' urgent concern over the potentially disastrous and already dire environmental problem of Florida's vanishing wetlands.

The only viable answer to that problem, he says, is the creation of ways to increase the dollar value of the remaining wetlands to Florida's citizens. That's where the harvest program comes in. If alligator hunters can draw cold hard cash as opposed to just recreational pleasure or aesthetic appreciation from the relatively pristine places in which they are being permitted to hunt, they will fight that much harder to keep those places the way they are. They'll make noise, support environmental groups, call their legislators. Jennings is quite explicit in stating that this is the greatest benefit to be derived from an annual gator harvest. It's good that people will have fun and adventures, he says, and it's good that the gator population will remain robust, but it's better that because of commercial gator hunting, some wetlands may become more valuable than the predominant income-producing Florida landscape of strip malls, fast-food joints, and billboards.

Well. Perhaps one should not be too surprised—people do say that those state wildlife guys are okay—but one is. Intelligence in government and concern for the long term are not common qualities of Florida's public service agencies. So applause, I think, is called for, and a certain small optimism.

There is one very dangerous cuckoo in the nest: the whole scheme, having been publicized so golly-gosh-upbeatedly by state, regional, national, and international news media, could become a bloody historical footnote in the heartbeat following the even more widely publicized moment when the first gator succeeds in turning the predatory tables on the first state-licensed hunter. But even that may not be the end of it. The vox populi doesn't really expect gator hunting to be *safe,* does it?

❂

Don and Bill and Eugene in our boat, and the two guys in Karen's boat, are hauling on the snare lines going down into the water—five grown men, each giving it his all—but nothing's happening. The gator just won't come up.

It's getting hairy, too. Our boat's listing badly enough toward the weight of the gator, but Karen's, smaller and closer to the water to begin with, is hardly an inch away from swamping. She's yelling at us: "One of you git over here! Git over here! Git on the far side here, or we're goin' over! One of you big guys! C'mon!! COME ON!!!"

Urgent as it is, though, Karen's plea is just one of many orders, appeals, and curses issuing from everybody with a communicable thought about the situation we're in. Nobody acts on it until the fifth wheel in our boat, the big-guy passenger myself, decides he really should do something.

I've struggled to my feet and am tensing to jump across the two or three feet of water between the boats when—no, it can't be, it really can't —this staggeringly huge, viciously clawed green-black reptilian foreleg thuds over the side of our boat about six inches from my shin.

The boat lurches down toward the water, and I lose my balance. I regain it by falling forward and grabbing the side of the boat where the gator is, thus pushing us all even closer toward swamping and giving me a split-second vision of something truly monstrous just beneath the surface, and then I recoil back upright. The boat follows.

Karen starts yelling at me again, but for now I can't do anything at all. That thing crooked over the side of the boat has me mesmerized. It's unbelievably ugly, and enormous. I'm trying to reconcile it with the proportions of the semicomatose creatures I've seen in zoos and tourist traps, and to the more threatening examples of the species I've encountered in the wild, in Louisiana bayous and Florida rivers and South Carolina swamps, but I can't. It's just too big, too black, too godawful nightmarishly mean. It doesn't look like it belongs in this world.

It's moving.

❂

The American alligator is a capable beast, able to fend for itself as soon as it hatches from its egg; it needs little parenting.

As an adult it needs little companionship, and being a highly adaptable, heavily armed, armor-plated predator invulnerable to any creature but man and its own kind, it can survive in solitary glory into its eighties or beyond, achieving truly gargantuan proportions the upper limits of which are open to question. The official record of alligators on the North American continent offers as its ultimate a nineteen-footer killed in Louisiana at the beginning of this century, but you can find ole boys more or less everywhere in Florida willing to swear to the past or present existence of even more impressive leviathans.

While the creature's absolute limit in footage is speculative, it is known that an alligator achieves its ultimate length during middle age. Thereafter its mass increases through the addition of girth. The biggest, oldest examples of the species can weigh more than a thousand pounds.

The adult life of the alligator features annual rituals of breeding (a springtime activity following which the bulls go their way and the sows retreat to nest, producing an average of forty eggs which hatch during the second half of August), and of course some fighting (bulls compete to breed, and all gators are highly territorial) and a lot of eating (a carnivore, the gator consumes what it can when it can), but the dominant theme of the creature's existence is internal climate control. An alligator spends most of its time doing whatever it must—basking in the sun or hiding in the shade, staying immersed in warm or cool water—to maintain a bodily temperature of eighty-five degrees Fahrenheit. In the spring and fall it is active during the daylight hours, hunting in waters warmed by the sun, while in the relentless heat of high summer it eschews daytime activity and hunts during the somewhat cooler Florida nights. In winter it hibernates.

An alligator cannot breathe under water, but it can alter its metabolic rate radically in order to reduce its oxygen requirement, and thus stay below the surface. In cool water it can go for up to an hour without breathing. In the shallow summertime waters of Lake Hancock it can manage a respectable ten or fifteen minutes.

It sustains itself on whatever meat, alive or dead, its habitat offers. In Florida that means a staple of fish complemented by whatever other relatively easy pickings happen by: small life-forms such as turtles and coons and possums and birds, and larger meals like hogs, dogs, deer, small cattle and horses, and the occasional human.

An alligator detects potential food via very acute senses of sight, smell, and hearing enhanced by underwater-vibration sensors in its lower jaw. It approaches and captures its prey with a combination of silent stealth and sudden blinding violence from close range, and disposes of it with admirable efficiency. Relatively small fish and birds and mammals are simply taken into its mouth with one snap of its jaws, and swallowed. Larger fish are clamped, then stunned or killed or dismembered with sawing-tearing sideways whips of its head, then swallowed either whole or in portions as large as the beast's impressively elastic gullet can accommodate, following which an industrial-strength digestive system goes to work. Typically, larger birds and mammals die by drowning rather than bloodletting; the gator will pull its prey beneath the water, hold it until it expires, and then detach and swallow whatever portion satisfies its immediate needs. If the remainder of its catch is substantial, it will store that meat in some safe underwater place, and depending on what comes more easily during the following period—catching fresh prey or feeding from its existing larder—it may or may not return for additional meals. This is the fate of most humans killed by alligators, the exceptions being those taken by the leviathans of the species and children caught by any sufficiently hungry large-ish beast. In such cases the person will be swallowed whole.

So much for how gators eat humans. The way humans bring gators to the table is something else again.

The answer to the question "How do you hunt an alligator?" is the same as the answer to "How do porcupines mate?" Very, very carefully.

Carefully? you ask. Are you kidding? Have you lost your mind as well as your command of the language? Do you call going out there in a fourteen-foot johnboat with a rod and reel and a homemade harpoon and a roll of electrical tape *careful?* Do you think it even remotely sensible to actually wrestle with one of the strongest, most agile, most dangerous predators on the planet before you're absolutely one hundred percent certain that it's stone-cold dead for ever and ever? Would you hunt a grizzly bear or a lion or a tiger this way? Why in God's name don't you just haul a twelve-gauge shotgun out there, pump four or five loads of double-ought buckshot into the reptile's teeny-weeny little brainpan, and *then* begin to think about getting it into the boat with you?

That's a simple enough question, but legal gator hunting in the modern world is not really a very simple business. The buckshot-in-the-brainpan days are now just a glimmer in the eyes of Florida's older ole boys and some fellas who are a tad reticent about what they've been up to in gator habitats in the years since '62. Now we have a hunting method almost as complex as the laws which govern it.

Just like the laws, though, the method makes sense. Developed by nuisance-gator trappers in the days when they had to take the semi-precious beasts alive for relocation farther away from civilization, and amended in the days of plenty thereafter to accommodate the accomplishment of a sure kill, it works. When you begin by actually catching the gator, you see ("catching" in this case meaning just that: securing the beast to the point where it can't escape), it is a virtual certainty that if you do things right from that point on, you will be able to kill it and keep it.

The problem, of course, is that by catching the gator, you have reduced its two options to one: it can no longer flee, so it must fight. It must try to kill you. Which of course is not beyond its means. It has terrible jaws, terrible claws, and a tail which can snap your legs like toothpicks, all mounted on a body of armor plate over muscle. In extremis, this predatory nightmare can move with explosive speed.

That's the deal. Now for the method itself.

The basic requirements are three people and a small open boat, something flat-bottomed, close to the water, and equipped with both an outboard gas motor for getting places and an electric trolling motor or two for semi-silent running when you get there; your basic bass boat, in other words. It has to be low to the water because you can't haul monster reptiles over a three-foot freeboard, and it has to be open because you need somewhere to put them once you've caught them. It also helps if your boat's bow is pointed rather than flat, because the fewer vibrations you set up cutting through the water, the better.

If you have to do your hunting in big weeds or vegetation-clogged waters, you need an airboat, which makes everything a lot harder; you can't really sneak around very easily when your power plant is an unsilenced automobile engine attached to an airplane propeller. Whatever kind of boat you use, though, you use it at night. You hunt in the dark.

Personnel-wise, it goes like this: one soul to drive the boat, one to work the light, and one to gig the gator.

The gig man is the key to it. Once you've spotted the gator you want by sweeping the beam of a high-intensity, hand-held light around some likely scenery (you see their eyes glowing red and figure out the approximate size of the gator by how far apart they are), you turn off the big light and the gig man takes over. Standing up in the bow of the boat, he holds the gator with the beam of a smaller, less intense, narrow-beam light attached to his forehead, and directs the boat towards it.

What's going on here is that all the gator can see is that light on the gig man's head—the light creates perceived darkness around and behind itself, masking the boat and crew—and it's curious. It wants to know what's happening.

If you're lucky and it's not, it won't find out until too late, until the gig man gets within range and strikes.

This is the ideal. What happens more often is that the gator hears or sees something anomalous—waves slapping against the boat, the straight metal pole of the gig or a section of boat or human glimpsed in direct or reflected light—and dives before you're right up on him. He goes down to the muddy bottom of the lake and slithers off in whatever direction seems most prudent to him.

When he does that, you still have a chance at him. His progress across the lake bed stirs up mud and vegetation, air is released, and a substantial bubble trail appears on the surface.

If you can find that trail on the dark surface of the water, you hold the big light on it, and follow. The gig man drops the gig, picks up a rod and reel equipped with a heavy four-pronged snatch hook, casts beyond and ahead of the tip of the bubble trail, and reels in for all he's worth. If he's guessed and cast and reeled just right, the hook will drag along the bottom, snag on the gator, and stick.

Now you've halfway got him. If he's any sort of respectable size, you're probably not going to be able to reel him in on the fishing rod, but if you keep the line taut and unfouled and unstrained by the gator's full strength—no easy trick when you're dealing with the changing relationship between a boat and an alligator moving in whatever direction his flee impulse dictates (back under your boat is a favorite)—you have a reasonable chance of keeping the hook in the beast and closing the distance between you to the point where you can stab the gig into him.

Now, all things being equal at this point—if you've hit him right and hard enough, and the gig's worked the way it's supposed to—you really have got him. The point of the gig has gone into him, separated from the gig pole, and turned sideways in the soft tissue under his thick, leathery hide. It's there to stay, and the heavy line attached to it is tied securely to your boat. You and your alligator are now firmly connected.

You are also in one hell of a fight. He's hurt, and he's mad, and he's desperate. His alligator afterburners have just kicked in, and he's running on a blast of adrenaline you don't even want to dream about; he's at the absolute peak of his powers. He's rolling, diving, thrashing, flailing his tail against the boat, whipping himself in circles trying to bite the line and whatever else comes within range of his jaws, lunging up at his tormentors, going totally crazy.

What you do at this point is size-dependent. If he's a little guy, six or seven foot or so, you can try hauling him up out of the water and going to the next step in the proceedings while he's still nuts. You'd be foolish, but you could choose that option.

With a big one, though, you have no choice. You just have to stay the hell away from him, hang on with your hands and feet and other valuable appendages as far from the water as you can possibly locate them, and wait however long it takes for him to burn himself out. If he's really big and you feel like risking it and are willing to accept the further damage it'll do to his hide, you might want to get another gig into him at this juncture. That'll give you double the leverage, and tire him out faster.

A tired big gator, however, is still an absolutely unacceptable boating companion, so when he's calmed down to the point where he'll stay in one place for more than a second or two, you take the next step in gator threat reduction.

For this you need a bang stick, the closest thing to a gun the law allows you to carry in your boat, a length of metal tubing with a cartridge and a spring-loaded firing mechanism at one end. When it's loaded, the bullet protrudes from the business end; to fire, you simply poke it sharply into your target. With a gator, you need a bang stick of substantial caliber, .357 Magnum or better, and you have to hit him where it counts, as close as possible to the spot where his spinal column meets the back of his skull.

This is by no means a risk-free operation. Despite the stressful, action-packed, and unpredictable nature of the ongoing moment, you have to pay careful attention to the virtues of timing and precision. If your cartridge goes off against that gator above water, you're likely to get hit by a potentially lethal spray of blood, hide, burning gunpowder, bullet fragments, bone chips, pieces of boat, and whatever other nastiness results from the uncontained explosion. Or your bullet could simply bounce off the gator's armor plate and come right back at you.

If on the other hand your cartridge detonates under water in the desired location, you are now a little closer to home. Although it is unlikely that even the most powerful cartridge a bang stick can be built to handle (a warmly loaded .44 Magnum) will do enough damage to a big alligator to actually kill it, your catch's lights should at least blink out for a while. If you don't spend too long thinking about the capabilities of a creature which does not immediately depart this mortal coil when you shoot it in the back of the head at point-blank range with a .44 Magnum, you'll probably have time to take the next steps in the threat reduction process.

The first step is the additional securing of the beast. You need to get stout snare lines around both ends of him, giving you more control of him should he exhibit further friskiness and facilitating the business of hauling him out of the water without tearing up his hide.

The second step is simple, but fraught with the stuff of nightmares:

you have to tape his jaws shut. A gator can exhibit the appearance of certain death for however long it pleases, waiting for its next good chance, and then come suddenly and apocalyptically alive. If that happens in your boat, you really want those jaws nonoperational.

So ha-ha, you tape them shut. Hold 'em with one hand and run the tape around 'em a few times with the other, or trust your buddy to hold them while you use both hands taping. Ideally, you get the gator onto his back and bend the back of his neck up over the side of the boat while you perform this trick. That gives you a better chance of holding on to him if he resists, or having him flip into the water away from you rather than lunging straight at you if he breaks loose.

If you manage to tape his jaws without bad things happening, you're getting there. Now all you have to do is pull him into your boat with you, and kill him.

Getting him into the boat can be awkward and effortful if he's a big guy, ten feet or more, but three people can usually manage it okay if they have the right attitude.

Killing him isn't that hard, either. You just have to be thorough about it. With as many hands and bodies as necessary restraining your gator, you have to pick up some sharp, strong implement—a good hatchet will do fine, as will a big wood chisel—and set about chopping or hammering through the hide and muscle and bone just behind his skull for as long as it takes to completely sever his spinal column.

Then, and only then, can you be certain that you have dead meat, not a live and explosive predator, in your boat.

●

On the eastern shore of Lake Hancock the harvesters are waiting for the magic moment when official dusk falls and it's legal to hunt: seven thirty-six P.M. tonight, says the young state wildlife biologist sitting on his trailered airboat in a cloud of mosquitoes with his armed nature-cop buddies. From then until one A.M., Hancock's gators are fair game.

There are plenty of them to go around. Hancock, a shallow, grassy-bottomed lake about seven miles by three and a half, is ringed with swamps and woods and weeds and old phosphate pits, ideal gator nesting and basking grounds, and it's stocked to bursting point with catfish, gar, and Nile perch. The wildlife guys figure that this habitat supports about fifteen hundred adult gators, but they acknowledge the intentionally conservative nature of their estimate and admit that while the locals' guess of four thousand seems high, there could easily be twenty-five hundred or so good-sized critters out there.

So far, the eight boats assigned to hunt on Hancock have taken forty-one of the lake's seventy-five-gator limit in three nights of hunting, most of them on the third night when the wind was low and approaches without the slap of waves against the boats were manageable. Tonight we'll see. It's breezy, but it might calm down after dark.

The hunters are a bunch somewhat more mixed than one might expect. Country boys from Eagle Lake and Eloise and Bartow and other nearby small towns predominate, but there are also two young insurance fast-trackers from Tampa, an ex-New Yorker living in Venice who's never hunted anything, let alone an alligator, and one young woman.

Here we have the result of the state's random-draw lottery, the legitimate entering of which did not (and obviously could not) demand that one have previous experience; while the majority of the applicants were country people, a significant minority of urbanites found the prospect of going up against an alligator too alluring to resist.

There is, however, a high degree of gator savvy out here tonight, some of it even legally acquired. Hancock was one of the sites of the state's experimental harvest program in '85, '86, and '87, so many of the locals have been hunting gators openly here for a while, and although the odds in the public lottery have worked against them, they are out here anyway; the urban initiates and locally inexperienced licensed "trappers" have most prudently hired them as their licensed "agents." Your average Hancock gator boat, then, is crewed by one nonlocal trapper, a couple of folks whose knowledge of this lake and its gators is impressively intimate, and perhaps a friend or other acquaintance going along for thrills.

You pick up some interesting tips and tidbits from the waiting hunters. There's scary stuff like what happens to your boat when the gig point doesn't separate from the gig pole and thus the gig becomes a weapon with which an enraged and desperate gator can beat the hell out of your boat as he fights for his life. There's historical stuff coming from the old-timers about how Hancock's never really had what you'd call a severe gator shortage, not even in '62; back in the twenties the critters were so abundant that one fella's daddy caught a hundred and four of them in one night alone. In those days a good hide sold for twenty-five cents a foot (when the price reached $2.50 a foot in the thirties, the locals "like went to heaven"), and you couldn't give the meat away with a gun; though Florida's Indians were partial to alligator snacks and had been for a long time (there are records from the 1500s of Ocalas smoking gator meat for winter provisions), not even the poorest cracker would touch the stuff. Nowadays, of course, your Grade-A gator hide is bringing $40 or $50 a foot wholesale, and the meat you sell to an alligator processing plant ends up on the menus of gourmet restaurants all over the world. Older gators, say the hunters, are tastier, "the difference between steak and veal," and gator barbecues are popular events around Eagle Lake.

Finally, there are the tales of the past three nights' hunting, and the expectations for this Monday night. They boil down to two essential items.

First, the record to beat tonight is twelve feet, ten inches and seven hundred and thirty pounds, these being the vital statistics of the bull captured and killed on Friday night by Timothy Thomas, who also took the biggest gator last year and is wearing, with brand-new pride, the "Dragon Slayer" baseball cap he had made in honor of that occasion.

Second, what we seem to have here on Hancock is a clan in competition with itself. There are no less than fifteen Thomases in the boats tonight, including Timothy's sister Karen and the patriarch of the clan, the Eagle Lake preacher/fish-business owner John Thomas. The only outsider presenting a serious challenge to Thomas hegemony appears to be Mr. Don Smith, gig man in the boat handled by Mr. Eugene Rewis and registered with the Florida Game and Fresh Water Fish Commission under the license of (local) trapper Mr. William Shattuck, who is working the big light and the second rod and reel tonight.

Messrs. Shattuck, Rewis, and Smith are a diverse trio. Bill, the lucky permit holder from Lakeland, is a dark, compact, early-forties feller who has his own business painting lines on parking lots. He's the silent type, his only concession to outward flamboyance a nicely turned Teddy Roosevelt mustache. Eugene, a rail-thin little deep-country fisherman who handles a boat with the touch of an angel, doesn't say much either, restricting his conversation to practical matters of moment. It's hard to tell exactly how old he is, because, as Don says, "Eugene's been rode hard and put up wet."

Don has no trouble saying things. The man will tell you stories till the cows are on the meat counter. Not surprisingly, he works in sales, representing Bethlehem Fabrication in Central Florida's phosphate-mining industry; on the side he runs a nice business selling gator-hunting equipment of his own design to hunters all over the state and beyond. He's a big, clean-shaven, towheaded man of thirty-three, married for the second time with three kids, and addicted to sunflower seeds in place of cigarettes. He met Bill when he went to the state's gator-hunting classes to sell his gigs and bang sticks, and he met Eugene when he was looking for a new fish house to clean and butcher his catch. The '88 harvest is Don's fourth year of legal hunting on Hancock.

Don has something of a reputation locally. Folks around the area know him well, of course, and deal with him a lot buying gigs and bang sticks and other gator stuff, and they seem to enjoy talking about him.

"Don's great on telling stories, y'know. Now and again one of 'em's true."

"Aw, hell, Don's all right. He ain't so bad. He just likes to make money, that's all."

"That he does. That he does."

"C'mon, now, Don's a good boy. He's got a good heart. You just have to wade through a lot of bullshit to get to it."

"Well, *my* waders ain't that high."

Dusk is approaching. Don isn't too sure about allowing a journalist into his boat, so he leaves the decision to chance; he flips a coin. I call it right, and a-harvesting we go.

❁

"Left, Eugene, left." A whisper.

The pitch of the trolling motors' hum changes slightly, the boat swings smoothly left, then straightens. Don stretches out his left hand, opens and closes it quickly, and the motors die. The boat drifts slowly toward the cattails. Don's little light stays riveted on the small log-like bumps and red-reflector eyes of the gator still surfaced ahead of us. Quite a big one, this, maybe nine or ten foot. Four or five hundred bucks' worth. The gig rises up over Don's left shoulder and poises ready.

Down to thirty feet now; no change.

Fifteen feet. The gig point swings carefully toward the water.

Ten feet, and LIGHT!! Bill's big one catching a sudden swirl off the bow, the gator going under, but ACTION!! not soon enough, Don plunging the gig fast and hard straight down at the shape slipping past him toward the stern of the boat, and *"Got 'im, Got 'im!!!"* and WHAM! an explosion. The gator's tail smashes against the boat, a flash of wide-open yellow-white jaws, water jumping up with a streak of bright red blood in it, the gator snap-rolling black-green-white-green-black-green-white, and then *"SHIT!!!!"* Nothing. Sudden calm.

"The fuckin' gig point didn't come off," says Don. "I had 'im, man, I had 'im—look, see that, see that blood there?—the goddam thing just didn't come off. Well I'll be damned. That was a good gator, too, weren't it, Eugene?"

"That were a good gator," says Eugene. "Gone now, though. Is that the gig you used the other night? That one worked all right, didn't it? Here, let me see that thing."

Don and Eugene examine the gig point, which is not just any old thing but a device proven effective and reliable by the many hunters who keep Don in pocket money by buying its clones from him. But they can't find a damn thing wrong with it. All they can think to do is replace it with an identical unit, and Don does that.

Just one of those things, then, and no point fretting over it. Let's move on.

No problem in that department. So far tonight we've heard four bang sticks in less than an hour of hunting, so it's sure enough happening on Hancock tonight. Not just for the Thomas boats, either; while Don's been messing with the gig in Bill's light, Eugene's been sweeping his own light over the water back out where we came from, and found us two more gators. He starts up the trolling motors and we head for what looks to be the bigger one.

❂

Alligator hunting is not a calm, cool, reflective sort of nature sport. It's not one of those deals where you spend most of your time standing or sitting silently someplace, waiting and looking, experiencing your environment, thinking about things. For the sole and simple reason that the supply of prey is spectacular, it's a lot more akin to— well, comparisons are difficult in this day and age. Perhaps buffalo hunting on the Western plains used to be like this, or African safaris in the bad old days, or (right, that's it!) shark fishing today in many Florida waters. There's no time to muse at all; you finish with one beast, look up, and there's the next one staring you in the face. If conditions are right, you're always working.

That's how it is tonight for Don and Bill and Eugene. They're going through gators like Presidents go through aides. While this is just swell from a participatory-recreational point of view, as a cash-crop project it stinks; the gators are all getting away.

It's a truly miserable tally so far:

We already know about Gator One.

Gator Two, out in the lake, gets away from a gig strike just as Gator One did. Inexplicable.

Gator Three, another pretty good one up against the weeds, goes under while we're still about fifty feet from him, but he seems to leave no bubble trail whatsoever. Don and Bill cast repeatedly in every direction for about ten minutes, but zip.

Gator Four leaves a bright, wide trail you could probably see from the space shuttle, but he goes under the boat, then out behind us, and cuts hard right through an outcrop of cattails. We have to go around them, and when we get to the other side, no gator. He's probably gone deeper into the weeds. This is annoying, as are the dense clouds of Boeing-sized mosquitoes gorging themselves on the good red blood we have so thoughtfully proffered.

Gators Five, Six, and Seven, out in the lake away from the bloodsuckers, go under and leave trails. We cast at them, but they're a lot better at this game than we seem to be. To be frank about it, Don isn't really casting so well tonight. There's the trail headed left away from us, nice and bright and obvious, with the gator on the bottom four feet in front of it—okay, Don, you know what to do—but splash! goes the snatch hook someplace entirely irrelevant, and it's about a minute and a half until Don can reel the thing in and cast again. By that time the gator's backtracked, or the trail's stopped, so we go over there and Don and Bill cast around the place—we *know* he's down there under the end of that trail someplace, he can't be anywhere else—but zip, zip, and zip. Nothing but one contact in which Don's hook bumps Gator Six but doesn't catch, and his next cast is too far off the mark to take advantage of the beast's thus-revealed prior location. Don starts mumbling about weird gigs and slow reels and overhunted gators and how well he did on Friday. Bill and Eugene say nothing.

The farce continues with Gators Eight through Twelve, all of them back up against the fringes of the weeds and swamps and tangled banks on Hancock's eastern shore. There's one gig strike which misses, and a great deal of casting and boat maneuvering to no avail at all. This is beginning to feel like we're the Ninth Incompetent Cavalry in a wagon circle; four thousand big fat happy Indians going round and round and round and round, and we can't even hit a horse.

But yes we can! Don gets that damned gig into Gator Thirteen, right up in the weeds, and the gig point separates as it should, and even though this is hardly the king of gators, probably under six feet, he belongs to us now.

He fights like they all do, of course—flying water and flailing nastiness all around for quite a few minutes—but he's just a little guy, no match for a two-hundred-pound human. Don doesn't bother to mess with the fine points. He just hauls him up on the single gig line coming out of the center of his belly, hands the line to Bill to hold, grabs him around the jaws, tapes him, and yanks him still thrashing into the boat. Then, with Bill holding him down, Don bends the gator's neck forward and down over the side of the boat and whacks on his spinal column with my hunting knife and his own hammer until, oh dear, the hammer jumps out of his hand and disappears into the lake.

What can you say? You just have to admit the truth according to Don: "I couldn't catch the clap in a cathouse tonight." Gator Thirteen *is* in the bag—even though he's still twitching, his lights are dimming to black and he's no problem at all—but he's no great shakes with that gig hole in the center of the most valuable part of his hide. Furthermore, our boat is no longer equipped with the means of killing the next gator we encounter. And both Don and Eugene have forgotten to bring ammo for the bang stick.

When we find Gator Fourteen off the mouth of Banana Creek, way on the other side of the lake, Don discovers that the light on his head (a nifty but somewhat cobbled-together affair featuring a rheostat with which he can dim the intensity of the bulb as he moves in on a gator, so that it appears the light is receding rather than approaching) has quit working altogether. Eugene tinkers with it, but in so doing he accidentally connects his big light, a forty-dollar unit, to the wrong pole on a twelve-volt battery and burns it out for good. He can't get Don's light working, either. Also, it's started to rain.

Well. Although this is a fine opportunity to revel in the lurid color and rich variety of country-boy curses, otherwise it's a total bust. There being no point in continuing the farce, and it being almost the end of legal hunting time anyway (the nature cops have already started buzzing around from boat to boat), Don bags it. Eugene fires up the gas engine and we head for the check-in point, where tonight's catch must be weighed and measured and examined and recorded and otherwise officially endorsed.

It's not a bad catch. The Thomases have done well tonight. Don doesn't stay to celebrate with them.

I stick around for a while, though, peering at sections of gator anatomy—this old guy's rounded, gapped, worn-down teeth and scarred-up back and missing tail tip, that young turk's handsome, as yet un-battle-damaged green-white belly hide, the fascinating cross-section of bone and nerve channels visible down amid the bloody pulp where John Thomas, Jr. chopped a ten-foot female's spinal column—and answering questions about how ole Don made out tonight. Don's bad news is well received.

To be continued Wednesday night. The hunters are happy enough about that, but the wildlife guys, who were hoping Hancock's quota would get filled tonight, aren't so pleased. Sitting around while the ole boys harvest isn't very exciting.

●

The gator harvest seems to be going okay on the statewide level. The ranking wildlife guys don't have any formal system for monitoring the events at every hunting location while they occur, but they're sure they'd hear informally about major screwups, law enforcement problems, or accidents, and they haven't heard of any yet. So that's good.

From my couch research during the past week or two, however, I've been forced to conclude that as a media event, the harvest leaves something to be desired. So far the typical video-news gator-hunting story, promo'd ad nauseam during every station break of the day, has been running thusly:

"Out on Lake [name], a very special Florida-style event is taking place," announces the minor-market celebrity at the Action Newsdesk. "Roving reporter Bob [name] is live on the scene with a very special report and a very special person. Bob, what can you tell us?"

Cut to Bob [name] by the side of a lake in the night, trying to control his haircut. A small boat is visible at the waterline. Beside Bob, standing at ease, eyes front, is Buford [name], a baccy-chewing, turkey-necked, somewhat florid gentleman of indeterminately advanced age, wearing a long-sleeved flannel shirt, suspenders, rubber boots, and an expression of tolerant disinterest. Or a young, beefy, mustachioed, baccy-chewing, bull-necked, somewhat florid gentleman wearing a Red Man gimme cap, a cammo T-shirt, rubber boots, and an expression of inadequately concealed hostility.

"I'm standing here with Buford [name], one of the lucky people chosen in [fifty-word upbeat account of the commercial alligator harvest]. . . . Tell me, Buford, how are they biting out there?"

Buford tells him: Good, okay, not so good, or they ain't there at all tonight, Bob, too much wind, it's that hurricane in Texas, see. Got an eight-footer last night, though, and five of 'em the night before that. That was all right. "An' they don't bite, Bob, or at least they don't bite no hooks!" (A little modest humor here.)

Bob, brightening, takes the cue: "Well, it certainly sounds exciting, and I guess it's kind of dangerous, too." Then he tucks his chin down into his chest, leans forward a little, gives his man a good hard Barbara Walters Soul Stare right between the eyes, and pops the Big

One: "Tell me, Buford, I guess what the viewers are wondering is, why do you do something like this? I mean, really?"

Now, what poor Bob prays for in his craven little showbiz heart is that ole Buford will say something along the lines of:

"Well, Bob, I got to kinda like the outdoor life while I was in the Nam, if you know what I mean, and things were kinda boring for quite a while after that. But now they're lettin' me come out here an' hunt gators, and really, it's almost as much fun as killin' gooks, y'know? I mean, these critters fight back better 'n people."

Or, "Well, Bob, y'see, I've got this problem with my manhood. I have to sleep with the light on, y'know, and I've got this real small weenie I'm scared to let the little woman see, so I spend a lot of time in the woods or out here on the lake handlin' phallic objects like guns and long metal poles with sharp ends. What I really enjoy is stickin' hard things into animals and makin' warm wet red holes before killin' 'em and eatin' 'em, and you can't beat gator hunting for that."

Or even something relatively mild-mannered like, "Well, Bob, it just ain't been too exciting around the house since they took *Dragnet* off the tube an' the missus put on that last hundred pounds, so frankly, I'll take any excuse I can get to spend a night out."

What Bob gets, though, are the following in-depth answers guaranteed quoted verbatim from Florida TV newscasts:

"It's fun."

"There's good money in them gators."

"Beats shoppin' at the meat counter, don't it?"

"Why not? I ain't got nothin' better to do."

"I want me some alligator boots, an' I can't afford to buy 'em."

"I'm too old for stock-car racing; this ain't so hard on you."

"My daddy taught me."

"It's a challenge."

"I ain't never done it before."

Such perfectly accurate but uncolorful home truths having been conveyed to the eager viewer, Bob and his anchor(s) thank each other enthusiastically for a while, and we go to Michelle's taped report on toddler tube surfing.

Sometimes, though, the TV guys actually get out there with the boats. One night on Hancock, just as Don and Bill and Eugene have gotten a real monster gator bottled up in a little cove near its home in a disused phosphate pit—when this thing hit the water on its way out to hunt, it sounded like the launching of the U.S.S. *Missouri*—Channel 13 shows up on a wildlife officer's airboat and floods the scene with light and noise. Hello, showbiz; good-bye, gator.

●

Make that gators. What was happening on Monday happens again on Wednesday. The equipment's back in shape—Don's brought his best coon-hunting headlight and a new hammer, I've brought a selection of hotter-than-average .357 ammo for the bang stick—but the gators just aren't ending up in our boat, or, for that matter, anyone else's. Maybe it's the wind. Maybe it's all the hunting they've been experiencing lately. Maybe they're extra intelligent on Wednesdays. Who knows? Whatever, it looks like tonight's headline is going to read: GATOR TEASES MAN, MAN ANGRY.

This kind of situation illustrates the limits of the legal hunting method. None of us, you see, would be having such bad luck and trouble if, say, we were allowed to find ourselves one of the hundreds of little month-old gators in the lake, pluck it out of the water, hold it up and slap it around a bit until it started squealing, and wait for Momma to come running.

That would work just great, guaranteed. So would bringing some tasty smallish critter along with us in the boat—any doggie would do fine, but a rabbit would be outstanding—and allowing it to communicate (the term "gator bait" really means something, you know, and so does "ass deep in alligators," a phrase which would describe our situation very nicely if we were to work the rabbit ploy). And of course we could get lucky very quickly if we were to haul our boat out of the lake and over a bank, and go hunting in one of those off-limits phosphate pits. Nobody doubts that there are sixteen-footers and bigger in the pits, "gators that'd *scare* you, boy."

Oh, well. Virtue is its own reward, and besides, there are far too many nature cops buzzing around the harvest. Those guys don't have much of a sense of humor.

Still and all, it's tempting, and easy. When Don finds us a baby gator in the lake, strictly to demonstrate how some bad fellas he doesn't know personally go about getting themselves good meat in this part of the world, the little guy does indeed squeal most appealingly, and loud splashes from the shoreline do indeed indicate rapid results. If we were serious about what we're doing, we'd really be on a roll right now. But Don, shrugging, lets the miniature gator go.

That little guy was cute. You can see why city people used to bring them back from Florida as pets. To my taste, though, he was a touch too reminiscent of the mature members of his species. Although he was barely fifteen inches from nose to tail tip, he was *strong*. Even with two hands clamped hard, one around his tail and the other encircling his neck and jaws, he was tough to hold on to. His tail whipped powerfully, and the jawbones pressing into my palm were hard and heavy, structurally massive. That critter was mean.

I'm having trouble accepting what I'm seeing, and what I'm doing. I've scrambled into Karen's boat, and now I'm sitting with my rump and upper body hanging out over the water on the side opposite the captive alligator, throwing my weight into the job of keeping the boat on a less than insanely dangerous keel. From this position I'm watching five strong men sweat to pull a monster into the boat with me.

As I watch, I'm beginning to comprehend a certain fact with truly distressing clarity. Should those fellas succeed in their labors, that alligator is going to end up pressed against my shins.

That worries me, because now I have seen how big it is. Don keeps saying that it's five hundred and thirty pounds—he's definite about that —but I don't believe him. I think he's underestimating intentionally because his pride's hurt, he's feeling bad about the fact that this behemoth belongs to little Karen and her trapper, who is of all things a Yankee and not even a country Yankee at that. The fact of the matter is that the alligator is longer than the boat.

Poundage and footage are irrelevant, though. The beast is simply too big, way too big. If he wanted to—and if he still has any fight in him, he surely will want to, because I'm going to be the first living thing he sees when he comes rolling over here into his new environment—he could spill my guts like an opened can of worms with one slash of his claws. One flick of that tail could pulverize every bone in my thighs and pelvis.

So I tell you, if that alligator's doing anything but counting sheep when he lands on my toes, I'm going over the side. They tell you not to do that—never ever to do that, because in the water you're just food, you have no chance at all—but I don't care. The way my adrenaline's running, I think I could make it back into Don's boat pretty damned fast.

●

It's getting really frustrating out here. The wind blowing in over Florida from the Atlantic is gusting healthily, and the alligators contemplating the light-studded stretch of calm water in the lee of the swampy woods on Hancock's eastern shore have been hunted hard these past few nights. They've grown very cautious about emerging from their sanctuaries to hunt in the lake beyond those lights.

Emerge they must, though, and so there is some action, even if it isn't thick and fast. Don and Bill and Eugene and Don's friend Jerry—another passenger, but no stranger to a rod and reel—are getting a reasonable, half-capacity dose of the going-around-in-circles game. Don's sunflower seed consumption rate and coffee intake are therefore about twice what they were on Monday night.

Perhaps that is why, when we get lucky as the final hour of the hunt approaches, he's a tad reckless in the threat reduction area. On the other hand, and more probably, the man could just be a cowboy born and bred.

What he does is haul a six-footer into the boat, this one gigged nicely through the horny, ugly, worthless armor-hide on its back. Don wrestles it belly-down and prepares to tape the jaws canted over the side of the boat, and then he screws up big time. He allows the critter to writhe away from him, out of his grasp entirely. The beast, right-side up, untaped and unrestrained by snare lines, is now loose in the boat.

It's a moment like this which teaches you forever that while there may be small alligators, there are no easy alligators. The sight of that six-footer going for blood, claws scrabbling for traction, jaws yawning open, sends five grown men into a squealing, girlish little ballet of evasion which would be really funny if (A) I weren't concentrating on dancing myself, and (B) I didn't know that one wrong step could introduce me to the wonderful world of prosthetic walking devices right here and now.

The point of our spastic fandango, realized instantly by everybody on board, is to get into the stern behind the cooler blocking the predator's progress in that direction, and I am happy to report that four of us accomplish our objective without incident despite the gator's best efforts and our boat's extreme gyrations around a fast-shifting center of gravity. Once there, we (putting this politely) await developments.

Don's dance took him in the direction opposite the rest of us, and that is fortunate. From his perch on the bow, behind the gator, he is able to retrieve the gig line running into its back. With the creature thus restrained he is able to move down the gig line, drop his weight onto its shoulders, and tape those jaws. And that's that, more or less. Connection between the alligator's brain and spinal column is lost a minute or so later, chop-chop.

Thank you, Don. It's been entertaining, but hysteria does not become us. We all sound better laughing in a lower octave than we have been these past few moments.

The next hour is anticlimactic, and fruitless. Once again we visit the Florida Game and Fresh Water Fish Commission check station with just one small gator. But at least the other boats haven't done much better. The biggest of the five alligators taken tonight was a mere ten-and-a-half-footer, five hundred pounds or so. No records broken tonight.

❂

I don't, it seems, have to go overboard, although that doesn't mean I don't want to. Everywhere I look there's alligator—rough, horny, stinking wet black-brown-green leather inches from my face, a stomach I could sleep in pressed softly against my shins, jaws four or five feet long stretching away to my right. Through the warm flesh pressed against my legs I can feel little tremors, synapses still firing through muscle. This monster's not thrashing, not resisting, but neither is he dead.

Kill him, then, and please-please do it fast.

Don seems to agree, because he doesn't lose a second working his way up that massive flank to the broad high plain of the head/neck area,

*jamming his wood chisel down through the surface tissue disruption
caused by Karen's two .44s, and whaling away with his hammer.*

*What follows isn't nearly as terrifying as what's gone before, and
neither is it particularly revolting if you've been around butchery or
surgery a few times; the stuff beneath the skin of all creatures, humans
included, is unpretty but also unsurprising. For some reason, though, I
have a hard time watching as Don hammers for a while, then one or
two of the other men haul back on the sides of the cut to get the meat out
of his way—diabolic field surgeons here, operating frantically to kill—
and then he goes to hammering again, and then again, and again
until the top of the chisel's handle is just a tiny factory-perfect circle deep
within that great irregular blood-bubbling organic gash.*

*It just goes on and on, this strenuous, sad, and brutal hammering of
death forever. But it ends. Karen's boat drifts quietly in the night, low
in dark water with the weight of a monster that's just meat and money
now.*

❂

Karen's gator is It, the record. An eleven-and-a-half-footer is caught
by a Thomas boat on Friday, and on Monday Don Smith kills a twelve-
foot bull, but no now-dead Hancock alligator lived as long on this
earth or achieved proportions as great as the monster pulled from the
lake into Karen's boat. When that beast died it was between eighty
and ninety years old, sixty or seventy years older than Karen. It
measured thirteen feet, four inches. It weighed seven hundred and
seventy pounds.

Today at the Thomas Fish House in Eagle Lake, it still does; butchery has not begun yet. The whole beast lies in solitary state amid
tables full of the variously stripped and portioned carcasses of its
lesser brethren. News photographers and grade-school children and
anyone else wishing to record or experience an extremity of nature
crowd around it. People have been flocking here all morning. It's
quite a wake.

The Thomases, blood-spattered and cheerful, accommodate their
guests informatively and entertainingly. They are very pleasant, well-
mannered, hospitable people, accepting of strangers, and if you spend
any time around them you know that they are also honest and honor-

able, that John Thomas's preaching is not a matter of words unconnected to personal values. He has raised good children here. The Thomases are, in short, the very personification of old country virtues.

They are also exactly the sort of people who should reap the bounty of the state of Florida's new relationship with its alligator population. The whole family works at the fish house or in the boats seine-netting for Nile perch on Lake Hancock, so they live with the gators, and like the gators they are sustained by the lake as it is today. Were Hancock to be drained, overpolluted, or destroyed in any other way, they like the gators would experience a painful end of life-giving things. Nothing would ever be the same.

The Thomases' September, now Gator Month, has become an exciting time: thrills, chills, and healthy sibling rivalries. Work goes on, of course, but it's a lot more about alligators, a lot less about fish. It's like a vacation, except that, God bless the Florida Game and Fresh Water Fish Commission, it pays its way and then some.

Karen poses beside the great dark body of the creature which came to life in her homeland as the twentieth century dawned. She is surrounded by awestruck children and brothers who may be a little jealous, but are grinning and laughing and joking anyway. She makes a tough-girl muscle for the photographer lady. Happy humans, happy times.

6

Narcotics North

Walt Murphree is standing alone in the Friday night rain on the corner of the ghetto boulevard, making staccato little noises—the drumbeat to "Bo Diddley," other rhythms from his rock & roll youth—and watching gutter-borne rainwater carry a used condom hesitantly through channels and around twigs and cigarette butts and clumps of dogshit and a discarded hypodermic needle toward the Greater Miami storm drainage system and the Atlantic Ocean beyond.

The condom slips through a grating into the netherworld and Walt looks up, past rubbernecking pimps and partygoers and assorted other citizens cruising slowly past him, at the Crime Scene men combing a lawn across the street for the most significant of the bullets fired tonight, the one which missed a Special Response Team man's head by a hair when he smashed his shotgun barrel through the crack house's jalousied window. Walt takes a couple of steps out into the street toward the Crime Scene men, one on his knees with the comb, the other holding the flashlight. Then he thinks better of it—

what's he going to say, "How're you doin'? Getting warm yet?"—and turns back toward the base house.

Not much happening there, either. The black-clad armored Special Response Team men are gathered around their green Econoline fussing with equipment, smoking, keeping to themselves, privately trying to assimilate another unacceptable lesson. Out by the curb, Walt's narcs are also all together, laughing about the big momma-beast in *Aliens* and going over tactics for Sunday's softball game. A couple of them are still picking around in the bushes for drugs and weapons with Bad John the Uniform, their favorite local "combat deputy." A few laughs there, too, and a mystery: a half-peeled, unripe banana with a miniature plastic palm tree emerging from its tip and three ten-milligram Valium tablets buried obscenely in the bruised shaft of the fruit.

Bad John holds this truly weird thing up in his surgical-gloved hand, shines his flashlight on it: "Anyone *hungry?*"

The narcs perk up—now, that's a *find*—and cluster around Bad John. Not Walt, though. He smiles, then walks over to the open rear window of a Metro Dade police cruiser containing the star of tonight's work, the shooter Abraham.

Maybe Abraham knows how lucky he is, maybe he doesn't. The latter possibility is more likely, for really, the man hasn't shown much evidence of intelligence so far tonight.

Until about an hour ago, Abraham was moving up in the world. Last year he was making ends meet by running girls and dealing a little grass on the side, maybe hustling the odd gram of coke or smack, but this year he's had it made. Like many a small-time operator blessed by the new down-market democratization of the cocaine trade, he was running a "base house." The place had become so popular that on many weekend nights his customers had to hang around on the street outside, waiting for a client to leave before there was space for them to enter, buy a rock or two of cocaine, and hunker down to smoke it in the filthy little living room.

So yes, crack's been good to Abraham. The trouble is, though, that he likes to consume his own merchandise, so he's acquired himself the mother of all crack habits to go along with his new status in the community. At times it makes him irrational, none too smart.

He was that way tonight. Business was brisk, the house was full of customers, and he was in the kitchen breaking out more rocks (having a little trouble doing it, he was so high) when bad things started happening and he just lost it.

It began when the first police submachinegun barrel smashed through one of his windows, and his back door started wrenching violently off its hinges, and suddenly they were coming from everywhere—big, black-clad, body-armored, face-painted, antenna-sprouting nightmares from warrior-cop hell, their weapons terrifyingly suited to the task of close-quarters threat suppression—and it went on from there: customers screaming, people flinging themselves to the floor, people trying to bolt through the windows; bedlam.

Now, Abraham did know what was happening. The seven men of a Metro Dade Department of Public Safety Special Response Team, backed by undercover narcs and uniformed officers, were executing a search warrant in the violently intimidating fashion Dade County narcs have long since learned to be the most effective antidote to gunplay in a jurisdiction armed to the teeth and driven by the dangerous passions of powder-enhanced machismo. Abraham had seen these lightning nighttime assaults before, on other houses at other times; in his neighborhood they'd started happening so frequently that they'd come to be perceived as regular entertainment by those not directly involved. What, then, could he have been thinking when he reacted the way he did? What logic could possibly have been running through the man's crack-smashed skull?

God only knows, but the end result of his thought processes was all too plain. He swung up his .38 Special revolver and fired three rounds, one-two-three, very fast, not bothering to aim. Then he just stood there, half shielded by a refrigerator capable of stopping a police 9-mm or .223 round about as effectively as a polyester tank top stops a switchblade, and thought about what to do next.

That was the point at which he became the beneficiary of two miracles.

The first was that the rounds he fired didn't hit anybody. One went up into the ceiling; the second blew straight through an outside wall and disappeared into the night; and the third flew across the crowded living room, punched through an interior wall into an equally busy bedroom, then exited through a jalousied window somewhere between an inch and a hairsbreadth from the left ear of an SRT shotgun man. Shards of glass from the shattered window sliced into this officer's neck and earlobe as he heard the bullet buzz past his head.

The second miracle, the fact that Abraham himself survived the aftermath of his shots, wasn't really a miracle at all. For the finite number of heartbeats during which he stood motionless with his gun up, he was not in cold hard tactical fact an immediate threat to anybody. Sure, if his gun had started to come down, they'd have taken him out—he'd probably have been gone before he even started falling, literally dead on his feet—but while he stood there making up his mind, he was probably safer than he'd been in his whole sick perilous life. He was in the sights of the coolest, most depressingly experienced police assault specialists anyone could ever hope to avoid meeting. None of them, not even the shotgun man with blood trickling down under his Kevlar assault vest and jolts of fear adrenaline surging through his veins, was going to squeeze a trigger unless he absolutely had to.

And none of them had to. With his customers crying and moaning and screaming and pleading with him, and the SRT sergeant offering a steady flow of quiet cool persuasion, Abraham reached his decision. He let himself be taken alive.

So again: can Abraham possibly understand how lucky he is to be watching Walt Murphree watch him right now? Sure, he'll do time this time, but if he'd done what he did tonight in Tampa or Houston or Buffalo or Los Angeles, or just about any other American city but Miami, he probably wouldn't have any time to do. They'd just have dropped him as soon as they got a shot; aimed for the kidneys, turned the stupid motherfucker's lights out, and had done with it. But here in Miami, primarily because they see so much action, the SRT guys are professionals, they're the best; they're It. Tac team cops from all over the world come to watch them work. They always go in first on a drug bust, and they almost never drop you unless they absolutely have to.

Walt just stands there looking at Abraham with a vaguely curious look on his face. He cocks his head from side to side, as if hoping that an altered viewing angle on Abraham's blackwall eyes will show him something he hasn't seen a thousand times before. Abraham just looks flatly back at him. This goes on for maybe a minute and a half until another cruiser pulls up with six-packs of cold soda, and Walt walks off to get himself a can.

●

Friday night in Miami. Oh, the wonder of it, the glamour, the danger, the lusts, the legends, the sheer wild dull-defying spirit of a whole city built for speed and to hell with the cost, to hell with the law, here's to everything the rest of America doesn't want in its own backyards (but certainly, most emphatically, wants somewhere) . . . Yes, Miami is a happening place, more Today than maybe any other city in the world. That's nice; you can just see Bebe Rebozo and Meyer Lansky and Juan Batista and even old Fidel himself boogying down on the astral plain, socked on gold dust served by senators and up to their eyebrows in showgirl muff, joining together in pride and affection for the sleek old whore they all helped launch into the modern world. It's good to see her alive and kicking so high.

And man, the old whore is beautiful. A tri-ethnic base community, a truly international city, Paree-cum-Hong Kong set in all that silver sand and lovely aqua blue, washed daily by the semitropical afternoon rains, sparkling green and gold and pink and white, definitely Western in the integrity of its fixtures and fittings but distinctly Oriental in other ways: the variety of its services, the diversity of its citizenry, the circumspection of its attitudes toward authority and legality, the violence of its contrasts, and of course, lest we forget for a moment modern Miami's most alluring aspect in our global TV culture, the violence of its violence.

It's not just any old violence, either. Miami's is violence with a beat, violence with flair, violence with style and statement, violence for fun so spontaneous and profit so effortlessly immense that it makes all other violence seem tawdry, petty, distressingly personal, unchicly irrelevant to a truly modern consciousness. Yes, even the city's much-storied mayhem, that impersonally balletic, positively awesome, almost mystical full-auto exercise in terminal transaction so celebrated by the camera's gyro-stabilized eye, is beautiful.

The new aesthetic has changed the city; not as much as has the cash-swollen underground economy of the drug trade from which it springs, but measurably. It has boosted tourism, internationalism, the city's media industries, its people's sense of their modernity, and also their sense of isolation. For if Miami's growth in the twentieth century has pulled it away from the state around it, drawing it slowly into greater kinship with Las Vegas and Shanghai and Monte Carlo and Paree than with Tampa and Orlando and Tallahassee, its modern evolution, since the sudden explosion of the cocaine trade and the Marielito immigrations and the consequent refurbishing of the city's publicity value, has detached it almost entirely. Now it is a place more in electronic space than in Florida.

You can feel this separateness as soon as I-95 begins to narrow and accelerate in its southward coastal plunge, or when Alligator Alley emerges from the Everglades' River of Grass into the treeless, half-finished condo complexes eating up the landscape as far north as Ft. Lauderdale. Traversing these border zones, you are moving out of cracker/yuppie/senior Florida, through the cathode-ray looking glass into a prime-time place of fantasy, wish fulfillment, and nightmare.

From the Florida side of the relationship, fear is the mainspring. When Anglos stick those angry little bumper stickers on their cars— WILL THE LAST AMERICAN TO LEAVE MIAMI PLEASE BRING THE FLAG?—they are expressing not only anti-black/Latino racism but a frightening, disorienting feeling that what goes on in Miami belongs in another world entirely, a separate and unknown socio-mental vortex to be avoided at all costs.

Even New York City, the traditional rotting urban nightmare of most Americans, pales by comparison. There, the danger is apparent and identifiable, and to some extent avoidable; junkies will mug you unless you exercise extreme caution in suspicious surroundings. But in this Miami of the popular imagination, nobody anywhere is ever safe. The possibility of Herb and Martha's disintegrating in a hail of heavy-metal pyrotechnics as they innocently impulse-purchase their way around the Galleria, or being spirited from their eggs diablo for inclusion in some bestial *Movie of the Week* punk-yuppie-terrorist-psychovet voodoo ritual, hovers constantly in the energized ozone of the lovely seductive seaside city. This is a place in which the stranger is visited constantly by seen-on-TV déjà vu—a stretch of car-chase highway here, a massacre-haunted mansion there—and where, despite your better judgment, you can find yourself scanning the facades of buildings for bullet craters, tracking the movements of stylish young men with unusual concentration, wishing perhaps that the law allowed you to carry at least a short-barreled shotgun loaded up tight with double-ought buck. Yeah . . . maybe one of those nice little ultra-badass flat gray jobs with a black neoprene pistol grip and a squeeze-activated flashlight under the barrel. Light 'em up, line 'em up, and blow 'em away. . . .

Such thinking, once commenced, is of course seductive, and in Miami today the romance of the TV city is on a self-fed upward power spiral. Extremes of reality are transformed into theater, which creates image, and the image creates a new reality in which the extremes become the totems. The totems are powerful. They attract people. People start to get ideas, act them out, personify the image.

Nobody is more familiar with all this than Walt Murphree, a Metro Dade Department of Public Safety lieutenant currently leading a street squad of ten undercover detectives working out of the Organized Crime Bureau's Narcotics North office.

Walt and his squad work the retail end of the Miami drug business, the hundreds of points at which the newly available rock cocaine hits the streets of the poverty-racked, explosive North Miami melting pot centered around Liberty City's hard-core ghetto.

In many ways the turf is not Miami-specific—it's just another urban American ghetto as far from TV reality as are Watts and Bedford-Stuyvesant—but in other ways which matter a lot to Walt and his narcs, it's unique. It is, for instance, a trend-setting ghetto. Being so close to the importation and distribution centers of the American drug trade, it serves as a handy test market for what may or may not sell in the nation at large. When the major dealers put their heads together and came up with crack (originally "base")—a product offering a major savings in process cost combined with an enormously enhanced repeat-purchase incentive and a magic opportunity to expand the supply network into the massive, previously unexploited low end of the marketplace—they performed their first consumer trials in Liberty City.

It was at that point that the ghetto really entered the modern world, really began to participate in the verve and excitement of Miami's romance with its TV self. Even in Liberty City, a miserable netherworld far from the blabbermouth cool of the cocaine discos and the sleazy suavity of the big-time Anglo/Latino players, the image began to matter.

Like tonight, for instance. After the shooting, when the SRT assault unit had secured Abraham and all of his customers, Walt and Dennis and Tommy and the other narcs entered the base house. From the outside, it was a typical cinderblock-and-clapboard North Miami bungalow. Inside it was also typical—dirty, smelly, full of cheap dilapidated furniture, every structural angle oddly askew—but it *was* a base house, a place where people came to smoke cocaine, and therefore it had been given The Look. Abraham himself had done it, painted every wall in the house pink or aqua. And even if he was just an eight-time-loser ex-pimp scratching around on the ass end of the cocaine supply chain, his clients welfare mothers and petty criminals and kids just learning how to go bad, he simply had to have himself the image. He had to have the things by which a modern Miami drug dealer has come to be defined; it was expected of him.

The things were lying on a half-rotted, piss-stained mattress under the front wall of the fetid little bedroom, just below the holes where two of the .38 rounds Abraham fired from his cockroach-infested kitchen had punched out into the street: a digital-lock Halliburton (not a copy), a cordless satin-gold Braun telephone, and an engraved, custom-plated Austrian 9-mm semiautomatic pistol which must have cost at least a grand and a half.

These things were all superfluous, unnecessary—the Halliburton was empty, the telephone's batteries were dead, the pistol had never been fired—but they were also the only beautiful objects in the whole sick, sad little house.

❁

Walt, a sturdy ex-Navy marine patrol pilot now approaching forty, is explaining how his squad works, and how it fits into the overall scheme of the Miami drug war.

First, he says, his is the Narcotics *North* Street Squad. This means that it operates on primarily American black, Jamaican, and Cuban turf, concentrating almost exclusively on the street-dealing end of the cocaine and marijuana industries. The Narcotics South Street Squad does a similar job, but in a somewhat more white/Latin suburban/rural environment.

Both Street Squads share offices with Major Case Squads which are charged with the task of making life difficult for gentlemen and ladies further up the supply channels than the street squads' clientele. Two more squads work out of OCB headquarters, one interdicting the flow of drugs through Miami International Airport and the other handling coordination between all the OCB units, plus the DEA, the FBI, the separate Miami, Hialeah, Miami Beach, and other local police departments, the Florida Highway Patrol, and all the other local, national, and international law-enforcement agencies involved with or affected by the flow of drugs through Dade County.

Often, though, the lines of demarcation blur in action. Just the other day, a pair of Narcotics South Street Squad detectives were going about their business (actually, they were buying canned goods at a Publix supermarket as part of a Thanksgiving food drive for the poor) when they noticed two men who "just had the look, you know?" The men got into a van, and the narcs followed them to a certain house, and bingo! That little piece of business ended up netting almost a million cash dollars, one house, one van, one truck, one Ferrari, two Mercedeses, a "go-fast" boat, and several drugpersons (one of whom, a nice middle-aged Latin lady, drove up to the house in the middle of the bust with $190,000 and a handgun).

All in all, the investigative and operational phases of that particular case, the kind of bust on which other detectives in other jurisdictions often spend weeks or even months, consumed about half of one shift's worth of time and manpower. The paperwork of course took somewhat longer; the squad had to work overtime reassembling shredded tally sheets to reveal a portrait of one little drug-money– processing house that cranked out between a million and a million-

and-a-half neatly sorted dollars a day, just another cottage industry like the one a few blocks away which specializes exclusively in repackaging broken or soaked or otherwise unpresentable kilos of cocaine. All the same, the whole affair was wrapped up within one working day.

Such instances—and there are many of them, all the time—illustrate the magnitude of the Metro Dade narcs' task. By their own admission the OCB narcs, and their colleagues in a large web of other law enforcement agencies, manage to intercept less (probably a lot less) than ten percent of the cocaine moving through their turf. And since that turf is Dade County, the Silicon Valley and Fort Knox and Grand Central Station of the American drug trade, that means that they are failing to intercept some ninety percent of the cocaine consumed in the entire United States, plus approximately half of Europe's intake. This is a place in which the DEA estimates that fully eighty percent of all wealth—eighty cents of every dollar moving on Dade County's streets—comes from drug profits.

The total number of Metro Dade Organized Crime Bureau detectives working narcotics is sixty-eight; that number is obviously, ridiculously inadequate.

What is adequate, though? Well, as Art Nehrbas, overall commander of the Metro Dade Organized Crime Bureau, puts it, "Who knows?"

"Look at it this way," he says. "About a year ago, the Narcotics South Major Case Squad made the biggest cocaine bust in the history of the world. They got two *tons* of pure, uncut rock cocaine. Do you have any idea how much cocaine that is? I'll tell you: it's enough to keep every cocaine consumer in this whole country high all day, every day, for six months.

"So that was great. I mean, we weren't dancing in the streets— we're not Pollyannas around here by any means—but we figured that two tons might just make a dent. We figured it might just drive up the street price for a while.

"It didn't. The street price had been falling for almost a year, and it just kept right on falling.

"So you see the size of the problem. The question is, how big does the solution need to be? And the answer is simple: it can never, ever, be big enough. Excuse my French, but there aren't enough narcs and there isn't enough money on this whole fucking planet to eliminate the situation we have here."

Which of course is the essential and unavoidable truth of all attempts to interfere with the immutable laws of supply and demand. It means that the OCB narcs really are ineffective in the Big Picture. But Nehrbas's honesty on the subject reveals something else: the fact that he is a realist. He at least is not playing any games.

Neither are his men and women. Walt Murphree, for example, knows exactly what his job is: to make his busts stick, and to keep his detectives alive. He also knows his role in the Big Picture of the drug war: to show the noncriminal citizens of North Miami that somebody cares, that although the police are almost impotent in the larger conflict, he and his squad *will* strap on their body armor, swallow their fear, and come out to do battle with the full-auto rock & roll assholes who just fortified the house next door, spread their cool around the neighborhood, and settled in to create some new need. Then they'll do it again when new dealers move in, or the old dealers pop back out of the courts' feeble grip, or the competition opens another house a few doors down the block. On average, they'll do it ten times a week.

It's an unglamorous, endlessly repetitive and almost insanely dangerous function, but it satisfies Walt. "We're in community relations," he says with a quiet little laugh, "and we're doing okay."

They are too. It takes a lot of time and effort, but sometimes they do end up making the solid citizens happy. There was for example the affair one of Walt's men describes during an afternoon tour of the ghetto.

It began with the pastor of a local church who'd finally had enough; his one and only stained-glass window had just been smashed by shell cases ejected from the silenced MAC-11 machine pistols of drug soldiers honing their marksmanship on the roof of his church.

He called Narcotics North, and the crew did their thing. A narc walked into the drug house across the street from the church that Tuesday afternoon, sweaty and hairy and dirty-looking as your average lowlife coke freak, unarmed and out of radio contact as usual, and made a buy. He and his partner went to court on Thursday and obtained a search warrant. On Friday afternoon the SRT leader assessed the house for entry/exit points, soft and hard cover, neighbor-safe and neighbor-threatening firing angles and the like. Then the narc team and the assault team congregated that same Friday night, made their very specific plan (one of four that particular evening), and went out, thirty of them in all, and did it.

It didn't go very well. "It was a fuckin' zoo," our man remembers. "There must have been a hundred people in the place. The dealers were Colombians, the worst; crazy machismo men, blaze-of-glory boys. But nobody fired a shot, which was really weird, because they could have murdered us with all that firepower. They were throwing their guns out the windows, down the stairwells, wherever they could get rid of them; just launching these loaded guns all over the place. I got hit in the balls with a .44 Magnum. A twelve-gauge landed on a deputy's foot and broke two of his toes.

"I mean, these guys were smart, is what it was. Somebody must have had it all worked out beforehand, and made the soldiers stick to it when it went down.

"They knew that if they opened up, see, we would too—it was nuts in there, we wouldn't have had any option—but we couldn't do a thing about them throwing their guns at us. We just had to dodge until they were all through, and then they surrendered. We got the guy who hit the deputy with the shotgun and charged him with assault with a deadly weapon, but the judge just laughed at us. Couldn't blame him, really. . . ."

It was a close-run thing, status-wise. The dealers and their customers won the legal game, as they usually do—of the sixty-seven suspects run through the courts during the next eighteen months, forty-eight walked free and clear; thirteen got probation; four got sentences of six months or under; one got two years; and one, the only man stupid or flustered or stoned enough to be caught with drugs actually in his hand, got five to seven in Raiford—but the narcs won the turf. The county bricked up the drug house, the narc force went back and busted six more new drug operations on the block over the next three months, and then it was over. The block has been clean for almost a year. It's just one block, of course, but hey, you do what you can do. The preacher certainly appreciated it.

●

Walt is unusual among the Dade County narcs (and indeed the Florida population at large) in that he is, as near as makes no difference, a hometown boy. He arrived in Miami at the age of four with his divorced mother and was raised by her and his grandmother in the Little River section of the city, just a mile or three from Liberty City and the other North-Central Miami neighborhoods which have degenerated slowly into ghettos during his thirty-four years in Florida. When he joined the department after a hitch in the Navy, he and his first wife moved farther north, outside the city proper to Broward County, where taxes and property values and crime statistics aren't so insane. He still lives there. So do most of his fellow cops, undercover narcs included. Because of budgetary restrictions and concern for the mental health of its officers, the department never demands that a detective live an "undercover," Sonny Crockett–type life. Only the Feds do that, and they don't do it a lot.

Walt is now three and a half years into his second marriage. His wife Karen, a stenographer in Metro Dade's homicide division, is expecting the couple's first child in three months. Walt figures that the new baby is a sign for him to quit smoking (done already), and also to break his Burger King addiction. His work, on the other hand, will continue as usual; he is committed to his narrow, practical cause in the ghetto.

Liberty City and the other poor areas comprising Walt's working turf were never scenic, never model neighborhoods, but back in his boyhood they had a lot they don't have today: some communal integrity, basically, a system in which neighbors and families and their clubs and churches looked out for one another, and did a lot of their own police work. There wasn't much trouble between blacks and Latins—they'd all been there awhile—and Anglos kept their distance.

It was quite a distance, too. The cops, all whites in those days, operated on the theory of containment, harassing ghetto residents when they strayed from their neighborhoods in undesirable directions, but involving themselves in the ghetto's internal crime problems only with great reluctance.

Walt began to know this turf in '71, during his rookie days on uniformed patrol. It is where, among other things, he received his first lessons in police survival. He'll never forget the day, five or six months after he first put on the uniform, when he walked up on a man in a stopped car who was waiting to greet him with a sawed-off shotgun. The instincts of his partner, a volunteer Senior Reserve officer with thirty years of street experience, were better than his; the older cop whipped out his revolver and drew down on the driver before the younger cop could walk into the shotgun's cone of fire. Therefore Walt survived to hear the bad man tell him just exactly what would have happened if he'd taken another few steps. Barely a year later, after he'd moved from the street into detective work, another man in another stopped car—this man wearing a good suit and driving a new Lincoln, seemingly the victim of a traffic accident or some other misfortune—reared up suddenly and stuck a pistol into his stomach. Walt survived all by himself that time. He distracted the man's attention, slapped the gun away, and wrestled him to the ground.

In his subsequent career there have been a few other life-threatening encounters Walt won't forget, but many more that have faded into interchangeable impressions. There's been so much gunfire in his life as a Metro Dade cop that he doesn't even remember the first time he heard shots fired in anger. Nor does he have any idea how many times he personally has been shot at; when the shooting starts, he explains, you have no way of knowing whether you're the target unless you get hit.

That's how it was when he ended up back in the Liberty City area during the riots of 1980. A lieutenant of detectives by then, he was pressed into service as the leader of a group of uniformed officers whose job was to penetrate the ghetto in "field force" during daylight hours, establish a perimeter around the location of wanted individuals, and attempt to take them into custody. He and his men received fire every day during that job.

Walt enjoyed certain aspects of that phase of his career. Other phases—general investigation, homicide, internal review—had their attractions, certainly, but none of them offered the challenges and rewards of leadership in extremis. None of them demanded the ability to think on his feet under the highest possible pressure, to react and adapt and improvise quickly and surely enough to survive the heat of law enforcement in second-by-second action. He found himself more professionally satisfied than he had ever been.

Given such proclivities, Walt couldn't be in a more suitable place, time, or line of work today, for today Liberty City and its environs are like any other American ghetto—half burned-out, ravaged by drugs, patrolled and serviced by cops and criminals of all races—only more so. Castro's Mariel castoffs, now working for the Colombians further up the cocaine supply chain, added a whole new dimension of violence to this melting pot, and the recently arrived Jamaican Rastas who own the marijuana market are just as bad. With these groups running the streets, relations between American blacks and the new Latins disintegrating into daily hostility and periodic mass violence, and the recent surge in the retail crack business fueling a major escalation in despair and need and bloody competition, North-Central Miami has become a nightmare more haunting than any other anywhere in the USA. A street narc could wish for no greater challenge.

Walt has led the Narcotics North Street Squad for almost six months now, and he does indeed find the job satisfying, both because it is so demanding and because he admires and enjoys the people who work for him. They are creative individuals, he says, real characters, every one of them exceptional: intelligent, adaptable, and brave. Every one of them goes out there every day and does things, like standing alone and unarmed in roomfuls of bad guys to buy drugs, which other cops would never even consider.

Walt doesn't know where his career will lead after he's worked two or three years in street narcotics, which is as long as most cops can take such an assignment. Major Case action, an obvious alternative, doesn't appeal to him. "Too many lawyers," he says. "Too many politicians, too much money up for grabs, too much stuff you can never be sure of. My job doesn't have a whole lot to recommend it, it's true, but at least I don't have to spend all my time waiting to get shot in the back, worrying it might be another man with a badge behind the gun."

Welcome to Miami. In some ways, it's true, it *is* like television.

It's worse, in fact. On TV you don't see the details—the flyblown mouth of the feud-dead drug soldier taped shut over a suffocating throatful of his own genitals; the swollen blue tongue of the coke-poisoned welfare mother convulsing to death in a flow of excrement on the bloody backseat of an undercover-narc car, most likely a rented four-door Ford or Chevy; the fear sweat on the blandly stupid face of a Friday-night white kid come to score in the ghetto—and you don't see cops who really admit what their limitations really are, who really don't give a flying fuck about beating the system but who are great cops anyway.

❂

It's 3 P.M. on a Tuesday in North Miami, the beginning of an undercover narc's workweek, but the squad room of Narcotics North is almost deserted.

There it is, then, in all its splendor: broken chairs with springs protruding from their cushions, rusty gray metal desks, thirty-year-old manual typewriters that were never very slick to begin with; peeling brown-and-cream institutional gloss paint; scarred, dirt-colored linoleum—your typical elite-unit New Wave glamour-cop quarters, skillfully located at the end of a cratered dirt road on a mosquito-plagued plot of trash land shared with a brand-new minimum-security correctional facility containing the majority of the state's short-term, first-time drug offenders. The windows of this building are so situated that approximately seventy-five percent of its shortly street-bound occupants can while away their time memorizing the faces of every undercover officer and the characteristics of every vehicle working out of or visiting the Narcotics North office.

The entertainment is slow today, though. Walt, Russ, Dennis, and Luz the secretary have the office to themselves; the other narcs on duty are in court, as they are most Tuesdays and often Thursdays too.

Tuesdays are slow days on the street, drug dealers' Sundays after the hectic action of the weekend and the universal Monday crash (the narcs, who typically buy during the week and bust on weekends, take their Sundays on Monday). Most of the big-time bad men are laid out somewhere in the bosom of their girlfriends or families; there's lots of concealed steel around the better domiciles and swimming pools of Miami on Tuesdays, lots of Rolex Submariners and cordless phones and six-pack coolers full of spare MAC-11 clips among the bouncing below-school-age bambinos. Most of the small-timers, Abraham's colleagues, are at the track or the jai alai fronton, doing their laundry, painting their living rooms pink, whatever.

As evening approaches, the Street Squad narcs begin to congregate at their office. Most of them don't make much of an impression, especially if a combination of TV exposure and erroneous rationale has led you to suppose that modern narcs must have The Look. If anything, their general appearance suggests a somewhat more protracted argument with a Mack truck and a slightly more extreme addiction to the fashion leadership of J.C. Penney than does the visual presence of the average working stiff.

That makes sense, of course. In the real world, most detectives eat trash and drink poison and smoke too much and never exercise, so they end up looking as reamed out as they are by the time they hit their mid-thirties. In the real world they don't make much money and the work is absolute hell on the threads, so they buy and wear the cheapest working clothes they can find. In the real world you don't need The Look to get on the good side of major drug dealers (what you need is the cash), and in the very specific real world of Narcotics North The Look is positively counterproductive. You're operating on turf where anything more respectable than an imitation-leather jacket and a pair of ratty Levi's screams either "CASEWORKER!" or "LANDLORD!" or "VICTIM!", and that's very bad. An undercover narc really doesn't need people running away from him or trying to mug him, now does he?

Of course, the unfortunate aspect of this fact of life is that if you're an Anglo, dressing to avoid one set of problems leads inevitably to another: your wardrobe now screams "NARC!" What business could any other category of raggedy-ass, hard-case white person possibly have on the ghetto street?

It's a pisser, all right, but at least you're not having to blow people away for trying to steal your wallet all the time, and in Narcotics North the term "undercover" is a joke anyway. The only detectives who have a ghost of a chance of remaining unknown in the ghetto are the blacks and Hispanics; that's why they're the only cops wearing ski masks during organized busts.

●

Visually, Dennis Reddington is a more or less typical Street Squad narc. He looks a little like a weasel after a rainstorm—the sharp thin cunning face, the long lank hair matted down with no discernible attempt at style—but there is also (appropriately) something of the bloodhound in those big, sad, bulbous, bloodshot eyes. From a distance he looks like just another street rat. He's an ex-Boston transit cop, fourth generation, born and bred a Fenway rat.

Surprising items come in shabby packages, though, and Dennis is a case in point. Since arriving on the Metro Dade force during its post-Mariel expansion, he has achieved great things. He's parlayed all sorts of street action into bigger and better cases worthy of state, federal, and international police attention.

For Dennis this kind of work was a wonderful tonic, just the kind of thing he'd been seeking ever since he first put on a uniform. He'd come to Miami in search of the things most people expect when they migrate from the cities of the North—more sun, better housing, an exotic atmosphere, a fresh start—and also for professional benefits. Better money was an important factor, of course, but even more important was the job's route into the front line of police work. Dennis could have signed up with just about any police agency in Florida (they're all expanding, desperate for quality recruits), and done very nicely for himself on many fronts, but like most other cops he knew that there was only one place where It was really At: Dade County, the eye of the storm, the Zone.

He loves it. Sprawled back in his funky old desk chair on a Friday afternoon, killing some time before the narc/SRT/uniform force assembles for its usual schedule of ghetto base-house busts, Dennis is the picture of contentment as he regales the press with colorful stories and modest, no-big-deal accounts of his spectacular successes. This is a role in which, to be fair, he has not cast himself; Walt did it originally, steered the original trickle of *Miami Vice*-inspired reporters toward the most outgoing of his detectives and continued to do so when Dennis handled the job so naturally, polishing his performances to a quote-dense T as the trickle became a flood.

Walt wasn't operating on instinct alone. He'd already seen more than a glimmer of Dennis's gift for media relations when Michael Mann's *Miami Vice* research team first showed up looking for some malleable reality. They glommed on to Dennis right away, and as the show began to take shape, it was Dennis and his then partner Tommy O'Keefe who took actors Don Johnson and Philip Michael Thomas out on the job with them, showed them the turf and told them the stories. Which of course means that in the predictably (extremely) tenuous interface between *Miami Vice* and the reality of an undercover Dade County narc's life, Dennis and Tommy are in fact the "real" Crockett and Tubbs.

Ridiculous, but true: scrawny, weasel-faced Dennis Reddington is the sexy Sonny Crockett, and cool Ricardo Tubbs somehow emerged from the sloppy, meatpacker-massive Irish-American bulk of the rude, crude, funny, multi-lusted Tommy O'Keefe.

When Dennis tells his repertoire of tales, they're great, full of impossibly rich drug dealers too stupid to remember the combinations to their Halliburtons, smarter drug dealers still not as smart as Dennis and Tommy, extremely smart drug dealers no narc will ever get anywhere near. There are all kinds of comedy—misunderstandings, farces, pratfalls, belly laughs, sick jokes, blacker-than-night ironies—and pathos aplenty; crooked cops, busted cops, terrified cops, wounded cops, unlucky cops, stupid cops, dead cops.

But this is all just the usual combat-narc stuff, basically unremarkable. It doesn't tell you much about Dennis. What does is the way he presents it all: the dramatic pauses, the sudden laughs, the merry twinkle in his big watery bloodhound eyes, the way he's enjoying himself.

Like when he's talking about his liaison work with the DEA and the Coast Guard, being staked out onshore below Coconut Grove as the Feds' planes track the drug boats roaring in from Bimini and the sailors' star shells light up the sky to the north, driving the bad guys south toward him and the foot-Feds and the black-clad boys with the serious toys. You stand there, says Dennis, watching the sky light up, and then you begin to hear the boats. They can be as far out as thirty miles, but the thunder of those mighty engines at full throttle—ninety, a hundred knots or more—still reaches you.

Dennis looks up. There's a light in his eyes; something special.

"You know," he says, "there's not another sound like that in the whole world."

As in 'You haven't lived till you've heard it,' Dennis?

"Right," he says. "Exactly. And you'll never, ever forget it. It's fuckin' *great.*"

Dennis is the only Narcotics North detective in whom any evidence of edge-romance is readily apparent. He's the only one who seems to find the context of his work, and the style of his enemies, as glamorous as your TV set would have you believe.

Just before leaving for the Liberty City precinct house where all the cops working busts tonight will assemble, Dennis gets a call from Michael Talbot, the actor who plays Detective Stanley Switek on *Miami Vice.* The two have become friends. Dennis hangs out on the set sometimes, pals around with Crockett and Tubbs and the girls. Maybe Talbot and he will go out drinking tonight when he's all through busting base houses.

Dennis rubs his hands together, grins from ear to ear. "All *right!*" he says.

●

No matter how many times his unit has been through it before and how well drilled their responses are, gunfire during an assault *always* scares Walt to death, just makes him crazy.

Tonight, for instance, they did everything right. The instant Abraham's three rounds popped off undramatically, muffled inside the base house, every one of the narcs and deputies was down, behind cover, guns flashing into their hands, safeties disengaging, front sights sweeping the house for hostile movement, half a dozen of them swiveling to face away from the house and guard the main force's back regardless of what went down at the focus of the action. Even so, though, Walt was crawling among them like some kind of demented spider, adrenalined almost speechless.

Even now that it's all over, and another potential worst-case scenario has ended in nothing more serious than a partially destroyed earlobe and a lot of frayed nerves (thank you, serious-toy boys), Walt's still flirting with hyperventilation. He's still too anxious for his own or anybody else's good.

"He's always like that," says Dennis. "You'd think he was our mother, the way he is when somebody shoots at us. It's nice in a way, really, but it can be a pain in the ass at times."

It takes at least half an hour before Walt calms down to his normal level, but that's okay. The strike force has lots of time now; there having been a shooting, everybody but a few of the uniformed officers has to wait around long after Abraham and his henchmen and customers have been taken away for processing—all that evidence to be collected, all those reports to be made and paperwork to be initiated —and the rest of the evening's scheduled busts are canceled. Abraham's done his colleagues and competitors a nice little favor tonight.

It is eleven o'clock, more than four hours since the SRT men flew from their darkened van toward Abraham's doors and windows, before Walt and six of his detectives get back to their office. It's looking good for Dennis's date with Talbot. If Walt calls it right, he can ditch the *Miami Herald* reporter he has invited along for the ride tonight and head for the bright lights of Coconut Grove.

But Walt doesn't call it right. There's a Rasta grass house three blocks from Abraham's place that was closed down when the strike force visited it, and Milt and Larry now report that it's reopened for business. Only two men are in the house. It's ripe for the taking.

Walt fusses with this one for a while. It's tough. The SRT unit is no longer available to him, and as a rule he really hates to work on entry situations without them, but here he is with six detectives and two hours' dead time before the end of the shift, and he himself is still sort of antsy, and it doesn't look like that tough a nut. Okay, he says, let's do it.

The plan is simple enough: a standard "buy and bust." Larry and Milt, both black men, will drop by the house and make the buy. They will be armed, and Larry will have an open walkie-talkie set on the Narcotics North frequency in his back pocket. He'll key it twice after the buy has been made, and then Walt and the four other detectives, waiting two blocks away with engines running but lights out, will come roaring in. Larry and Milt will grab the surprised dealers as they react to the shock of seeing the first car come hauling ass around the corner of the block, then the reinforcements will pile out of the cars, and that will be that. There are a few gray areas in this plan, but it will have to do.

Dennis is not amused. Not only does he have to call Talbot and fudge about whether he'll be able to make it, but the *Herald* reporter wants to go along on the bust, so he will have to play a less than starring role in the events to come, tag along at the back of the three-car procession where the reporter will be able to observe in relative safety.

That's the way it goes, Walt tells him; you can't be a cowboy with a reporter in tow. Dennis grumbles, but there's nothing he can do. That *is* the way it is.

❁

At 12:03 A.M., Walt and Tommy are in position in their car. Two more narcs are in a car in front of them, and Dennis and his reporter are behind. Walt, controlling his adrenaline with deep, measured breaths, has his walkie-talkie glued to his ear, the volume turned low. There are static-broken bursts of talk—Larry and Milt are making the buy—and then, suddenly, horrifyingly, the radio erupts with a shout and a series of loud, confused scuffling noises.

Walt drops the radio, stomps on the gas pedal, and wrenches the car away from the curb. Tommy, suddenly very pale, rips his handgun from its holster and thrusts it out the window as the car accelerates—then whips the gun back, cursing, as Dennis's car skids past. Dennis hurtles to the front of the police column, then slews suddenly left around the corner of the next block.

The car in front of Walt and Tommy follows, and so do Walt and Tommy. The grass house should be halfway down the block on Tommy's side of the car. Tommy thrusts his gun out the window again and reaches for his door handle with his other hand as the car starts braking, but even before it skids to a halt, he's yelling.

"Back. Back! *Go back! GO BACK!*"

The grass house isn't there. It's not on this block at all. It's on the *next* block.

Walt throws the Chevy into reverse, hurling it back in its tracks. As he does so, there's a burst of noise from the radio, this one worse than the first: someone yelling, "Down! Down!", then a sudden, sharp blast—an explosion—and then silence. Walt starts roaring rhythmically.

"No-no-no-no-no-no-no-no-no-no-no . . ."

The Chevy careens backward half a block, forward one more block, then screams left, in the lead now, the other two cars somewhere behind, and hurtles toward the grass house.

And there they are, out in the front yard. Milt is bent over one man, tightening the flex cuffs. The other man is already secured, flat on his face with his wrists cuffed behind him. Larry is squatting on his haunches, facing toward the street, with a shotgun resting barrel-up against his left shoulder.

Okay. It's okay. No blood, no corpses, no officer down. Thank God.

As Walt and Tommy burst from their car, Larry raises his right hand in an exaggerated United States Cavalry salute.

"Howdy, strangers," he says in a deadpan Western drawl. It doesn't sound very funny, and it isn't meant to.

●

Walt slouches wearily behind the wheel of the Chevy in a rain-swept Burger King parking lot at 3 A.M., feeling sick and depressed and resentful. Shamed, too. A diet-breaking Whopper with fries and a chocolate milk shake hasn't helped. If anything, it's made him feel even worse about himself.

He didn't do well with Dennis after the bust. Berating him like that wasn't right. It was after all he who set Dennis on the course which led to what happened tonight, or at least it was he who didn't see the danger until Dennis was too far along.

Dennis screwed up badly tonight. He just wasn't paying attention, is what it was. If he'd been paying attention, he wouldn't have fumbled the Transmit button of his radio; that's what caused static on the unit in Larry's pocket, thereby telling the Rastas that they were in the act of selling grass to cops. And if Dennis had been on the ball, he wouldn't have reacted to the results of that first mistake by rushing to the fore of the relief column and leading it down the wrong block. His comrades in the lead car knew exactly where the grass house was, but in the heat of the moment, with Dennis suddenly taking the lead from them, they repeated his mistake by acting on instinct.

The bottom line tonight is that Dennis was more interested in impressing that reporter, in burnishing the legend of his life on the edge in the great hip brutal glittering city, than in what was really happening on the sad, all too ordinary ghetto street of the moment. While he dealt in legend, reality nearly killed his friends.

As it happened, Larry was able to grab that Rasta-man's shotgun before he could use it, and no shots were fired. The explosion we heard on our walkie-talkie must have been something striking Larry's unit as things got suddenly physical. But really, it was too close by far. One-on-one is not the way to go in a situation like that.

Walt's anger was spent hours ago. What's left now is how much he feels for Dennis, and fears for him. But there's nothing he can do tonight. He puts his car in gear for the drive to his suburb, and begins trying to let go of his work before he gets home.

7

The King of Contra Rock

Outside the smart cheap little Deco hotel the new American melting pot is bubbling hot and hard. If he wanted to, Alfonso could draw back the window shades at his elbow and watch a whole world's stew of dreams and desires and stories and histories thickening slowly in the sweet soft South Beach night.

He could look out past a palm frond or two, the intervening air sensuous with the scent of orange trees and alien spices, and watch old Jews rocking silently on another hotel's veranda straight across the street. He could see them staring impassively at pairs of young male Germans, pale and unfashionable, checking in from Cologne or Essen or Stuttgart or Düsseldorf via Miami International Airport for a fortnight of fun in the New World honeypot, and he could wonder what specific memories stir at the sight of them behind tired ancient middle-European eyes; where, and with what consequences, very similar young men came long ago into the lives now drawing to a close at the end of the refugee road across the street.

Then too Alfonso could cast his gaze toward the brilliance of Col-

lins Avenue one block east, the black emptiness of the Atlantic two blocks beyond, and see the rainbow dazzle of a human kaleidoscope in the night: the strolling Italians and Egyptians and Swedes and Saudi Arabians, the Haitians and Jamaicans and other Caribbean blacks, the Brazilians and Chileans and Argentines, the Latins and Indians from everywhere in Central America; the suave slim self-possessed French gliding almost disdainfully and the eager knobby-kneed Brits pecking hungrily through the riot of nightlife like dim suburban sparrows loosed suddenly into a magic jungle, the girls and boys from Ohio and Omaha somewhere between these two extremes, titillated but also terrified by an American city which demands that you emerge from the cocoon of your automobile to actually walk its streets, literally rub shoulders with blacks and Jews and Latins and even Anglos who could have come from anywhere, be anybody.

And really, the polyglot energy of South Beach does boggle the mind, stagger the senses, kick your curiosity into hyperdrive. Even the people who make this place their home, the declining Holocaust Jews and thriving Cuban Marielitos—even the motivating-renovating yuppies who may one day drive its property values beyond the reach of anyone but people exactly like themselves—feel its human heat. So it is not at all surprising that in South Beach (and indeed anywhere in Greater Miami) the opening question in a conversation between strangers is not the all-American "What do you do?" or New York City's "Where's your apartment?", but an infinitely more interesting and essential inquiry: "Where did you come from, and how and why?"

That's the question Alfonso is waiting for.

❂

Before the saga of his answer unfolds, first impressions first: a newspaper photograph and a Miami-datelined UPI wire story in the *Tampa Tribune,* mid-1987. One wild card and loony story among the many on any Florida day.

This was a beauty, though, a rare little gem. In the photograph stood a wild big bearded boar of a man, as mean and nasty as the Mini-14 with the thirty-round clip in his left hand (his right caressing a Fender Jazzmaster guitar supported by a strap doubling as a bandolier). Behind him stood three other men, not quite as threatening but no peaceniks either in their camouflage fatigues and stony stares, and behind them a rough thatched roof, palm trees, jungle foliage. This, the caption told us, was Wolf and the Pack; the Wolf himself, Alfonso Lobo, front and center.

The headline too was startling—*Nicaraguan Releases Contra Anthem*—and the story no less so. Lobo's song "Freedom Fighter," in which parallels were drawn quite explicitly between the counterrevolutionary guerrillas in Nicaragua, the *Mujaheddin* in Afghanistan, and individuals such as Lech Walesa, the Pope, and Jesus Christ, had evidently attracted the attention of Pentagon officials who found much to praise in it. One such person, an "operations research analyst" by name James Tyvoll, opined that the song was indeed "very catchy. We were hoping that it would be picked up commercially."

Well, make my day. There was Contra Rock in this wonderful world, and it had captured the hearts and minds of the Cold War Warriors, and it even had a king. He was alive and well and living, where else, in Miami.

Here we are, then, one year later, live and in person with His Majesty. Face to face with the Wolf himself.

The man is perfect for the part—a passionate pyrotechnic of a person, not a calm or studied man, not an introvert. Everything about him is big and bold, loud and proud, fast and furious. Squeezed near a South Beach window into an inadequate hotel chair with his belly butting up against an undersized table, he is a creature at the mercy of his energy; his story, punctuated by sudden tank-like lurches of his body and the mortar-bomb thump of his fists on the table, assaults the ear in bursts and volleys and explosions from every quadrant of the field.

In this our first encounter his story's a mess, a jumble of information as vivid but nonsensical as a combatant's moment-by-moment perception of a firefight. Here in one moment is Alfonso the privileged Nicaraguan ruling-class teenager on the lam from his studies in Swinging London, up to his ears in tough tender English girls and jamming at the Bag 'O Nails Club with Jimi Hendrix (Jimi *Hendrix?*). Here he is again, one gathers somewhat later in life, making a killing dealing Massey-Ferguson tractors in a pre-Sandinista Nicaraguan rural economy. Next he's leaving New Orleans to accompany Carlos

Santana and his band on tour, or becoming "like a son" to a French count in Provence (he's already that to the dictator Somoza back home). Then suddenly he's getting horsewhipped by mounted *flics* in the Paris students' strike of '68, then trying to make sure John Belushi doesn't overdose before noon in New York, or protecting Mick and Bianca Jagger from earthquake-loosened masonry in stricken Managua, then making another killing, this time in the seafood business, and then watching his whole operation go broke in Apalachicola, Florida, because the locals don't like Hispanics (the Klan sends notes, and once a bullet). He's wanting to study nuclear chemistry but studying psychobiology and mathematics and mechanics instead, and finding any kind of study harder and harder as he begins to realize that all he really wants is to play guitar. Then he's doing that in all sorts of places with all sorts of people: Hendrix, of course, but also unknown black bluesmen in New Orleans and flamenco masters in Managua and salsa addicts in Miami and generals and politicians in the Pentagon and the White House.

Finally, after he's replayed portions of his most recent life on videotape—he's come with a leather case containing a mini VCR and TV monitor—he thrusts the image of a life-pivotal moment under my nose. It's another newspaper clipping, this one datelined Costa Rica, 1971.

The caption, fortunately, identifies him by name. Otherwise you'd never know him. He's younger and slimmer, and he's clean-shaven, and then too the face of the young man supported by two police officers in the photo is contorted by pain, his image disfigured by the peculiar newsprint-gray Rorschachs stamped all over it. This is blood, a great deal of it. Six .45 caliber bullets' worth, to be precise. One in his thigh; one in his left hand, which it ravaged; and four in his guts for a total of eighteen separate intestinal punctures and a half-destroyed liver.

But obviously, no banana. The target is still here before us today, bursting with life. He thrusts to his feet and pulls up his shirt, and there they are: four large ugly scar-brown craters to remind him, as if he needed any prompting, of how he personally grew to fear, hate, and finally fight the World Communist Conspiracy. Like the overwhelming majority of his fellow immigrants in South Florida, and for very similar reasons, the Wolf is a Republican.

◉

There are, depending on who is making the estimate, between one and two hundred thousand Nicaraguans in the Greater Miami area. Alfonso himself leans toward the higher figure, which implies both a formula of one "illegal" to every "legal" and a vision of Nicaragua's internal condition which would logically drive very large numbers of its citizens into exile.

But more on that, one of Alfonso's favorite subjects, anon. The most reasonable guess is that Greater Miami's Nicaraguan population is somewhere between a hundred and twenty thousand, and a hundred and fifty thousand. There are in addition some half a million Nicaraguan refugees in California. Altogether, between the overthrow of the Somoza regime by leftist Sandinista guerillas in 1979 and the date of this writing (August 1988), approximately one million of the country's citizens, or slightly more than a third of its entire population, have left their homes to seek refuge in the United States or neighboring Central American countries.

Again depending on the ideology of the individual making the judgment, Miami's Nicaraguans are either the cream or the scum of the nation. In chronological order of immigration—basically the richest and/or most immediately imperiled got out first—they are (or rather were) politicians and the military elite and Somoza's national guard and police torturers; major landowners and industrialists; doctors and lawyers and educators and other members of the professional class; middle-level entrepreneurs; small businesspersons; small landowners; and finally anybody else who at some point found something overwhelmingly distasteful and/or life-threatening about the Sandinista style of government. These days, with Nicaragua virtually empty of non-Sandinista citizens of any significant worldly means and the economy of the country in chaos, the Miami refugee reception center deals primarily with destitute members of the rural working population at the rate of some four or five hundred a month.

As one might expect, for in the main the exiles are educated capitalists whose departure from their homeland was not entirely voluntary (rather than the opposite: illiterates seeking relief from a Third World economy in the richest nation on earth), Miami's Nicaraguans are doing quite well for themselves. They are making deals, setting up small businesses, practicing their professions (some even legally, although like any other immigrant group in this country the dishwashing-doctor syndrome is hardly unknown to them, and neither is the phenomenon of, say, a dentist operating at cut rates out of a closet in his home). They are, in short, working. Although there are of course some very bad, dangerous men within their ranks (high-level mass murderers and foot-slogging mutilators with a lot of blood on their hands and a burning desire for more, political gangsters involved in all manner of free-lance or U.S.-sponsored arms dealing and drug running and other international *realpolitik* nastiness), the common-criminal element in the community is small, and Nicaraguans do not appear in any significant number on the area's welfare rolls.

In many ways, then, the majority of Miami's Nicaraguans are model immigrants, a boon to the vitality of Uncle Sam's economy and the future of his gene pool. While it is true that Uncle has an odd way of recognizing this reality, denying most Nicaraguans the right to apply for U.S. citizenship on political refugee grounds (now *there's* a hot potato), his logic has some substance. Considerable energy and U.S. resources are after all being expended toward the goal of removing the factor which drove these people from their homeland in the first place, and unlike the Cuban case, the outcome of that process is still regarded, both on high in Washington and on the streets of Miami's Little Nicaragua, as an open question—so why grant easy U.S. citizenship to people who might be going home if U.S. policy succeeds? To do so would imply, indirectly but very clearly indeed, official acknowledgment that U.S. policy is not expected to succeed. And really, the feeling of a quite substantial majority of Miami's Nicaraguans is that given the chance, given a capitalist homeland to return to, they would in fact pack up and depart the Home of the Brave.

So these people are not at heart, where it counts, an immigrant community. They are a community in exile, the latest such group in a city with a complex, longstanding netherworld of coup plots and assassination plans and secret funding and paramilitary training and all the other seething symptoms of the violent intersection where international politics meets the business of diplomacy by other means. They themselves liken their condition to that of the Free French in World War II London or South Florida's Cubans before the counter-revolutionary death knell at the Bay of Pigs, not to the Puerto Ricans in today's New York or the Mexicans in Los Angeles or the Haitians and Jamaicans or indeed the present-day Cubans who walk the streets of Miami with them. Within their ranks, then, the most significant feeling toward the homeland is not nostalgia of one sort or another but tension, expectation, the anxious knife-edge between hope and despair. This is a community living in the dynamic unknown of its future, not the stale familiar grave of its past—and so it has the mobilizing energy of a common political cause in addition to the economic vitality of other educated New World newcomers like the Vietnamese.

Alfonso Lobo, in whom these qualities are immediately and often spectacularly apparent, says that he himself wants to go home. Truthfully, he asks, who wouldn't? The physical Nicaragua is a beautiful country—mountains and lakes and beaches and rivers, just gorgeous. It's a rich country—an agricultural paradise, bountiful and productive like no other anywhere near it. It's a *big* country—not the overpopulated postage stamp of its jealous neighbors Costa Rica and El Salvador, but a place where a man can ride his horse for days without seeing another soul, hunt valleys and fish lakes which haven't felt the touch of humanity for years. And the human Nicaragua is also rich, rich in the things of the soul: music, poetry, art, love. Its citizens are creative people, the artistic aristocracy of Central America.

Alfonso is of course somewhat partisan in these assessments, but the people with whom he is most often in violent disagreement echo his thoughts. One of the rallying cries of North American political opposition to the activities of the Contras is that the "freedom fighters" (and therefore their North American sponsors) are waging war on a nation of poets. Likewise the accounts of Yanqui journalists returning from Sandinista-orchestrated fact-finding tours display an appreciation of the country's physical beauty every bit as profound as their admiration of its government's socialist virtue. And then too, says Alfonso, the Russians and Cubans and Czechs and East Germans now occupying the homes of the exiled indigenous aristocracy are quite obviously aware of Nicaragua's potential for feeding peoples far beyond its borders. In *their* vision of the future, he says, the nation's function will be to feed the Central American socialist armies which, subsequent to the possible tumbling of certain dominoes in a certain order, will grow into U.S.-threatening millions if all goes according to plan.

By all accounts, then, Alfonso's homeland really is quite the place. And yes, it annoys him most terribly that as he sees Nicaragua today, only Sandinistas and Soviet bloc advisers and their guests of the world's press get to wine and dine and rut and strut their way around the lovely country's most alluring pleasure spots. He just hates to think that at this very moment, while he and I talk in this South Beach hotel room, some loutish KGB major could be rolling some sweet young well-bred honey from *his* little sister's high school yearbook around *his* old bedroom—or worse yet, one of his own school chums, now a state-sponsored Latin-lover public information officer, could be dispensing similar treatment to some second-string Barbara Walters he's been fucking silly ever since she got off the plane from Bloomingdale's.

But although this subject is very relevant to an understanding of Alfonso, and there's nothing like the combination of sex and revolution (or counterrevolution) to stir the most basic passions in a man, we digress. The main thrust of our story must concern not the Nicaragua of the present or future, but Nicaragua yesterday, Miami today, and Alfonso's journey from one to the other.

Some ordered chronology here, beginning at the beginning: Alfonso's roots, the genus of his people.

They were, originally (or at least as far as his knowledge goes) Sephardic Jews practicing high finance in post-Medieval Spain, the days of Castilian might and seagoing conquest, the era during which the ambitions of the English and French and Dutch were but minor footnotes to the power of the great Iberian monarchs.

It was the first radical shift in that relationship between the nautical powers of Europe's Imperial Age, Francis Drake's savage underdog mauling of the Spanish Armada in the English Channel beyond Portsmouth, that reshaped the destiny of Alfonso's people. The towering Spanish men-of-war which succumbed to Drake's mean little fireships or foundered in flight up the wild North Sea had been paid for with loans made by the Lobos, and when they didn't come home—neither the ships themselves nor their anticipated cargo, the plunder of a looted and subjugated England from which the Lobos's repayment was to be made—the Catholic Crown resorted to a not-uncommon method of welching on its debt in all good Christian conscience: King Philip issued a crowd-pleasing edict stripping all Jews of their property and declaring them personae non gratae in his realm.

The Lobos had an answer for that. They took themselves to Rome, converted to the One True Faith, ingratiated themselves with the Pope (who at the time was chronically eager for ways of bringing his temporal power vis-à-vis Spain in line with his spiritual supremacy), and then, with his blessing, returned to the Spanish court loaded for royalty.

History does not record the King's personal reaction to this deliciously deft employment of his own religious legerdemain (though "*!@#&%+!!!!!" reads the same in any age or language), but it is known beyond a doubt that now he faced a sticky professional situation.

He simply couldn't pay the Lobos. The Crown had no cash and couldn't get it, for by this time the English devastation of its navy, an asset representing by far the most enormous single investment made by a Christian nation at that point in history, had extended even beyond the vessel of state; the whole economy was splintered and smashed, shipping water from sternpost to bowsprit. More or less everybody in Spain was broke.

His Highness was however no fool. He still had significant assets in the form of his oceangoing surrogates' existing claims to large parts and parcels of the South American and southern North American continents. He also had an ongoing problem arranging for the colonization of all those millions of square miles. Finally, he knew that these born-again Lobos represented the promise of an unbearable thorn in the royal flesh until somehow they could be satisfied. So, intelligently, he wove these strands together and got rid of his debt, part of his colonial personnel problem, and the troublesome Lobos in one grand gesture: he granted them land in the Americas. That's how various branches of the family ended up with multiple millions of New World acres in what are now southerly states of the union or sovereign nations all over the South American continent. Alfonso's branch received a healthy portion of rich, beautiful Nicaragua.

Alfonso's antecedents farmed and ranched—Nicaragua is prime cattle country—but, with the entrepreneurial impulse running in their blood, the sons of the elders also diversified into all manner of enterprise. Alfonso's father, for instance, made his personal fortune importing and distributing tractors (initially the English Massey-Fergusons in which Alfonso himself later traded) and other tough, reasonably priced vehicles suited to the Central American rural market; it was he who converted Nicaraguan agriculture from donkey power to gasoline. That's not all he did, either. Equipped with a North American university education (he holds degrees in both agriculture and law), he was a powerful force in Nicaraguan agriculture as a whole, and he became a very prominent politician. In the final year of Somoza's rule he was the leader of Nicaragua's Liberal Party and a close confidant of the President.

All of which made young Alfonso, the firstborn son of this gentleman, quite the exceptional young Nicaraguan; very definitely a child of wealth and privilege, quite possibly a future President or President-maker himself.

Such however was not Alfonso's own vision of his destiny in this world. The first guitar of his life came into his hands at the age of four, and it wasn't long before his quite-evident talent and the joy he felt with those strings under his fingers convinced him that he was a musician born if not bred (only later did he discover that this proclivity was also a gift of the blood: the greatest flamenco guitarist of seventeenth-century Spain had been a Lobo).

Other qualities of character, manifest with increasing vigor as the boy became a preteen-ager, also indicated against a career in conventional politics or for that matter any calling requiring decorum, respectability, deference to authority, that kind of thing. The kid was a rebel, a teacher teaser, a troublemaker, an individualist, a real pain in the genteel bottoms of the nuns and priests and laypersons charged with preparing the golden children of the Nicaraguan elite for their bright right futures. He had a big mouth and a lively wit to go with it, and—this being the latter half of the twentieth century A.D.—he was also a carrier of the youth pandemic of the age: he had a bad, bad case of the rock & roll fever, the boogie-woogie flu.

Yes. Young Alfonso cared a lot about getting his hands on a Tele or a Strat or a bank of Marshall amps or the new Spencer Davis Group 45 some other feedback-fixated young aristocrat had carried home like the Grail itself from New York or Paris or wherever else his parents had sent him in search of the necessary cosmopolitan polish; cared hardly at all about less amazing, potent, head-splitting phenomena. Except of course the direct rather than electrically amplified expression of his sex drive, which, as previously hinted, moved from fantasy into reality when his parents sent him after his own world-class education to Swinging London. Alfonso's subsequent Anglophilia is at no time more evident than in those moments when he recalls a certain adventurous English rose, a certain Kensington staircase. . . .

But although the man's most visceral connection to the sap-strong spring of his adulthood is the memory of moments in places—a French basement, a London blues pub, this stage in Managua or that in New Orleans—it was the itinerary of his largely unremembered formal education that brought those experiences into his life. France was languages (and knowledge of his mother's roots); England was mathematics in London, mechanical engineering in Coventry; the United States a distracted catch-up blur of biology and business administration and related subjects at Georgia Tech and in New Orleans.

The music of course was everywhere, and so were its accompaniments: like most other Western youths in the millrace of the sixties, Alfonso plunged through the sociophilosophical rapids between "I Wanna Hold Your Hand" and "White Rabbit," negotiated the buoyant channel between cellar-cool wet English Watney's and high dry Mexican marijuana, began crisp and eager in an innocent pageboy bob, ended bedraggled and stained with the secondhand earth tones of U.S. Army surplus, splashed with the tie-dyes of psychedelia. In that '71 newsprint photograph of his, a picture of a bloodstained longhair in the grip of police—a pig 'n hippie sandwich à la Berkeley, à la Jim

Morrison, à la Kent State—he could have been any child of that violently turbulent age.

He was not, though, and it was not the Establishment that pounded him on its rocks. It was the Revolution itself; not the Euro-American parlor game of words and music and sticks and stones, but the real dead-serious thing. The bullets which spilled Alfonso's blood weren't strays or mistakes, errant instruments of authoritarian overreaction; they were the everyday currency of armed revolutionary transaction, and they were aimed intentionally and personally at *him.* The Sandinista who identified him on the commercial flight taking him home from the U.S. to Nicaragua for Christmas had been a high school friend, and the Sandinista who shepherded him into first class, strapped him into a seat near the crew cabin, and fired seven rounds at him knew exactly who he was: a son of the elite, a favorite of Somoza, and, with his music and his hippie ways, a nationally known and celebrated symbol of enlightenment bestirring within the ranks of the Nicaraguan ruling class. The assassination of Alfonso Lobo—for that is clearly what was being attempted; you don't stand three feet from a man and empty a Government Model .45 automatic into him with the intention of simply hurting, chastising, or otherwise discomforting him—was a revolutionary act designed to demonstrate that while The Beast may change its coloration, The People were not to be fooled.

That act was also an accident of sorts, or at least an instance of blown timing and bad judgment. It had been the three-man unit's intent to kidnap Alfonso and the airliner containing him to Cuba, there to hold him hostage for the purpose of acquiring revolutionary finance from his parents and/or the Somoza government, but that's not how things worked out. The flight crew began the ruination of the Sandinistas' day by convincing them that a refueling stop in Costa Rica was necessary; the Costa Rican authorities continued the process by stalling their demands for fuel or another airplane; and then the victim of the plot—well, he didn't behave himself, either. Perhaps if Alfonso had exhibited the appropriate degree of fear or contrition, if he'd pissed in his pants and groveled for his life, the Sandinista with the .45 might have decided to spare him when the options started disappearing. As it was, he restrained neither his outrage nor his contempt, and so it is quite possible that the bullets he took were fired in the heat of personal passion as opposed to the cold light of revolutionary logic.

We'll never really know. The man who shot him was himself ventilated—terminally—when, after a horrific few minutes in which his half-slaughtered but now totally enraged target made a vigorous attempt to tear him limb from limb, he exposed himself to the fire of Costa Rican cops while (finally) heaving wrecked and bloody Alfonso out through the airliner's door to the concrete below.

A news photographer recorded Alfonso's pain in the next moments, but the psychic tribulation which followed was an internal, invisible affair. Alfonso will be the first to admit that yes, some benefits did accrue from his introduction to Central American revolutionary politics in action as opposed to theory—as he puts it, "I allowed the beautiful women of Costa Rica to comfort me in my anguish"— but his mangled fretting hand was a source of very troubling feelings. So was an entirely new, depressing vision of his place in this world.

Very simply, after that Judas finger on the flight home for Christmas, he no longer knew who his friends were. That's why he recuperated and convalesced in Costa Rica instead of Nicaragua; he was safer there from murder behind a smile. So although he did return to Nicaragua after a while, in a very real sense the Wolf's exile began in '71, not with the final physical exodus of himself and his family in '79. Seventy-one was the year the destruction of the home in his head really began.

Physically, though, Alfonso's recovery was a triumph. North American surgeons reconstructed his hand with eighteen separate operations, and Alfonso himself built on the results of their labors with hour after hour and month after month of constant, often wildly painful exercise. So in a mere five years he had his fretting hand back in full: ugly, but functional; incredible, according to those privy to the original X rays and the statistics for recovery from devastation such as had been visited on Alfonso's bones, but the very opposite of a miracle.

No such luck, however, with the long counterrevolutionary struggle back home. The despot Somoza did not have Alfonso's stomach for excruciating remedies, visiting upon his rebellious subjects much energetic repression and many truly bestial varieties of torture and death but no genuinely thorough, all-encompassing, totally ruthless campaign of extermination. When Jimmy Carter knocked the stout beams of Yanqui support from under his ruling house, the intellectual-turned-guerilla-fighter Sandinistas toppled the whole rotten edifice.

According to Alfonso, most members of the Nicaraguan ruling class felt no particular regret that Somoza was gone. They too had grown sick of him, outraged by his and his family's takeover of what could otherwise have been a thriving capitalist economy with room for everybody. But they enjoyed the new alternative even less. Suddenly they were no longer big fish in the Nicaraguan pond. In the tried-and-true tradition of violent socialist takeover, their assets were assumed by the sharks of state in the name of the teeming minnows, and they themselves became a prey species.

Alfonso's memories of those final days are still vivid. As he and I stroll the wee-hours sidewalk of Collins Avenue in the South Beach night—no tourists now, just feral-eyed Marielitos and nightclub trendies capering in the blithe oblivion of sex and drugs and rock & roll—he remembers both the process and the particulars: how his family's house and land and trucks and tractors and bank accounts were taken, and the faces of the men who came to take them; how he and some of his cowboys rounded up his cattle herd to drive it all the way into Costa Rica, and the contours of the little valley his grandfather had once made him memorize as the entry point to just such a desperate endeavor; how Sandinista emissaries crossed into his Costa Rican sanctuary to retrieve the herd and failed, and what the mutilated corpse of his foreman looked like after their visit; how he returned to Nicaragua one more time to liberate the bright pink '67 Mercedes limousine in which he and his musician friends had traveled and laughed and accepted the accolades of the nation's rock & roll fans ever since he first rescued the vehicle from a rusty death in Somoza's government motor pool, and the sight of just two bullet holes drilled through the trunk after his wild ride of squealing springs and scattering roadblocks and strong German steel hurtling through the rural night.

The cattle herd, a good and valuable one, sustained Alfonso through the early days of his exile, but it was the denial of his limo to Nicaragua's new elite that piqued his émigré spirits; no bloody

Belorussian komissar would be whisked from Managua's airport to the jewels in Nicaragua's crown in *that* great national symbol of free music, love, and enterprise.

Alfonso is reminiscing happily about the high times had in the vehicle—the usual musicians' stories, risqué and rank, thick with the doings of great indigenous spirits and visiting stars whose names we should perhaps not mention in the context of hearsay—when a more current event captures our attention. On the wee-hours boulevard at our side a Miami Beach police cruiser crawls to a halt, projects a hiccup of static from the loudspeaker on its roof, and then conveys the amplified message of authority to a listless little congregation of Marielitos hanging loose in the light of a twenty-four-hour bodega: "YOU HAVE ONE MINUTE TO LEAVE, OR YOU ARE GOING TO JAIL!"

Alfonso stands there, staring at this as yet motionless tableau of resentful Hispanic faces and cold clean Anglo steel, of authority interacting with the underclass; this little oversight of probable cause and freedom of assembly and other trifles promised in the Bill of Rights.

Perhaps the scene puts him in mind of his motherland in either of its political realities, Somoza's secret-police past or the Sandinistas' state-controlled present. Certainly it causes him to reflect on the condition of the most common alternative to those forms of government, democracy, here in action on a grass-roots level before his eyes. "I didn't know we were in Moscow," he says quietly. "I thought I had made my home in the Land of the Free."

In fact, Alfonso makes his home in Kendall, within the walls of a recent addition to that substantial suburb, an enormous subdivision known as The Hammock: ten-thousand-plus acres and fifty thousand or so homes around a five-mile-long artificial lake on land that used to be the Everglades.

Not at all a bad address, this. There's no underclass of any kind in The Hammock, just a *Leave It to Beaver* spell of well-kept lawns and two-car garages and healthy school-bound children, even if (this being Miami in the modern era) the children do come in a spectrum of skin colors somewhat wider than the all-American middle-class norm.

Lo the lovely two-story Lobo home, then, and lo the extremely attractive three-generational Lobo family: the demure and gorgeous wife, the two spirited but perfectly mannered children, the handsome kindly grandparents; the kids experts in local gossip and what wildlife The Hammock still sustains, their parents active in community affairs, Grandma and Grandpa (surprisingly young) vigorous and patrician; Grandpa still involved in his agricultural work but on a consulting basis only, absorbed in his free time with exotic home plantings which of course interest his granddaughter inordinately. Here in short suburban Nirvana, the kind of life any self-respecting American would defend to the death.

But lo! too the starkly functional Yamaha electronic keyboard with its industrial-strength speakers in one corner of the living room (no Early American or Spanish Moderne parlor-music piece *that),* and mark well the family mementos: little Alfonso's school yearbooks full of friends now banished, vanished, tortured, raped, mutilated, or murdered, and other friends who own these horrors as deeds committed (some for Somoza and/or the Contras, a significant number for the Sandinistas, a substantial minority for both). Lend an ear, too, to the conversations over dinner about the relative merits of socialized and private medicine in countries around the globe, about the perceived vulgarity of Cuban women relative to the Nicaraguan norm (all that makeup, that teased or bleached hair, those tight dresses which do not perhaps offend the Lobo males but most certainly provoke the disdain of the ladies at the table). Listen to the talk which begins once the womenfolk, most un-Anglo-contemporarily, have cleared the table around the men and retired to their private places.

Alfonso and his father appear to get along just fine. The older Lobo seems proud of the younger's talents, more tolerant of his modern ways than in earlier years (once he banished the boy from the house for smoking marijuana; Somoza himself took him in), and more overtly loving than even the best-adjusted Yanqui dads. For his part the younger Lobo challenges with vigor but also a certain affection, forgiving if not forgetting some strife and clearly remembering some kindnesses too. These two men are intimate, alive together; they have not grown to be strangers.

They can for instance coexist comfortably under one roof despite the conflict in their personal politics which, notwithstanding the older Lobo's attempt to head it off by persuading his son into an exposition of sweet Nicaraguan folk laments lovingly finger-picked in the flamenco style, erupts at the table as this night grows long—as once again the communal future rattles the windows of the émigrés' today.

The bone of contention is very simple. The father hopes that the Sandinistas can be reasoned with, pressured diplomatically, enlightened without violence, and he is unmoving in his belief that any rearrangement of Nicaraguan politics must be ruled by international law and the scales of eternal justice. The son prays for whatever it takes to see the murdering dogs into their graves.

The debate seethes and simmers, twists and turns, until Alfonso grows weary of it and makes his move. Shifting into Spanish, he rakes his father with a fast verbal volley the meaning of which cannot be obscured by any amount of linguistic incomprehension: *Shut the fuck up, Dad,* he's saying, *the man's here to write about ME!*

Dad smiles, shrugs, falls silent, and after a seemly interval bids us good night. Alfonso charges forward for a while, scattering scumbag Sandinistas and even a few culpable Contras and CIA chiefs (they don't have it right either, he thinks), until his passions are subverted by his biological clock. It is very late, and in the morning he must have at least a partially clear head. You can't deal fish without one.

Fish. Well, seafood really; lobsters and shrimp and the like aren't fish. Seafood paid for the house in Kendall, seafood finances the Lobo lifestyle entirely, seafood paid even for the recording of "Freedom Fighter." Alfonso says "I am drawn to seafood. It calls to me. It is one of the big things in my life; the other is music. Of course there is a conflict between them—am I a seafood broker, or am I a musician? —but also, one helps the other."

What he means is that music saves him from being just a businessman, and fish gives him freedom. Seafood brokerage is not an absorbing profession—not agriculture or education, not the law, not professional politics—and if a man is sharp and forceful, as Alfonso is, he need not devote the greater part of his psychic energy to it, take it to bed with him. Also, though for a smallish operator like Alfonso the trade does involve time spent schlepping and sweating—deliveries here, collections there, the occasional hard-deadlined packing and shipping work—most of it happens on the telephone. So the administrative overhead is low, and when things work right, when for instance you're able to connect one unusually large source of supply with a suitably hungry and correctly timed single demand, it is possible to make your weekly or even monthly nut in an afternoon; and at such times you can walk away for a while, leave it alone until you have to get back on the blower and put a new deal together.

Of course you've got to know what you're about, and Alfonso does. He's been moving *les poissons* for a while now, beginning almost ten years ago in New Orleans with a sweet little deal which opened his eyes to the possibilities of the trade: a straight profit of three dollars a pound on lobsters bought from a fisherman and sold to a restaurant.

He's made a lot of cash since then, and lost it too; he had to walk away from about a million when his substantial full-time wholesaling business in Apalachicola got the deep-freeze treatment from the locals and finally (accidentally, it seems) burned to the ground. But in a way that disaster was a blessing. It got him out of daily drudgery and moved him to Miami, where all the Lobos are happier than they were in pretty but unwelcoming Apalachicola.

It also taught him to value his freedom more highly. When a South Beach Marielito entrepreneur elevated him from the ranks of the totally broke by fronting him five thousand in cash with no security but his word as an honest man (twentieth-century Anglo ways not yet having subverted émigré brotherhood), he went back into the business as a determined free-lancer.

So yes, seafood has been good to Alfonso, and he appreciates it. He has warm feelings toward it. Inspecting a particularly lustrous local redfish or a dozen exceptionally well-meated Venezuelan hopper shrimp, his eyes light up with almost the same sweet heat which illuminates his regard of a blue metal-flake Fender Jazz Bass from the pre-CBS fifties, or one of the dark subtle Nicaraguan beauties he can mark in any multiethnic Miami crowd. He can even eulogize the product of his trade and see the cosmic benefit of what he does; rolling toward South Beach in the Lobowagon of the moment, a massive Chrysler suited to his personal bulk, he discourses quite eloquently and knowledgeably on the health benefits of fish oils and the potential of the planet's enormous so-called trash-fish resources for feeding Third World billions. "That's why I got into seafood," he says. "I wanted to get into a good business, but I also wanted to do something that would benefit people, help feed the hunger of humanity." Despite his personal animosity toward Nicaragua's socialists and his conviction that the USSR really is the Evil Empire, Alfonso is no enemy of the teeming masses.

But enough, perhaps, of fish. Or maybe not, for the subject really is crucial to the Wolf. He struggles with it constantly, forever flip-flopping between appreciation of the security it brings him and the notion that he really ought to give it up, move on, embrace fully and forever his destiny as a musician. "Which one of all these guys is really me?" he asks. "The businessman, the politician, the musician, the chef, the man who writes poetry? I am very conflicted on this subject, and I change from minute to minute."

At least he knows why this is so, however. "It is very much part of being a Leo," he explains. "We go to extremes. We're very volatile as far as temper. I can go from being Saint Francis of Assisi one day to being Napoléon the next; I can be very peaceful for a month, and then all of a sudden I get into a bad temper. But then, you know, I often realize that the reason is that I haven't played guitar, I have been neglecting my music. When I play music, you see, I'm happy. Music to me is like a drug. I can pick up my guitar and go to my room and play, and I sweat out all the venom."

So is Alfonso's music the salve of his savage business-political breast, or is it his real life's work? Even the cover of his *Freedom Fighter* E.P. record addresses this burning question; he saw fit to make the final words of the liner notes a message from his good friend Rocky Aoki, owner of the Benihana of Tokyo restaurant chain (and intercontinental balloonist, power-boat racer, all-around daredevil and risk taker): "Get out of the seafood business, Alfonso!"

But without fish there would not have been any record on which to print that advice, now would there? Or then again there might have been a dozen albums by now, and no fish at all.

❁

The Lobowagon is in South Beach now, parked on the motivating-renovating trend strip across from the public portion of the island's oceanfront, and Alfonso is entirely out of fish, into music. Camo clothing and a Rambo headband have transformed him into the Wolf just as similar touches have made the savage Pack out of his mild-mannered musicians, and together the boys are running through a loose-limbed little afternoon jam at the quintessentially funky-but-chic Tropics Club.

Wolf and the Pack are not by any stretch of the imagination the Tropics' typical entertainment, big hairy hooligans in camo being about as far toward the antithesis of South Floridian urban hip as it is possible to get. Therefore, when Alfonso starts the band's brew cooking with a slow low burn of primal Chicago blues guitar (busting, I'd bet, the Tropics' twelve-bar cherry), the all-chic wait staff and the almost equally modish customers give each other dubious looks, but —wouldn't you know it—the kitchen staff emerges en masse from behind the scenes and digs it.

And yes, it's diggable. The *Freedom Fighter* record is very strong in a snaky, swampy, slightly sinister groove (New Orleans midnight-downtown funk-jazz-blues, basically), but that's a studio cut, not a live-in-person acid test; this right here, the first few bars of un-rehearsed interaction in a far from ideal situation—without a home crowd, with a bass player brand new to the group, without their seminal percussionist Chepito Arias, who's off playing with Santana somewhere—is hard evidence that Wolf and the Pack can cut it. Sounds good, sounds good; Alfonso's all right, leading well and finger-picking with feeling. The music has soul.

He moves out of his blues and into "Hey Jude," which quite frankly turns out to be something of a mess except for the guitar and trombone solos, but is fun all the same if like Alfonso you're in the mood for a meander down an English memory lane (and anyway, even Paul McCartney himself screws the pooch on this one now and again). Then he and the boys put it all together in a fine long supple percussion-driven weave of all kinds of stuff. Basically, it sounds like what might happen if Keith Richards and Jerry Garcia and the Blood, Sweat and Tears horn section were to run into each other somewhere in Central America, hire themselves a local rhythm section, and jam up a few Santana tunes. Which isn't at all surprising when you consider the roots of Alfonso's vision: the blues, sixties and seventies Euro-American rock, and the discrete Nicaraguan percussive tradition (not salsa or any other Caribbean form) in which he's been involved since childhood, notably with his old friend the absent Chepito Arias, who was in fact a cofounder of the Latin-rock band Carlos Santana named after himself.

Those then are the ingredients from which the music of Contra Rock has fomented in Alfonso's mental still. The result is not an uninteresting or unmoving potion. Even in the diluted form served at the Tropics, its powers are obvious.

But Wolf and the Pack's jam is over before it really gets cooked. The Wolf's musicians don't have any more time to spend on the Pack today. Since Alfonso has set his sights high, refusing to spend his musical energies in the subsistence work available on the local club scene, their involvement with him is speculative—unpaid—and right now each of them has some other life-supporting studio gig or club date or personal project to get to. So one by one they effect the sartorial transformation from jungle fighter to civilian, and go their separate ways.

Ditto with their leader. He too must now attend to certain matters which press.

●

The first is fish, or rather money from fish. Alfonso has to collect payment for the most recent deal he worked with his old Marielito benefactor, and so the Lobowagon lumbers away from the oceanfront trend strip toward the little streets of South Beach's Cuban interior, Alfonso explaining that while Marielitos do in general honor their debts, sending them invoices is not an effective means of collection; personal visits, allowing the opportunity for socializing, haggling, or even argument, are much more successful and much preferred.

Such is certainly the case with the gentleman he is seeking today, a man whose parlaying of one small bodega into a medium-sized fortune has featured a disregard of formal paperwork that would cause instant cardiac arrest in the average Yanqui business breast. "He's a millionaire, an entrepreneurial *genius,* but he doesn't even read English!"

says Alfonso. "He gets papers from the city or whoever, he gives them to me and I do them for him!"

Which works out just fine. The millionaire gets a free intermediary with the Anglo world; and Alfonso gets both a fast handy market for less-than-premium-grade seafood and, when he really needs it, an instant cash banker. No muss no fuss, then—but the personal touch is an absolute requirement in this partnership. Alfonso must show up and dance for every seafood penny.

No luck today, though. The man isn't around, so Alfonso cashes a fifty-dollar walking-around-money check with the clerk behind the bodega's counter, picks up a few Cuban delicacies, waves adios, and moves on toward the next item on his schedule.

This is a matter of greater import, a real biggie for Alfonso. Well, more precisely, it's for the Wolf: a meeting with the president of the Nicaraguan Bankers Association to discuss financing for a massive peace concert, hosted by Wolf and the Pack, which Alfonso wants to stage at the new Miami Arena.

Peace, that is; not victory. Having been singed by the political heat accompanying the Pentagon's embrace of "Freedom Fighter"—even the local Hispanic radio stations wouldn't give airtime to such a hot potato, and the only major record company whose interest was piqued made it very clear that the political content of any Wolf and the Pack music sold under its label should be zero—Alfonso has loosened his embrace of partisan positions and broadened his appeal; surely, he hopes, the goal of "peace" in Nicaragua is inoffensive to anybody. And besides, he says, peace is what he personally wants: that and a free Nicaragua run by and for Nicaraguans, for he dislikes the idea of his homeland ruled by some dupe of the White House and the CIA with almost the same vigor that accompanies his disapproval of the current regime. So really, the publicity won for him by "Freedom Fighter" was a mixed blessing. Sometimes he almost wishes Ronald Reagan's attention had never been drawn to his cassette of the song back in '83, that the President had never extolled him as a symbol of Nicaraguan resistance and copped his song title as gilding for the Contras' bloody lily (if indeed that is what happened; while Alfonso presents convincing evidence that Reagan's first use of the term occurred shortly after he or one of his handlers heard the song, the White House stops short of acknowledging such a debt).

Whatever. The waters through which these issues of fact and philosophy must be examined are hardly crystal-clear, and we must accept the ambivalences and even the contradictions which move in their shadows and in Alfonso's heart. Peace is now the word—and really, is one peace concert orchestrated by a camo-clad anti-Sandinista musician any more an ambivalent event than another staged by pro-Sandinista MTV liberals? Alfonso doesn't think so.

Neither, it seems, does his banking connection. Straight off he likes this peace concert idea. Not that the idea is presented straight off, of course. Before the bottom line is addressed, there are the usual pleasantries.

They seem sincere. This young banker, a gentleman in whom the blood of Castilian gentry quite obviously moves, is not apparently one of those members of the émigré elite who still regard Alfonso as a class renegade, a guitar-bashing ally of the Great Unwashed. The gentleman is in fact something of a fan. His first question when Alfonso made contact was "Are you *the* Alfonso Lobo?" And now, in this first meeting, as he sits there in his banker suit watching the big hairy ball of energy before him, the light in his eyes suggests that he is not entirely immune to the lure of sex and drugs and rock & roll, that back in Managua he wouldn't have said no to an experience of the pink limo lifestyle.

So okay, the meeting looks good. Alfonso presents his package and makes his pitch (out come his videos, his press clips, his letters from the White House), and the banker nods along, pops the odd question (Can Alfonso deliver Santana for the concert? No, he can't, Carlos is too expensive, but he and Chepito and the Pack can surely do Santana's tunes), and concludes that well, certainly, the necessary finance can be found this way or that: through his bank, through private Nicaraguan investors, no problem. And while we're talking peace and music and the like, how might Alfonso feel about donating his musical services to a big upcoming fund-raising dinner in honor of Enrique Bolaños, "a democratic guy with big balls" whose continued residence in and vocal opposition to the Sandinistas' version of Nicaragua mark him as the prime contender for the national leader spot should events ever conspire to create a vacancy. Sure, says Alfonso; anytime, he'd be honored. He'll sing his new song for peace.

That seems to wrap things up nicely for now, so the talk veers back toward fond memories and mutual acquaintances until the banker recalls that Alfonso is in the seafood as well as the music business, and remembers too that he knows another fellow in that line of work. This fellow, he believes, is in the fishing end of things, and is Alfonso not a wholesaler? Would he like perhaps to be introduced? Why certainly, Alfonso replies, by all means, and the two men go off toward a telephone.

In a little while the banker comes back alone, and the flavor of the occasion undergoes a radical change. What we have now is an interview, initiated abruptly at his suggestion, on the subject of the Nicaraguan condition in both Miami and Managua.

The message of this interview is not surprising—the Sandinistas are brilliant politicians but vicious World Communist Conspiracy thugs all the same, the Miami émigrés are respectable hardworking champions of democracy, Enrique Bolaños and the nonviolent internal Nicaraguan opposition of which he is the figurehead are viable, shamefully neglected alternatives to either the Sandinistas or the Contras—but the style of its delivery is a revelation. The banker's performance is wonderful, riveting; he has transformed himself from a smoothly casual middleman into a fireball of charisma. The relentless eye contact, the poetic repetition, the steady rise in vocal volume, the climactic impassioned appeal to the heart—here we have an expert ideologue and rabble-rouser, a mini Martin Luther King. If I were a PAC in search of a candidate, I'd look no further.

I'm still sort of stunned when Alfonso returns, looking pleased with himself, and the mood reverts to business as usual, specifically the leave-taking rituals. We gather around the banker's desk to exchange business cards and the sort of promises and invitations that are not meant or interpreted as binding. As we do these things I glance down and notice, along with the usual family snapshots that grace most executive offices, something you don't see too often in too many glass towers: lifelike little plastic models of Soviet military personnel, one of them a lean mean hawk-nosed officer of the KGB.

On our way to the Lobowagon Alfonso declares himself well

pleased. A seemly stroking of the mutual interests has been negotiated very politely, and what could be a nice relationship over Florida lobsters has begun, and (although who knows the degree of real sincerity behind the words of practiced middlemen, bankers especially?) the peace concert has advanced another step toward reality.

"I think this fellow is a good connection," says Alfonso. "I think he will treat me right, and you know why? Because I think I can help him as much as he can help me. He has political ambitions, you know."

To this somewhat redundant observation I must add a couple more. Firstly, the visit has been a little disorienting. This time in the glass tower with a powerful, utterly executive-conventional gentleman who conducts his business in Spanish as he looks out over the heart of a great American city has been an oddly novel experience. For while our TV sets have acquainted us with several clear images of South Florida Hispanics—the show person, the welfare mother, the busboy, the migrant worker, the cocaine cowboy—they have not prepared us for this one, or for the unassailable reality behind it: that in Miami it is a commonplace. Spanish-speaking gentlemen occupy many of the catbird seats over the city, and moreover they belong there, for the labor of Hispanics built this city, and in the modern era, in the years since the revolution in Cuba, their energy gave it new life. They came to the graveyard of the United States, and they resurrected it into the nation's international powerhouse, the economic hub of the two American continents and a whole world beyond. So really, if a city can be said to belong to one group above all others, today's Miami is theirs. The fact that the sharing of this notion in Anglo Florida is likely to get you nothing more than a hot knuckle sandwich or a cold quick freeze does not invalidate its accuracy.

The second observation is smaller, more personal. Fret as he might about his divided professional life, the combination of music, politics, and fish is good for Alfonso. He would not, perhaps, be fully himself as a specialist.

Consider for instance what comes next in his day: a visit to a concrete, specific, and very probably workable vision of a fully integrated future for the Wolf.

The location of this vision, familiar to many of us as a backdrop to televised Sonny Crockett car chases and political protests and civic folderol (notably the annual Orange Bowl parade and the more recently inaugurated Miami Grand Prix), is the semiderelict stretch of the city of Miami's downtown bayfront property known as Bicentennial Park. It is here, on sun-scorched grass and litter-strewn concrete currently occupied by a tiny proportion of the city's homeless or otherwise footloose population, that Alfonso wishes to center his energies. With a little money from the city for some cleanup and repair work and a more considerable sum from private investors or financial institutions of his choice, he will bring a full-size Mississippi riverboat to this place, park it alongside a handy pier, and operate it as the center of a dancing, wining, fish-dining, music-listening, water-sporting fun spot capable of bringing twenty-four-hour light to the drab urban darkness. This will be a great thing, Alfonso thinks. The indigents and alcoholics of the park will get employment keeping the grounds up (Alfonso doesn't require references or fear the unfortunate); nightlife trendies will get a suave bright wee-hours breakfast spot (Miami is strangely lacking in such amenities); moms and dads and kids and tourists will get fine or budget waterfront dining and outdoor/indoor recreation; the Orange Bowl parade and the Miami Grand Prix will get a new, videogenic headquarters; the city will get tax revenue and a cheap facelift in place of an eyesore; and Alfonso himself will get (A) a guaranteed high-volume seafood outlet, (B) a headquarters and bandstand for Wolf and the Pack, and (C) more money, power, and local influence. Fish will serve music will serve politics; all will be enhanced; Alfonso's light will burn brightly.

Sitting beside him as the prow of the Lobowagon nudges around the current reality of Bicentennial Park—winos and trash pickers staring blankly from beneath scruffy palms, city scum undulating against broken piers on wavelets of greasy water—one can grasp the logic of his vision with ease. This sorry spot, surrounded as it is by the bright new renovations and multimillion-dollar waterfront leisure developments of Miami's economic renaissance, is an obvious target for somebody's entrepreneurial acumen. One wonders why, in fact, in a city so richly endowed with international capital and densely populated by supercompetitive corporate players, nobody else has perceived and acted upon this opportunity, why the backhoes are not already at work. Alfonso's scenario gives the distinct impression of being almost too good to be true.

But maybe it's real, maybe this little stretch of coast *is* clear. Maybe this really *is* one of those land-of-opportunity inlets through which the energy of the new citizen can be released to build a financial empire, found a dynasty, become another in a long proud historic series of realized American dreams.

So far, Alfonso's Bicentennial Park ambition is intangible, its financing only a broad conception and its interface with the city of Miami a matter of future negotiation. The riverboat itself is real, however—it's sitting unused in Corpus Christi at the moment—and so is Alfonso's connection to its owners. They have another boat, a fifty-six-foot sportfisherman, docked at the downtown Miamarina, of which the Wolf and his family and friends have free run in exchange for routine maintenance.

Not a bad little perk to the Lobo lifestyle, that, although it is difficult to imagine Alfonso approaching the vessel in any truly recreational spirit; like most of the other boats sharing its berth, this grand toy is more likely to be the locus of wheel greasing and deal mongering than a source of simple pleasures. It's marvelous how malleable a man can become with a rod and a beer at hand and you in total command of his schedule.

Today, a Friday, the last of my days with the Wolf, we visit the boat only to prepare it for an outing with "some men" tomorrow. Alfonso stays long enough to direct his maid and his fishing boat's captain in their labors, and then he and I retire into the air-conditioned comfort of a bar in the adjacent big, brassy, brand-new Bayside spending complex. Business is brisk today; the din of pleasure and consumption roars from the multinational flow around us, forcing us to almost shout at each other from neighboring bar stools.

We strain our vocal cords about all kinds of things: rock & roll records we love (we agree on most except Blood, Sweat and Tears' hits, which never moved me personally); the Swinging London we both knew (though I at a less comfortably funded level than he); the relative destructiveness of gunshot wounds (though I know a man who survived an amazing thirteen 9-mm submachinegun hits, I've never before met or even heard of anybody taking six big fat .45s and living to walk, talk, and boogie); and, as the road begins to call to me and more significant matters must therefore be addressed, we talk about the specific nature of Anglo-to-Latino prejudice in Florida today. Alfonso says it's simple: some Anglos still bridle at the mere sound of Spanish spoken, but in Miami anyway, the prejudice of the overwhelming majority is keyed by physical rather than cultural factors. A man or woman with dark brown skin and/or Indian facial features, " a hondo type of person," endures a great deal more discrimination than his or her lighter-skinned or Spanish-featured brothers and sisters. In this respect, Miami is no different from Managua, or anywhere. Alfonso himself has very little trouble.

At this point there remains only one question. We have already asked our immigrant stranger where he came from and how he got here. Now we need to know the answer to the third and final standard question: what he thinks of his new country, how *he* sees *us*.

"Well, personally, the U.S. has been very good for me," he says. "Being here has meant that I can have my own life, that I do not have to live in the shadow of my father, that I am not a well-known person —you know, a symbol of things I may or may not really be. So yes, that is liberating. Here I am me. I was reborn here.

"But you know, the United States has incredible energy, amazing power and wealth, but it is like that old saying, 'A sleeping giant,' except that it is not sleeping. It is wide-awake, but its people are dreaming.

"Compared to other peoples, you see, North Americans are very naive. They are impressed by physical things: cars, stereos, boats; they are not impressed by spiritual things, the things of the mind and the heart. They are ignorant, too. They do not know languages, they do not know what is happening in the world; they do not even know where these places are that they hear about in the news. I think that is what worries me the most: some of the leaders know and care about world politics, but the people don't. They think they're invulnerable. So often, when I am in places like this one, or the Tropics Club, anywhere like that, and I see all these people having such a good time, I think to myself, 'Here you are—dancing and drinking and taking your drugs and spending your money, and meanwhile the Russians are marching to kick your ass.'

"I don't like to say that to people out loud, you know, but the other night I was in a disco, and this American guy I know comes up to me and says, 'What are you looking so serious about? Why aren't you having a good time?' So I told him: everybody there was totally oblivious to the world situation, couldn't care less, while in Russia and Cuba and Nicaragua, people were working day and night to take everything away from them. And you know what he told me? He said, 'Man, you're on a bad trip.'"

"No, my friend," Alfonso says, staring hard at me, conscious of our time running out and the tape rolling in my little machine. "It is not I who am on a bad trip. It is you. You do not know how bad your lives could be. You know you are lucky, but you have no idea how lucky you *really* are. I am in reality. I do not think world politics are a joke, or a bore, and I do not believe in luck. The difference between us, you see, is that *I* have seen countries fall, and I don't like it when I see that. Make that the end of your story, my friend."

We shake hands and wish each other well. I go to my car. The exile Lobo goes back to preparing his boat for an outing with some men.

ABOUT THE AUTHOR

Patrick Carr's journalism has appeared in *The Village Voice,* the *New York Times, Southern, Rolling Stone* and *Country Music.* His last book was *Gun People.* He lives with his wife in Tampa.